THE
PURPOSE
OF YOUR LIFE

THE
PURPOSE
OF YOUR LIFE

FINDING YOUR PLACE IN THE WORLD
USING SYNCHRONICITY, INTUITION, AND
UNCOMMON SENSE

Carol Adrienne

EAGLE BROOK
WILLIAM MORROW AND COMPANY, INC.
NEW YORK

Published by Eagle Brook
An Imprint of William Morrow and Company, Inc.
1350 Avenue of the Americas, New York, N.Y. 10019

It is the policy of William Morrow and Company, Inc., and its imprints
and affiliates, recognizing the importance of preserving what has been written,
to print the books we publish on acid-free paper,
and we exert our best efforts to that end.

Library of Congress Cataloging-in-Publication Data
Adrienne, Carol.
The purpose of your life : finding your place in the world using synchronicity,
intuition, and uncommon sense / by Carol Adrienne.—1st ed.
p.   cm.
ISBN 0-688-15512-X
1. Vocation.   2. Spiritual life.   3. Coincidence.   4. Intuition.
5. Adrienne, Carol.   I. Title.
BL629.A37   1998
131—dc21   97-36912
CIP

Printed in the United States of America

First Edition

4   5   6   7   8   9   10

BOOK DESIGN BY OKSANA KUSHNIR

www.williammorrow.com

I first met Carol Adrienne while contemplating a study guide for *The Celestine Prophecy*. At the time, I was lukewarm about the idea, wondering whether a guide to the novel would overintellectualize the concepts. Once I got to know Carol, however, my concerns were quickly put to rest. Besides her skill at understanding people and being able to relate to many different life perspectives, she has a knack for bringing every conversation down to earth, and focusing on experience itself. After that discussion, the guide to *The Celestine Prophecy* did come into being and, chiefly because of Carol's writing, became one of the most popular study guides of all time.

As much as anyone, Carol has her finger on the pulse of current evolution. In terms of popular psychology, we humans are integrating the left and right hemispheres of our brains, which only means that we are rediscovering the mystery in our individual lives. Most of us grew up thinking that we lived in a physical world that was ordinary and explained and actually devoid of spiritual mystery. In this world we tended to overly intellectualize goals and to expect only ordinary opportunities to come our way.

Then, as a result of new discoveries and popular books, a new image of the universe around us has begun to take shape. We now expect miracles and small coincidental events to pop up everywhere, opening up magical, destined opportunities that we thought we could only dream about. What's more, we expect to suddenly crystallize in our minds a greater sense of calling and mission, toward which all this mysterious guidance leads.

What makes this new image so poignant is that we are pulling into consciousness what has always been occurring in the lives of human beings. Those who have made the greatest contributions in history have always done so with a higher sense of destiny and an increased perception of guidance. At some level these people knew that we must face life like detectives—gleaning the meanings, the silver linings, the windows of opportunity, that lie hidden in what occurs around us.

At this point in history, we know that this mysterious life is not just for the geniuses among us; it is waiting there for all of us, no matter where we live, no matter what our education happens to be, and, above all, no matter what kind of childhood we've had. The only thing that matters is that we find a way to open ourselves up to this experience. And that means facing the individual ways we keep ourselves out of it.

Increasing the synchronicity in our lives, for instance, is what we tend to talk about and aim for, but in order to put ourselves in the right place for these destined events to occur, we must get in touch with our intuitions. And as you will see in this book, if we are preoccupying ourselves with negative thoughts about our own abilities, or revenge thoughts about others, or with anything else that serves ourselves, then there is no room for other images and urges to appear—the ones that spontaneously form in the back of our minds. These are our intuitive thoughts and they come to guide us, always suggesting that we do something, go somewhere, or search for a new bit of information. When we risk following them, we move into just the right spot for the synchronicity to unfold and lead us forward.

Getting past our preoccupations can truly bring us to a greater sense of the self we are, the genius we all share, and the knowledge that every event in our lives, whether we have labeled it positive or negative, has uniquely prepared us to be where we are now, poised to pursue a path of service.

Yet again, merely hearing all this at the intellectual level—even if we believe it completely—is not enough. Our challenge is to integrate this spiritual life into everyday existence, to clear ourselves until we can experience it fully.

With this book, Carol guides us succinctly through this process . . . and that has always been her special gift.

ACKNOWLEDGMENTS

I would like to thank my editor Joann Davis for inviting me to write on the topic closest to my heart, and my agent, Candice Fuhrman, for her constant support of my work.

The heart of this book lies in the stories that were so graciously contributed by the people whom I interviewed. I thank them all for showing up at just the right moment with such clarity and generosity of spirit. I also want to thank certain individuals for their unique contributions and viewpoints: Zenobia Barlow, Joan Jovan, Elizabeth Jenkins, Virginia Lawson, Mary Patric, Virginia Talucci, Patricia Whitt, Natasha Downing, Stephen Rose, Dr. Selma Lewis, Penney Peirce, Nancy Rosanoff, Sharon Franquemont, Dr. Marcia Emery, Dr. Joyce Petschek, Larry Collins, Steve Winfield, Larry Leigon, Donna Hale, Bill Voelker, Richard Wolski, Valerie Vollmer, Stefani McKinzie, Wendy Topping, Arlene Thompson, Elizabeth Maglio, Valorie Thomas, Amy Aldrich, Lorraine Sykes, and Georgia Rogers — and James Redfield. I also want to recognize the contribution of all my teachers along the way, and my invisible companions who have no doubt had many a good laugh at my peregrinations.

SPECIAL ACKNOWLEDGMENT TO

THOSE WHOSE PATH INCLUDED BEING

A woman who loves horses
A word wizard working to end illiteracy
A female executive in a corner corporate office
An urban planner, Buddhist, and publisher of spiritual art
An adaptable beauty who has survived multiple setbacks
A teacher who became a comedian
A master innovator of gem cutting
A positive-thinking Miss America
A Zen master offering incense and flowers with the Dalai Lama at Auschwitz
An Iowa soybean farmer of esoteric persuasion
An artist and the wife of a famous director
A networker, organizer, and Peace Corps volunteer in Africa
An office equipment recycler
An environmental allergies consultant
A Buddhist nun, spiritual teacher, and tap-dancing mother
A holistic financial crisis healer
An Irish Vedic astrologer and herbal healer
A fallen goddess

Imagine you have been invited as a guest to a salon of the above-named exceptionally interesting and creative ordinary people. You have a chance to speak to each one of them for a few moments about how they have found, or are finding, their unique contribution in the world. This book is your invitation.

CONTENTS

THE PURPOSE OF THIS BOOK

My goal for this book is to inspire you to become aware of and appreciate the fullness of who you are. I know that a book is only a tool, but books have the power to take us many places — in this dimension and beyond. I would like you to think of this book as an introduction — first, to a host of people whose stories may touch your own life; and second, and most important, to your own self-discovery.

My intention is to create a field of interaction among you, me, and the universal field of intelligence that will begin to create a momentum of energy, catalyzing the recognition of your purpose, if that is as yet unclear to you. In order to do that, I am counting on your own desire to know yourself as part of the current of energy flowing between you and the book. The book is based on the perennial philosophies by which humanity has long navigated the unpredictable shallows and depths of life. My hope is that by bringing you the stories of real people, some inner knowing and recognition of your own path will be touched.

The book is based on my own lived experience both personally and professionally. As you will see in Chapter 1, I have taken the winding road to my present occupation as a teacher, writer, and facilitator of workshops on spiritually and life purpose. Along the way, I have discovered, tested, and taught certain principles and techniques that I feel are eminently practical for helping us to find our place in the world.

It is my intention that this book provide a matrix of information to feed your soul — as much as any book can be a stimulus to insights.

We make sense of our world by telling each other stories. Some of the stories in the book will move you. Some will not. Stories connect us to each other's experience regardless of time, place, or culture. According to scholar and mythologist Joseph Campbell, the first stories, or ancient myths, were designed to put the mind in accord with the body, and a person's way of life in accord with the dictates of nature.

Stories are understood as a whole, and from them we extract a meaning that is relevant to our own concerns. Each story will, however, work on your psyche in a particular way. What I learn from a story may be similar or completely different from what you learn, depending on our backgrounds, our current situations, our vocabulary, our hopes and fears, and our ability to listen—and our inherent life purpose. Maybe at a later time, a story you had not thought much about will suddenly come to mind just when you could use some support.

The right side of the brain, our intuitive and imaginative side, learns best by stories. The left side, rational and deductive in its reasoning, connects easily to techniques, principles, explanations, and step-by-step processes. This book provides both avenues to help you find your place in the world.

HOW TO USE THIS BOOK

Read the book at random or all the way through. It is organized using a mix of stories, principles, suggestions, and personal questions. Hopefully, one of these methods may set off the intuitions that are ready to come forth from your intention to know yourself better.

Life is found in relationships with people, places, and things. I hope to create a relationship with you and this environment of ideas, fueled by your desire to know yourself. Two states of mind will help this process. The first is a strong intention to open up to the unfolding purpose inherent in you. The second is the capacity to live without knowing what your purpose is, yet be ready to do what is asked of you.

THE SEQUENCE OF THE CHAPTERS

Part One: Principles for Finding Your Place in the World
Chapter 1, "The Call and the Journey—My Story," gives you a brief history of my own path, and demonstrates a progression of synchronicities (meaningful coincidences, which we will discuss at length), mind-sets, catalyzing events, and the joys and despair of my unfolding

purpose. This is the background from which I have pulled together the principles I feel are relevant for the search for one's path. I have sincerely tried to include what I have found to be most important, but no one person's point of view can ever include everything—so please feel free to question and revise these ideas based on your own experience.

Chapter 2, "You Are a Self-Organizing System," establishes the domain of the book—that we are a self-organizing energy field with an inherent purpose for existing. We will learn what life purpose is and is not. You will see that your life purpose is already in progress, even though you may currently feel absolutely convinced otherwise. This chapter begins to address the idea of realigning with that purpose, and explores how to engage with it more *consciously*.

In Chapter 3, "Taking a Stand Moves You into Place," we address two facets of our path. The first is that we cannot drift aimlessly—hoping to keep every option open—because we will wind up doing nothing in the name of "being open." It will be necessary to take an initial stand or to choose a focus, and then follow the feedback that comes from doing that. Without some kind of focus, you will not be able to engage your life deeply enough to let the synchronicities take you where you need to go. One of my students, Bill Voelker, likes the statement he once heard, "You can have anything you want, but you can't have everything." Throughout life, you must choose and select. Paradoxically, being both focused and open are not incongruent.

Second, as you will see in our story of Zen master Kwong-roshi, sometimes circumstances force us into taking a stand, and that can affect the rest of our life. Circumstances may clarify who we are and what is important for this life and how we are going to live with integrity.

Chapter 4, "Anything Is Possible," introduces one of the most important foundational beliefs for catalyzing the emergence of your life purpose—and that is that almost all limitations exist as beliefs in our minds. This part of the book encourages you to trust your unfolding purpose. Anything is possible if you have a deep belief in God and Her infinite possibilities—miracles. If you merely give lip service to this idea, you may find a time-delay in the accomplishment of your goals.

Chapter 5, "The Magnetic Force Field of Your Life Purpose,"

considers life from the new metaphors of quantum physics — that we exist more accurately as a field of energy/consciousness, which acts and reacts within the collective field of energy/consciousness. As long as you are alive on the earth, things are going to happen to you and through you. Usually, a book on life purpose takes the stance that you must "find" your purpose in the outer world, and then set goals to achieve it. In this book, we propose the theory that you are immersed in a complex of personal energy patterns that magnetize purposeful people, places, and events into your life. Chapter 5 has an analysis sheet for you to use to begin to describe the components of your own attracting field.

Chapter 6, "Synchronicities Unfold Your Purpose," describes how there are no accidents, and that certain events bring information and opportunities, and open new doorways into your purpose.

Part Two: Techniques

Chapter 7, "Intention and Nonattachment," provides practical techniques for living your purpose on a daily basis — even if you have not clearly grasped what it is. Even if you cannot articulate your purpose, you can initiate its unfolding more quickly if you have a strong desire to be shown what it is! Therefore, we see *intention* as an initial stage of the unfolding. In the deepest metaphysical and scientific levels of understanding, we learn, in the words of physician and author Leonard Laskow, that "in the subtle realms (of cellular communication) *intention is action*" (my emphasis).[1]

Chapter 8, "Using Intuition to Follow the Movement of Your Life Purpose," helps you understand and practice this nonphysical sensing faculty that is the key to knowing what to do when.

In Chapter 9, "Increasing Creativity and Developing Your Abilities," our purpose is to offer some easy ways to play with your inner images. Finding and living your life purpose requires that you venture into uncharted territory. You will, at times, have to let go of conventions and the opinions of other people. You will have to have confidence in your creative power and in your power of interpretation of the messages from your intuition and inherent in synchronicities.

In order to strengthen your intuitive side, the book offers you a variety of simple ways to increase your creativity. These practices have at least three purposes. The first is to help you evoke who you are so that you can see things about yourself you would not otherwise have access to with your everyday mind-set. The second is to give you easy-to-use tools for allowing your intuition to speak to you on definite issues. The third is to entertain you: The exercises are fun. When you are relaxed and having fun, you are more likely to attract like energy!

Part Three: Deep Water

Chapter 10, "In the Void," helps you deal with the difficulties of being in "the desert"—an inevitable part of the spiritual path. The void is a natural and necessary part of our life cycle. It forces us to change, or to accept those things which we cannot change. The void fosters growth at a deep level, and germinates the seeds of our life purpose.

Chapter 11, "The Shadow and Life Purpose," describes how we might tap into the parts of ourselves that we have turned away from, and the common pitfalls of how we spend our energy around other people in counterproductive ways. The purpose for this chapter is to heighten our conscious awareness of these patterns so that we can change our behavior. There is an analysis sheet to help you determine just how much energy you spend this way.

Chapter 12, "Transforming Obstacles," shows you how the problems you face may contain seeds of growth that may change your outlook in life or provide you with new ways of handling barriers. You will learn rational and intuitive ways to work interactively with and release the creative energy of your obstacle.

Part Four: Being There

In Chapter 13, "Doing What You Love—and Were Meant to Do," you are reminded to follow your heart, and keep your mind open so that you, too, can live the purpose you hold inside.

I discovered that people are not really afraid of dying; they're afraid of not ever having lived, not ever having deeply considered their life's higher purpose, and not ever having stepped into that purpose and at least tried to make a difference in this world.

JOSEPH JAWORSKI

PART ONE

PRINCIPLES FOR FINDING YOUR PLACE IN THE WORLD

CHAPTER 1

The Call and the Journey—My Story

You are born with a character; it is given, a gift, as the old stories say, from the guardians upon your birth. . . . Each person enters the world called.

JAMES HILLMAN

The reason that this book is being written, I believe, is that one day I "snapped." In August of 1993, at the moment that it happened—that I snapped—I was standing in the exact middle of my very small cottage in the East Bay hills of Richmond, California.

The first time I saw this house, I thought to myself, "This place looks like a writer's cottage." I assumed it had been a summer cottage, built in the 1940s, for people who came over to the East Bay from San Francisco. From the tiny front porch on which I have tried to grow purple pansies and pink geraniums, I can see the Golden Gate Bridge. If the pine trees and bushes were not planted in front of the house, I would be able to see Mount Tamalpais, the magnificent mountain spirit of Marin County. The entire front wall of the cottage has small-paned windows, which make me feel as if I'm sitting on a sun porch, and not in a "real" room. I see clients here, and write looking out from these windows, which offer both vista and wooded nature. I am very happy working here.

This living room and work area, the space where I snapped, holds my computer, file cabinets, chests of drawers, and tables on which I have placed vessels and vases collected from my travels—vessels that

I have reproduced in pastels, in drawings framed on my living room walls. There is a small, green-striped couch, which doubles as guest bed, the back of which is draped with a red Peruvian weaving. Supported on the window ledges are Mexican pottery, pictures of my children and their spouses, candles, and a prim and serious picture of me at age two resembling Shirley Temple—my mother's archetypal model of the perfect child. Besides a few exuberant houseplants, the only other significant feature of this room is an overcrowded bookshelf and stacks of books that do not fit on the shelves.

I now see that definitive moment in August of 1993, as painful as it was, as a turning point that allowed my perception of myself and my life's work to come into harmony. At the time, of course, I had no idea that my life was going to change dramatically. I only knew that *something* had to change, or I was going to have to seriously rethink how I was to make my living and stay sane. I had turned fifty-two that year and was living alone, struggling to make sense of a career that seemed to be slipping away under my feet. I had no idea that the intention that I was affirming that day—to live in alignment with my artistic nature and my deep metaphysical values and interests—would actually lead to what I now see as my life purpose.

Since 1976, I had been living a dual life. On the one hand, I skirted the edges of regular mainstream life, raising two children as a single parent, and working in administrative positions, usually for directors of education or health-oriented nonprofit organizations. On the other hand, I considered myself an artist, and a student of the psychospiritual nature of life. From the age of nineteen, my goal had been to avoid suburbia and "the ordinary." During the years I was a single working mother, I tried to choose work that seemed to have social value. I was probably what I would now call a "classic under-earner," but that may just be another label for being a college-educated woman with no heart for the corporate ladder.

In the beginning, when I was four or five years old, my main preoccupation was playing house. Around the age of seven, I decided I would be a secretary like my mother had been before she began to take over the administrative and design duties for my father, who was a building contractor. I would sit at the coffee table—my desk—and play with pads of paper and pens and pencils, shuffling the pieces of paper, hitting them together to make sharp, crisp stacks, and talk to myself in a very serious way. Excellent training for my later years.

When I was in the fifth grade, our school put on a carnival and after that my only thought was to be a Gypsy fortune-teller. At night, I would lie in bed, and when I wasn't listening for B-52s to bomb my house and start World War III, I would fantasize myself traveling around the world doing something important and being by myself on adventures. Interestingly, my life now includes a great deal of travel—lecturing and conducting workshops—and I usually travel alone. I have kept house all my life, and I have been both a secretary and a fortune-teller. Did my early fantasies create these experiences? Or were the fantasies a premonition of my later years?

In seventh grade, I remember, I was so bored in history class that I started writing little adventure stories starring myself and giving them to my friends to read. I had always been an avid reader, borrowing my grandmother's Book-of-the-Month Club selections. After about the age of fifteen, I decided to define myself as an artist. I suppose I chose artist because my first happy memories involved sitting on the couch with a new box of Christmas crayons. I still adore the act of painting and the sensuality of color. I could eat paint. Color is a visual vitamin to me.

While I thoroughly enjoyed the social life in my high school art class, my favorite class was English. I couldn't wait to be given essay assignments on any subject. When I graduated from high school, my English teacher told my parents that he thought I could become a professional writer. Did I take this seriously at the time? No. It turned out that I was the valedictorian of my class, but I had had no idea what that even was until the principal informed me that I would be required to give a speech. There are no words to describe the terror I felt standing before my assembled peers, friends, and family on the day of graduation. Years later, I realized that I had left my body, because when I said, "Hello," I looked around in bewilderment to find out who had spoken. I literally did not know that I had spoken. While my academic record was good, my parents had no intention of sending me to college. Why send a girl to college, they said.

I have often wondered why it never once occurred to me to pursue writing as a career, even though that was probably the easiest and most exceptional thing I had ever done. I guess it was too easy. Because I had other opinions about my self-worth, I could not even see my strengths until years and years later. Today, writing has become a *very* large part of my work, and is one of the most fun and financially rewarding activities that I've ever done.

As I write this, I realize how compartmentalized my thinking was in those early years. How odd it was to have decided that I wanted to be an artist, and at the same time had two self-defeating, negative beliefs. The first belief was that artists don't make money. The second was that I probably would never be "good enough" to be a professional artist. How odd to have decided that art was what I naturally resonated with, and yet never, ever, to have considered going to art school. By the age of nineteen, apparently I had made an internal assumption, without knowing why or how, that I was somehow not destined to be successful. The possibility that an artist could grow and develop—that one might persevere and become successful over time, even late in life—never occurred to me. I never gave myself permission to make mistakes or explore possibilities. Somehow, looking back, I think I must have believed that one had to emerge from being a teenager complete, perfect, with one's talent fully formed so that one dominated one's chosen field, was better than anyone else, unique and sought after by people just because one was so absolutely special. If you weren't that, forget it. You were out of the running. Better be a secretary because the rest of it would never happen.

I married at the age of twenty. My husband and I were both students at the Berkeley campus of the University of California, and I had just discovered psychology. While I was fascinated with the field, the required college psychology course involving statistics was incomprehensible to me. At that moment, I took my first art history class and was introduced to the subtleties of Renaissance symbolism. For that I am eternally grateful. It was in my study of early Netherlandish art that I began to awaken to the excitement of discovering a deeper level of meaning beyond the literal. Medieval and Renaissance painters routinely embedded all kinds of symbols (oranges to indicate wealth or connections to the south, or slippers and small dogs to indicate marital fidelity) in these deliciously mysterious and beautifully composed interior scenes of sacred and profane life. Art and beauty often rescued me from melancholy. The power of symbols as messages became a deeply planted seed in my soul.

In 1963, I graduated in art history from UC in the midst of the Free Speech Movement, and the social upheaval of the times. The import of what was happening hardly made a dent on me because I was basically introverted, lonely, and depressed. Since I had grown up in an unsophisticated and culturally deprived environment, I was avid to change my entire self. The first three years of married life were very hard for me, and I remember feeling almost as if I didn't exist. I remember reading newsmagazines in the university library so that I would be able to make dinner conversation with my husband and his engineering friends. I was so shy at that time that I didn't know how to make friends of my own. Besides, I had deluded myself, in an effort to individuate from my mother, that women were less interesting than men and to be avoided at all costs. Really.

After my divorce eight years later, I moved to San Francisco. My life centered on rearing my two small children, making new friends, creating landscapes with the batik resistance technique, and working part-time. I hungrily entered into a bohemian lifestyle.

The most important event in finding my life's purpose was about to happen in 1974, two weeks before my thirty-third birthday. For a year and a half, I had been managing a large and very busy catering company. I literally worked day and night. Because I was so rarely home, I often had to leave my children, Sigrid and Gunther, with a baby-sitter. Leaving them alone so much was not working. They rebelled and were starting to become uncontrollable. In the first week of January, my friend Zenobia Barlow and I decided to visit Santa Fe, New Mexico, for a week's vacation. We were both exhausted from our work.

As we drove from the airport in Albuquerque up to Santa Fe, I began to notice something strange. The landscape looked very familiar to me, although I had never been there before. The surrounding red hills dotted with little green bushes resembled my latest paintings. Had I made this place up? Both of us were enthralled from the moment we arrived in Santa Fe—a not uncommon occurrence with visitors to this area. We began to meet people in the most synchronistic way. Within a week, we were talking about moving there. Even the smell of the fireplace piñon smoke exhilarated me. I was entranced.

The long and short of it is that when I returned home to California, following my intuition, I quit my lucrative but demanding job. To the amazement of my friends, I sold most of my furniture, and shipped the rest of my belongings to New Mexico. I packed myself and the kids into my old blue Volkswagen square-back, and drove the three of us to Santa Fe.

The synchronicities confirming my decision began the moment I arrived. The small kitchenette motel we stayed in turned out to be two blocks from the house I would end up renting for a year. One of the most amazing coincidences happened that first Sunday. Even though I was tired and new in town, I decided to go out to the International Folk Art Museum to see an Indian movie. As I sat down, I noticed that the walls were hung with many batik paintings. Batik painting had been my own art medium for several years. As I waited for the movie to begin, I soon realized that I knew the two people sitting in the seats directly in front of me. Patti Nelson, the former secretary of my ex-husband, was sitting with her boyfriend. Only minutes after I sat down, Patty turned around, saw me, and her eyes opened wide. "Carol!" she said. "We were just talking about you because of all these batiks. We were wondering how you were doing, and where you were!"

From then on, my time in Santa Fe unfolded as if in a movie. I worked at various jobs to scratch out a living at a time when beginning wages were about two dollars an hour. I worked as an artist's model, and was a waitress in both a Mexican and an Italian restaurant. I learned to handcraft silver jewelry, and managed a Southwest jewelry and artifact store. Most of my friends were artists and spiritual seekers. During this time, I serendipitously reconnected with two sisters whom I had met in 1971, when they moved from New York to San Francisco. I had, in fact, invited them that year to stay with me for three months in my flat. Oddly enough, one of them had moved, unbeknownst to me, to Santa Fe. Knowing what I know now, I would have to say they must have been members of my soul group, part of whose mission was to introduce me to the next person who would help connect me to my destiny. One of the sisters kept insisting that I must meet her friend Ruth Drayer. As usual when someone wants you to meet their friend, you are not quite sure if that is going to be a good idea. However, one day I did meet Ruth Drayer, who seemed a very nice person. She had two children the same ages as mine, and they all went to the same school; she and I hit it off.

During my initial conversation with Ruth, I casually mentioned that I had been thinking strongly of changing my last name, since I was no longer married. I explained that I had been feeling for some time that I did not want to keep my current name, nor did I want to return to my maiden name. Ruth immediately suggested that the system of numerology could help harmonize a new name with my birthday to ensure an appropriate new path of destiny. She offered to do a chart for me, and I somewhat skeptically agreed. Little did I know that this was one of the most important moments of my life, and would put me on the path of my life's work.

The moment I laid eyes on the little handwritten chart she had calculated for me based on my birth name and birth date, something *literally* clicked in my head. I was entranced by a system that would allow me to understand myself and other people, and perhaps to divine what the purpose of our life was supposed to be. We worked out a couple of names that had occurred to me, and I finally chose Adrienne as my last name. I had always liked the name, and had given it to my daughter as a middle name. The symbolic potential of this name promised a destiny involving art and a psychological and spiritual orientation, with perhaps the chance to inspire others through public speaking and the media. Even though this path seemed highly unlikely at that time, I liked the idea that it seemed to emphasize art and metaphysics. After that, I was hooked on numerology and what it seemed to reveal about people. I began to study all the books on the subject that I could find, and experimented on every person who came into my life. The system proved so accurate that I kept moving deeper into it. It was something I could not let go.

As I would learn through my study of personal cycles, I had moved to Santa Fe in a "nine" personal year, which meant that I was really *completing* a cycle rather than starting a new one. However, the influence of the nine also greatly *expanded* my spiritual development. I now realize that the purpose for moving to Santa Fe was to meet Ruth and be introduced to numerology, a major piece of my life path as a teacher and counselor. There is no question in my mind that I was born to use this system and develop practices to help people remember who they really are.

The moment that I "found" numerology, I knew I was supposed to leave and return to California. I felt a little sheepish about returning after having moved away. I was afraid that my friends would think I didn't know what I was doing, which was true. However, before leaving New Mexico, a clear intuitive message flashed across my brain—one of the first I clearly remember having—"You must now go back to school." I had absolutely no desire to go back to school. In fact, I actively resisted the idea because I was already working hard as a single mother, and did not need one more thing to do. Or so I thought.

However, the "nine" year was over, and it was time to leave and start something entirely new. I repacked my belongings, and we returned to California. We stayed with a friend in Berkeley, and I tried to figure out what I was supposed to do next. The idea of graduate school dominated my thoughts, but I was very confused. I had no idea what it was that I was supposed to study. I knew that it was going to have to be something mental—as compared with art—because by now my passion was for all subjects metaphysical. I began to search for a graduate program that seemed right. Was it parapsychology? No. I didn't really care that much about ghostly appearances. Was it psychology? That was close, but psychology didn't include the mysterious, esoteric side of life that intrigued me. Finally, I found a transpersonal program at Sonoma State University in northern California. Miraculously, I was accepted into the program the week before the semester started. My daughter had gone to live with her father that year, so my son and I moved up to an awful student apartment near the campus. I soon found, however, that no matter how hard I tried, I could not find a part-time job. This lack of flow around how to support myself loomed larger each day. I felt as if I were swimming upstream. Even though the synchronicity of securing a position in the graduate program seemed to indicate this was the right place to be, I was forced to give up and return to Oakland. Once there, I synchronistically met two other house-seekers, and we immediately found a beautiful, large house near Lake Merritt in Oakland. The landlords had turned down several offers to rent this place at a higher rent than the asking price, but had given it to us as soon as we met them. Within a week, I found a boring receptionist job to pay the rent. Later I would realize that the obstacles I had faced in Sonoma were evidence that the universe was rearranging the furniture in my life, but I had no inkling of that at the time.

A few months went by. I worked at my job, which I didn't like at all, studied numerology, and continued to do a few charts. I did a little sewing on the side to increase my income. One day, out of the blue, I received a call from my old friend Zenobia Barlow, who was by now living in Petaluma, California. Zenobia and I had been out of contact for over a year when she was traveling around the world with her new husband. She told me over the phone, "I found a very interesting psychology program up here at Sonoma State. It's called archetypal psychology. I want to take this program, and I think you should go, too. Let's do this program together!" I explained that I had already made an attempt to go to school there in the other program, but she remained adamant. The program was new — a type of depth psychology, based on the work of Swiss psychologist Carl Jung. It turned out to be exactly what I had been seeking, with its emphasis on symbolism and core, collective forces within the human psyche. The time had come to put in the next piece of my puzzle.

During the next two years, everything I needed fell into place for me — a perfect house, and a variety of part-time jobs. I did whatever it took to keep myself and my family fed while I went to school. Our professor was especially drawn to the work of Jungian psychologist and author James Hillman, whose book *Revisioning Psychology* had recently been published.

To make a living, I took a variety of odd jobs. I cleaned houses, baby-sat, or did temporary office work. For a while, I cooked meals for my friends Eleanor and Francis Coppola at their home in the Napa Valley. I had met both Zenobia and Eleanor years before in San Francisco, when we had formed one of the newly emerging "women's groups." At the time, Eleanor's husband, Francis, was making the movie *The Godfather*. She and I and Zenobia had continued our friendship as, oddly enough, we had all moved to the country north of San Francisco.

During this period, I oscillated between the intense scrutiny of psychological process and the minutiae of household tasks in my "day" jobs. The sheer boredom of the mundane tasks forced me to turn my attention inward. In quiet afternoons dusting a client's collection of precious glass objects or cleaning toilets, I had time to think. There was a richness to this time because of the pace and variety of outer tasks, and the depth of the inner work that I was doing. With what I was learning in my studies, and the unexpected encounters with people from all streams of life, I practiced staying in the moment. I enjoyed spending a little time with some of the older people I worked for who were homebound. For example, with one family I took care of their two children and their grandmother, Connie, who was in the beginning stages of Alzheimer's disease. Sometimes I would write down the things Connie said because they were full of poetry. Another woman, an invalid for whom I cleaned, regaled me with fascinating stories of her early life in many exotic locations. I became friends with a ninety-year-old man, Mr. Wright, and took him out for steak and martinis one evening.

I kept a diary, and took to writing bare, haiku poetry. My intellectual life during those years was a patchwork of vivid psychological ideas; it included my intense study of Jung, Hillman, and other Jungian writers, as well as books on the symbolism of tarot, dream analysis, and numbers. At the same time, I was also a mom, bringing up two bright and active teenagers, all the while continuing my painting, and trying to find some time for a social life. I didn't have time to think about my life purpose, because I was living so intensely.

As I paid attention to symbols and dreams, and became aware of how every day synchronicity was leading me down my life path, my inner world exploded. As I prepared to select a subject for my master's thesis, I discovered that I could identify four major forces working within me that seemed to be running my life. Therefore, I began to track these subpersonalities through dreams, intuitions, passions, and practical events, and eventually wrote my master's thesis on these four archetypal voices that I felt were living inside me and driving me with their own specific agendas. The four interior personalities I found were: *the Director, the Odalisque, Little Carol,* and the dominant one — *the Mother Juggler.* My life purpose seemed to be in the hands of these four subpersonalities. The Director, a clear, objective masculine voice — my *animus* — kept me focused on finishing my projects and heading into new territory. He frequently showed up as a major dominant male in my dreams. In guided visualizations, he was the voice of assertiveness and dynamic risk-taking. The Odalisque, clearly my *anima,* or inner feminine voice, and often traditionally represented in art as a reclining nude temptress, was easy to recognize throughout my life. Languid, earthy, sensual, and dramatic, the Odalisque conjured up my passion for painting, my relationships with men, and my intrigue with the exotic and metaphysical. It was she who loved color, romance, candlelight, and fantasy. Little Carol was the inner child who, despite her fears and insecurities, was a plucky and bright little thing. She came to me in memories and old photographs, and reminded me of the fun we had planned to have once I became an adult. In my mind, I saw her poised with a slight scowl into the sun and her hand on her hip in the same stance my beloved grandmother often took; she waited impatiently for our next adventure together. Last, the Mother Juggler was the one who actually ran my whole show. Driven, practical, and organized, she got the jobs, cooked the food, drove the car, and handled things in a timely fashion.

In 1976, I completed my master's degree and thought, "Well, now I have two useless degrees—art history and archetypal psychology." Obviously, I could not see any way to put this newfound knowledge to work in the "real world." I had perfunctorily tried to continue my education by getting a license in marriage and family counseling, but absolutely nothing flowed when I tried to begin that process. I also did not feel a passion to be a therapist.

The moment that I mentioned at the beginning of this story, the moment when I *snapped*, however, did not happen in the midst of all this chaos, but was to come about seventeen years after these struggles, these identity crises, and all the patience-developing episodes of creativity and family life. There was, of course, a prelude to it.

In the years between 1976 and 1993, my life centered around my children, producing art, studying metaphysics, and doing intuitive counseling. The stacks of books next to my bed continued to topple and spread out on the floor. During the day, I would sometimes work on a client's numerology chart in spare moments at the office (keeping the chart under the desk blotter). I continued to take in housemates to help with the rent. My favorite and most illustrious housemate was Anne Lamott, the novelist. She stayed for a year while working on her second book, *Rosie*. Many times I would be upstairs painting in my bedroom studio, and Annie would be hammering away on her old typewriter on our screened front porch overlooking a rock quarry. The quarry was an apt metaphor as we both chiseled away at the boulders of our creativity.

A major turning point in my career took place unobtrusively one beautiful summer afternoon, as I was sitting beneath the oak trees in my little numerology booth at the Renaissance Faire (produced each year in northern California by the Living History Center, a lively collection of artists, actors, musicians, dancers, food vendors, and seers). A man strolled by, and my sign caught his eye. He paused a moment before saying, "Numerology could be put onto a computer program, you know." He offered to put me in touch with a software programmer, and disappeared from my life. The suggestion stuck, and I decided to pursue the idea. Having to write my ideas down necessitated my learning to use the computer—thank God. The data manager at the nonprofit organization I worked for began to teach me word processing after hours. Thus was born what would turn out to be, not a computer program, but my first book on numerology. I forced myself to plug away at this project with little or no encouragement from outside sources. Since I was never able to find a software publisher, I put the manuscript aside for several years.

When I was forty-one, after twelve years of being single, I married C., a wonderful, warm, and funny younger man. I was still painting, working at office jobs, and was building a substantial part-time numerology practice. Life was good. I had been looking for work in the newspaper one day, and a small ad offering a part-time position in a public relations agency leapt out at me. My subsequent meeting with Candice Fuhrman, who had put the ad in the paper, turned out to be on the same level as my destined meeting with Ruth Drayer. I did a little numerology reading for her and convinced her that our numbers would work well together! She laughed and hired me. Years later, she and I are still friends, and she is also now my literary agent, and was responsible for turning my forgotten numerology manuscript into *The Numerology Kit*, my first book.

During the six years C. and I were together, we created a blended and extended family that made me feel, much of the time, that life was really great. We had been married four years, when my daughter, Sigrid, left for college at UCLA, followed shortly by my son, Gunther. With the children gone, and C.'s work requiring him to be more and more frequently in San Francisco, I began to feel an urge to move to San Francisco. We began to talk seriously about moving.

One evening during this period, I happened to notice a small, but palpable, lump in my left breast. The next morning, I immediately called the doctor for a checkup. After examining me, he told me it was probably nothing serious, and that "we will watch it." Over the next several months, I got two other opinions from breast cancer experts, and received the same message: "Let's wait and see," and "I don't think there is anything to worry about," they said. The urge to move grew stronger. I was driven by the need to find a new home.

Almost in response to this inner urge to move, the lump grew larger. By this time, nine or ten months had passed. At last my surgeon did a biopsy in his office. Within minutes he had a diagnosis of breast cancer. We had no way of knowing at that moment that it had already spread to eight lymph nodes. My first thought was "I am not going to die of this. I am going to learn something." My second thought was to go over to the Center for Attitudinal Healing in Tiburon and get some books on cancer and what to do about it. My remedy for everything, it seems, is to get a book. Eleanor Coppola had come with me that day to keep me company. I told her the news in the waiting room.

After the diagnosis, life began to seem like a series of chunks. Over the next year, there would be the chunk of moving to San Francisco, the chunk of starting chemotherapy, the chunk of surgery, the chunk of radiation, and the chunk of divorce. From the beginning of my diagnosis, the synchronicities were amazing. I felt completely guided and supported by the universe as it worked through my family and friends. On the weekend that C. and I moved out of the house I had lived in for ten years, I started an initial dose of chemotherapy so massive that I have little memory of how we made that move except that my boss, contractor Michael Conroy, brought in his construction crew to move us out. Once in San Francisco, Zenobia's husband, O. B. Wetzell, brought in *his* construction crew to move us into the new house. On Valentine's Day, 1988, I had a modified radical mastectomy. In March, C. told me he wanted a divorce. Obviously, I was struck numb. I couldn't wrap my mind around this idea, but he was adamant about moving on. His mother had died of breast cancer when he was fifteen, and apparently he could not face the uncertain road ahead. He moved out.

I resumed chemotherapy, but was too sick to take any kind of job. Lying on the couch during the day, reading, replaying the scenes of the last few months, I had plenty of time to wonder about the deeper meaning behind these events. My spiritual work allowed me to focus on three questions: What was the message in the cancer coming at this time in my life? What constellation of attitudes, expectations, karma, unconscious choices, and physical, mental and emotional toxicities had created this glitch in my system? And what was I going to do about my future?

Within a month or so of C.'s moving out, one of my closest friends, Kathryn, moved in to share the house with me to help pay the rent. Kathryn was enormously helpful in resolving some serious money issues, and keeping up my spirits. In addition, she took it upon herself to keep me from looking at the classifieds to find a new job! "Carol," she would say over our morning cup of tea, "you have a special talent. People love getting readings from you. You cannot go back to a regular job. You'll find a way." Or some variation on that theme. We got so we could laugh about it. My sneaking a look at the classifieds became like "having a slip," a term we borrowed from Alcoholics Anonymous, because looking for another office job was my old pattern of settling for something out of fear. We both knew it was time for me to create a full-time counseling practice.

That summer, my first book, *The Numerology Kit*, came out. I gave a talk at a bookstore with my head wrapped in a scarf because I was still bald from my treatments. Following the publication of the book, I knew the time had come to create a full-time counseling practice. I knew in my heart that my years of "making do" by taking administrative jobs was over. I believe the cancer had come to awaken me to my spiritual path, and to force me to realize the old ways were no longer working.

I set to work to write a brochure, and printed new business cards. I asked clients for referrals. People called for appointments. It seemed that the universe was supporting my new determination to succeed at what I loved to do—talk to people about their lives, and use my intuitive gifts!

I began to look for places to speak to promote my counseling business, and joined a few networking organizations. For example, I'll never forget the first time I went to a meeting of an organization for professional saleswomen. I walked into the banquet room knowing no one, and tried to work up the courage to begin introducing myself to people. I was desperately shy. Everyone seemed so polished and professional. All I saw were well-dressed successful women with long, manicured fingernails, who all seemed to be full of energy for what they were doing. When someone asked me what I did, I answered in a soft little voice, "I'm a numerologist"—such a tiny little whisper that they usually misheard me and thought I had said I was a neurologist! I felt completely intimidated because I saw myself as an outsider, practicing an uncommon vocation in a mainstream world. Part of what kept me going through this initial phase of "coming out" was knowing that the cancer had been a wake-up call urging me to stay focused on what I had come here to do. I knew that when I worked with people, something shifted for them and they went away with more faith in themselves and a belief that what they had to offer was important.

I gave them what I could not always give myself. Later, after reading *The Celestine Prophecy* and reflecting on its insights about the control dramas, I realized how much of my life had been dominated by the aloof control drama—while I timidly waited to be discovered!

Frankly, I persevered at building a practice because I had no other choice. In a grand attempt to expand my contacts, I became a member of the San Francisco Chamber of Commerce. That is where I met Leyla Bentley, whose own adventure we shall hear in Chapter 6. Because of Leyla's own interest in numerology and her genuine interest in other people's success, she made me feel completely welcome. I joined the hearty ranks of entrepreneurs and up-and-coming retailers and cellular phone salespeople. In my desire to fit in, I sometimes wished that *I* was selling cellular phones. Numerology was not very well known in those days—not as well known as astrology. I found myself explaining over and over again to people that numerology was an ancient system of character analysis that spoke to one's purpose and lessons in life. To someone whose worldview relied on scientific "proof" or strictly fundamental religious precepts, numerology was often labeled as New Age flakiness or perhaps "the work of the devil."

Small successes beckoned me forward on this path that I had chosen, although, to be honest, it felt more like it had chosen me. My innate attraction to metaphysics was stronger than my desire to fit in, but just barely. I really struggled. Sometimes I whined to myself, asking rhetorically, "Just because I am interested in something, does that mean I have to make a living at it?" And for that matter, I wondered, what about my art? I had thought art was my life purpose, but as much as I loved doing it, it didn't give me the same kind of fulfillment as the counseling did. I found that I needed the human flow of energy that was created in a counseling session, even though I also loved sitting by myself for hours and painting little squares of color.

I continued painting because I loved to do it. Every now and then—miraculously—just when I needed it most, a painting would sell.

This time of stepping forward and claiming my identity was a critical crossroads where my inborn purpose relentlessly took charge, with little regard for my health, security, safety, caution, timidity, or care about what "they" think. My inherent purpose was going to have its way or else. Like a hungry tiger, my inner drive to know about the mystery of life continued to create some truly amazing encounters with teachers that gave me exactly the pieces I needed for the next step in counseling and teaching. I began to look forward to what would happen next, and gradually the tension lessened, and I stopped waiting for the other shoe to drop. It seemed like all the shoes had already dropped anyway with the divorce, the cancer, the kids off to college, the financial difficulties, and the exigencies of being in business for myself. I literally began to breathe again.

As my purpose grew more clear, I would get frail little intuitions in the middle of the night about new ideas and exercises for workshops. Inch by inch it came into my awareness to offer ongoing classes on life purpose. I started to envision a curriculum for these classes during the dark hours of the morning. I consulted the tarot and the I Ching and listened to the incredible wisdom that seemed to come just when I needed support.

Things kept happening to take me to the next step, and the next. My job seemed to be to listen to these intuitions that flooded through me in the dark, to follow through on the ideas, to keep listening, to keep putting one foot in front of the other and trust that I was creating a livelihood that would sustain me. And get well—on all levels.

During this time, both my parents died within a year of one another. Perhaps I was feeling a bit numb by this time, but their deaths seemed to clear a pathway. Even though our relationship had been close, I felt released from the ties to the old life, and having to reconcile our widely diverging values. Hardworking, practical, fun-loving, and successful, they had also been politically and culturally conservative, and uninterested in abstract ideas, philosophy, or spirituality. I think my mother grokked me the best when she said, after hearing of one of my adventures, "Carol, you are better than TV!" Their influence gave me an ability to laugh at myself, an early and deep contact with and love of nature, and a strong ability for organization and punctuality.

A few months after finishing the last of my radiation treatments, I felt it was time for me to move from San Francisco. Once again, I had no idea where to go. Not only was I uncertain where to live, but I also needed to increase my income. All of a sudden, the gains of the last two years seemed ephemeral. Had I gained this foothold only to lose it? It turned out that Necessity was going to prod me to take the next step on my path.

Similar to the intuition I had to go to graduate school, I awoke one day with the clear thought: "Maybe I could make some money helping someone to write a book." I have no idea why this thought came to me, or how I thought I could do this since I had virtually no experience. Nevertheless, I called my friend Candice, since she was the only person I knew who was connected to books and writing, and told her, "If you hear of anyone who needs help writing, let me know." *Before the end of that day,* she called me back. She had "just happened" to hear about a doctor who was looking for a ghostwriter. I was amazed at the speed by which my intention had been answered. As it happened, he shared many of my own metaphysical interests. Even though this was a completely new challenge, I knew without doubt that this writing project was the next step for me. Incidentally, he never once asked me for a resume, nor did he request any samples of my writing.

In the months that followed, I successfully completed his book while continuing my counseling practice. Amazingly, another opportunity to organize and cowrite a book—this time on financial management—came my way. It was during this period that temptation knocked once again. Or had it ever ceased?

With the best of intentions, I decided to go into partnership with the author of the second book. I highly respected and resonated with her work. Charismatic and strong, she had developed an excellent process for working with people on their most problematic area—money. I began to do the work myself on my own finances, which had been in disarray since my divorce. I found it very healing and empowering.

I loved the idea of working with an ally, a partner. I'd have support in building a new business. I wouldn't be alone. I could help people in a very tangible way. I began to see this path as the answer to my feelings of isolation and struggle. I knew it would be a big commitment, and that I would only be able to schedule my own numerology clients after business hours. I never considered that I would actually stop doing intuitive readings. Interestingly, I fell right back into my old pattern of half commitment, figuring I could do both types of counseling. I began to talk myself into this new career. It seemed to have so much promise. I trusted that this new business was going to be successful, and I felt sure that I had what it took to do the work. The only problem was that this type of work was in my own shadow area — that is, the area in which I had the least strength. The language of numbers, so familiar to me as qualities and spiritual descriptions, was like a dense fog of terror when it came to talking about investments, interest rates, checkbook balances, and periodic payments. Some days, I was so panicked about how to handle a difficult case, it was like those old dreams of standing naked in front of your high school locker with your clothes inside, not being able to remember the combination.

I was out of my element. Completely. After a few months, my colleague picked up on my distress, of course; and yet I struggled to put a good face on it. I tried to rationalize my sense of being out of control. I argued that I needed more training (I did). I discussed my cases with her. I took copious notes. I continued to feel overwhelmed, and yet I had invested so much of my heart, time, money, and energy into the decision to work at this business, I couldn't imagine quitting. I felt I would be lost, as if this was my last chance to make it in the world. I was determined to succeed in spite of my feelings of inadequacy, which were not diminishing with time, but growing worse.

Suddenly, I became aware of how I had slipped into classic codependency, people-pleasing, denial, and addiction to control. I was *willing* myself to overcome my entire nature and deny my own natural gifts and talents in favor of something that intellectually seemed to be more desirable and "real." One night, driving home in the rain, tears streamed down my face, and I literally didn't care if I lived or died.

It was the next day that I finally snapped.

I stood in the middle of my living room and screamed at the universe, "I am an artist. I am a writer, and I am a numerologist! That's who I am, God. If I can't make it as that, then I don't know what else to do. You're going to have to help me out because this is who I am and this is what I do." I said it a couple of times really loud so that She would be sure to hear me. I stamped my foot for emphasis. I had really had it. I was absolutely up against the wall of my own self, face-to-face with my will. I was trying to be something I wasn't, and it wasn't working.

The next day, I had a meeting with my colleague and told her I was quitting. That came as no surprise to her because she had finally realized the kind of agony I was in. And what she didn't know, I told her. By the time we parted, we had managed to regain our sense of humor about the whole ludicrous thing. We hugged and cried, and shook our heads slowly like people who have suddenly seen some kind of truth and wondered why it took them so long to recognize the obvious—like people who are exhausted from a long hike over unexpectedly rough terrain and are ready to head home.

That next week, the universe responded to my declaration with a flood of abundance. My phone started ringing. Clients I hadn't heard from in months or years called for an update reading. New clients called who were referrals from old clients. I was asked to give a presentation somewhere. Without any new advertising or effort on my part, I made more than twice my usual income that month from my counseling practice. I had turned a corner. I had got myself back again.

What the heck was going on? I now see that this was only the beginning.

Two months after I made my "declaration" to the universe, I was invited to Mexico and managed to meet some wonderful people who helped me broaden my work to people there. During the first week after returning from Mexico, in August of 1993, two different friends suggested that I read a new book, *The Celestine Prophecy*, by James Redfield. Over the years, I have learned to listen when people tell me things, so I went out and bought the book. At this time, his self-published book had been out only a few months, and was already being passed furiously from hand to hand, without publicity of any kind. There was no way to know, at that moment, how popular this book was to become.

Like almost everybody else, I was immediately swept up in the adventure, and resonated with the concepts. I, too, underlined the principles, and began to think about my own life in terms of this philosophy. The book describes the journey of an unnamed character who is mysteriously led to Peru in search of an ancient manuscript. One by one, he discovers the insights of the manuscript, which describes the transformation of consciousness that has been taking place in the late twentieth century. It talks about how more and more people are realizing that they are part of a larger world vision. Although written as a fable, the book draws upon universal principles and perennial wisdom, and brilliantly puts into sequence many of the truths that we have instinctively noticed in our own lives. The book tells us that each of us is born with an *inherent* purpose, which can be discovered by watching where synchronicities lead us. Our purpose can be seen in (1) our natural inclinations; (2) our childhood dreams and goals; (3) continual intuitions; and (4) our nighttime dreams that guide us. The book asks us to notice how we gain or lose energy around other people, and to notice any habitual behavior that we fall into in order to maintain a feeling of control in our interactions. It also reminds us that our soul had certain intentions for this lifetime. In order to fulfill those intentions, we selected the parents and the early circumstances that would help us develop along certain lines. By looking at our parents and seeing the paths they had been on, we might better understand that we were the *product* of those two streams of experience, which gave us a unique perspective that would continue to be developed by our own choices and actions. It predicted that if we lived by these new insights, our interpersonal relationships would change and we would begin to live more authentic lives in alignment with what we had come here to do. If each of us was doing his or her purpose, the whole culture would shift and we would make more inspired decisions for living harmoniously in balance with the earth. It was a big vision.

Apparently, these ideas made sense to a lot of people. *The Celestine Prophecy* turned out to be the top-selling book in the *entire world* for the years 1995 and 1996. My own belief is that the book was a trigger. The time had come for this material to be widely known, and those of us interested in working to further the spiritual path woke up to the call of the book. I also believe that we—all people who resonate with this new spirituality—form a kind of soul group or brother/sisterhood. I believe we are beginning to meet the members of our soul group in order to do work together.

But in 1993, all I knew was that I, too, was responding to this material, and wanted to try it out in my own work. I decided to write a simple questionnaire to use with my clients, reviewing the lessons learned from having their particular parents,. The idea was to find out the characteristics of the parents one had, and to look for the *deeper purpose* in why *those* people were chosen by us to be our parents (or caretakers). Why was it necessary to have that particular parent, and what clues about one's life purpose might be afforded from examining the lives of one's early caretakers? Another crucial insight was to look at ways that we try to get energy from other people. I found, for example, that my tendency to be aloof and isolated had created many of my painful experiences and faulty thinking. It explained so much.

I found that by asking my clients a few questions about the lives of their parents, we quickly gained insights about their own life purpose, especially in relationship to the blueprint for their lives in their numerology charts.

Perhaps two or three weeks passed after I had started experimenting with the nine *Celestine* insights. One day, Candice called. We chatted casually about mundane things for a while. After about thirty minutes, just about the time when I was thinking I should hang up and get back to work, I had a fleeting thought: "Tell her about the book." I said, "I've just read a new book, and it has really changed my practice." I have no idea why I thought to say this as it wasn't relevant to anything in our prior conversation. Taking a cue from *her* intuition, she asked me if the author was self-published, and I said, yes, he was. She remarked that she might call the author—James Redfield—to see if he was interested in having an agent. I was surprised. I would not have thought of calling him myself, but I gave her the number from the back of the book.

Miraculously—because he is a very private person—she reached James after persistent calling. She congratulated him on the success of his book. Interestingly, even though he declined her offer of representation, something made her persist. Coming up with an idea on the spot, she mentioned that people might like to have a guidebook to work with the ideas in the novel. True to form, James said, seeing perhaps the synchronicity of her call, "Well, maybe that is why you are calling. A guidebook might be a good idea, but I don't have time to write it." Shortly thereafter, she was back on the phone to me, retelling the story. At first I didn't understand the implications of what she was telling me. Then she suggested that I write a proposal for a guidebook on how to apply the insights in everyday life—something that would be practical and help people use the insights for their own growth. Needless to say, I was taken aback (becoming aloof again!), but at the same time, I was excited by the prospect of such a project.

As I followed up on her suggestion to write the proposal in the days to come, I began to get a glimmer of the road I had been on. I almost felt I could physically turn around and see my past journey in a new light. I began to see that all the work I had done with writing, with creating my life purpose groups, designing exercises, and learning to organize ideas and explain concepts had helped develop the skills I needed to respond to this incredible new challenge.

Four months later, James and Salle Redfield met with Candice and myself to discuss writing the book together. He agreed to work with me, and we worked closely together on the phone for the next four months. It has been a pleasure to collaborate with James, and I feel we were both guided in our work in getting out the first book, *The Celestine Prophecy: An Experiential Guide*, in a relatively short period of time. Later, following the publication of his sequel, *The Tenth Insight: Holding the Vision*, James asked me to coauthor *The Tenth Insight: Holding the Vision: An Experiential Guide*.

Since 1994, I have traveled nationally and internationally, applying the insights of the *Celestine* material to everyday life and life purpose. I have heard countless fascinating stories of synchronicity and the amazing things that have come from following one's intuition—and uncommon sense. I am convinced more than ever that each of us must be alert for the tiny intuitions and ideas that show us where we need to pay attention, and what we need to develop. Even when we feel blocked and stagnant—as I have certainly been many times—I believe that we are simply at one particular *stage* of the unfolding life purpose that we came to fulfill.

Part of our process together in this book will be to keep an eye out for the patterns that our purpose has been weaving, and for the signals of the life to come. I absolutely believe that each of us is capable of living a meaningful and fulfilling life if we are willing to put the work into it. Sometimes it will even be and feel effortless.

No matter what situation you are in right now, there is a purpose to that situation, and I believe that you are not off the mark. You may not want to stay in a particular situation for long, but a meaningful purpose has brought you to this place. By working with the specific conditions in front of you, you will begin to discover things about yourself that will give you clues to the next step. Your job will be to look, listen, feel, choose, and act.

I do think there are inklings about what works for us. Not what works for our mother. Not what works for our husband, our neighbor, our boss, or our friends. Since I have been tracking these events in my own life, and cross-referencing them to metaphysical laws, I have found that these universal truths do help us in our search for ourselves. These same perennial *forces* have sustained bewildered human beings for thousands of years. The wonderful thing is that if we do *our* part in becoming ourselves, our human part, the grander scale gets accomplished, too. Welcome.

Let's begin.

CHAPTER 2

You Are a Self-Organizing System

⌒∞⌒

*There is no type of a priori intervention that can transform the system
or turn it masterfully in a desired direction. The system is spinning
itself into existence. It creates itself, including its future direction and
capabilities, by exercising its freedom to choose what to notice. It is
not volume or quantity that stirs any system. It is interest and meaning. If the system decides that something is meaningful, it absorbs
this information into itself.*

MARGARET J. WHEATLEY AND MYRON KELLNER-ROGERS[1]

THE CALL

"I want to know what my life purpose is." "I'm so confused, I know
there is something that I'm supposed to be doing, but I don't know
what it is." "If only I could get some clarity, then I could take action."

These comments or some variation of them have been the most
important concerns of clients in my practice during the past twenty-
two years. I recently heard these statements from a seventeen-year-old
boy who was talking about life to his girlfriend. It was ten-thirty at
night and the two of them were standing in the parking lot behind
the bookstore where I had just finished giving a lecture. "I'm so confused," he said, seizing the opportunity as I walked back to my car
to express something he hadn't been able to say in front of the other
people in the group. "I'm reading Meher Baba and Rilke, and looking
into Sufism. I don't know if I should be writing, or pursuing my
music, or even staying in school. But I know I want to find my direction and get started on it." His breathless waterfall of heartfelt
desire both touched and overwhelmed me as I knew how important
and how monumental this life question was for him.

Similarly, an exquisitely educated, and enormously gifted eighty-six-year-old woman said to me when inquiring about a life reading, "I want to know what my true career is. I know I have all these gifts — people are always telling me I should write my life story or teach young people — but I don't know which way to go." The strength of her determination to find her path at such an advanced level of experience in life was magnificent to me.

I have also heard the question from a fifty-six-year-old woman who had just been promoted to the corner office of a utility company. She now had every benefit and status symbol, and had come to talk about what her true purpose in life was, and where she could find something truly meaningful at this stage of life. I've heard the question from hundreds of people who are in jobs they don't like because the jobs don't align with their values. Or from people in careers they fought hard to attain, but now want to leave. Or from people who think they might have been meant for the monastery, but are instead driving seniors for a living, or moving furniture, or running a business. I've heard the question from people who have five-dollar-an-hour jobs, terribly difficult and draining jobs — and no jobs at all.

YOUR PURPOSE IS ALREADY IN PROGRESS

A Metaview

Have you had the experience of working around the house and going into another room, only to realize that you had forgotten what you were going to do?

That is what happens to us when we are born.

It is a necessary condition that we are born with no conscious memory of what we set out to do. Why? If it's true that we do live many lifetimes, then each life has its own purpose and set of experiences. Some of those experiences are left unresolved. This is what the Eastern traditions call karma. Karma, obviously, is a multidimensional complex of forces beyond any simple explanation. Karma is action. An action has consequences. Our identity comes from past actions, which create memories. Those memories create desires, which give rise to new choices and new actions. Let's say, as an example, that in one life you were a talented musician who died at age eighteen in a drunken brawl over a woman. You never got the chance to develop your talent. Your soul really wanted to experience the ecstasies of playing music, but was unfulfilled. Not to mention that you died full of rage and jealousy. That unresolved energy pattern still exists at the energetic level of your being, when you exist without a physical body in between earthly lives. This unfinished business or karma must be completed in another life. Both physics and metaphysics recognize that matter and energy continually transform, but are neither created nor lost.

> "In the lives of many people it is possible to find a unifying purpose that justifies the things they do day in, day out—a goal that like a magnetic field attracts their psychic energy, a goal upon which all lesser goals depend. . . . Without such a purpose, even the best-ordered consciousness lacks meaning."
> Mihaly Csikszentmihalyi[2]

Your soul, selecting a purpose for your life, may choose to postpone working on this karma or may choose this lifetime to work through it. Therefore, we cannot possibly enter a new lifetime burdened by all the memories and feelings of our past actions — some of which might have been pretty grim. Who wants to start out with all that rage? Not consciously, of course. However, we may very well select those same souls (our lover, our foe) to work with again — perhaps this time as a parent!

To grow in consciousness is to become more aware of the consequences of your actions. As you fulfill desires, you find that you seek an ever-greater fulfillment — which becomes the desire for union with All-That-Is, or God. In the experience of unity with God, the personal will (the creator of karma) surrenders to the divine will. We are then open to being of service, using our individuality in the service of something greater than our own desires. Our desire, in fact, responds to a higher source. At this level, we are, without striving to be, not attached to any specific outcome, because we trust that there will always be something to be learned. In a state of surrender, we move into direct relationship with God, being open to Her in all Her manifestations — love, joy, service, pain, or suffering. Our individual proclivities easily find work in the archetypal paths of mother, father, teacher, healer, artist, leader, peacemaker, provider, and prophet. At the level of synchronistic flow, we enter our dharma, or path of service. We live in integrity and we are guided by our values.

In looking at life with this metaview — the bigger spiritual picture — it is very important to look with nonjudgmental eyes. First, none of us chose to live a miserable life. Second, we cannot judge the value of a life based only on societal values and external appearances. One soul may be rejoicing in the experiences lived as a homeless person, and another person's purpose may be achieved in helping them. We can only grow in consciousness as long as we can maintain the ability to see beyond our conditioned judgments. We cannot get caught up in labels, for example believing that a life lived as an educated, wealthy person is of more value than one lived in dire circumstances. Even though someone's experience is painful or challenging, it is neither bad nor wrong. Each life, because it is unique, is of equal value. We all dance the dance together.

A Close-up View

If you picked up this book—curious about what it might tell you about your own life purpose—you may be feeling vaguely restless. You may be feeling that time is passing, and that you are not far enough along in something that seems "meaningful." You may be longing for work that has shape and promise, and that makes you look forward to getting up in the morning. Perhaps even more than a desire for more money or status, you have a desire to be recognized and seen. I believe that what you are feeling—that urgency for change, that confusion about what to do, that desire for "clarity"—is coming from the soul's own purpose, which *is* being fulfilled even as you read these words.

At this moment, you are in a *stage* of your developing purpose, and *you are not off track*, no matter how blocked you currently feel. Your calling has already made itself known through what *motivates* you (past and present), what *attracts* you, what you *resist*, and what *frustrates* you. Your calling may have made a brief appearance between the ages of three and eight, or revealed itself in adolescence through a sudden interest. Your calling can also be glimpsed in what you admire in others. It can be seen in those abilities you have that you don't even think are special. You are almost always working on purpose when you lose track of time.

Some part of your purpose is also being served as you deal with obstacles and problems (resolving obstacles brings you great power and knowledge of a *specific* kind—necessary for your *specific* purpose). A piece of your life purpose may be fulfilled by the knowing that results from pain, struggle, and illness. However, if your life is *only* a mountain of continual obstacles, then you are going to have to take another look at the kind of beliefs you have about life. Generally, when you are on the right path, things flow. When you are attracting nothing but obstacles, you need to stop and ask yourself, "What do I need to change in my thinking?"

Beyond any narrow category of occupation, the purpose of our life is to develop our capacity to love. Our purpose is to create life out of *who* we are and who we are becoming.

Enterpreneur, artistic person.

SEEING THE INTANGIBLE IN THE TANGIBLE

Elmer Schettler is a soybean farmer in Iowa. But Elmer has a deeper ground that he is tending. In one of our conversations, I asked him, "How do we know when we are doing our life purpose?" Always direct and to the point, Elmer replied, "Look around. Each of us is doing it. Our life purpose is a moving dynamic. I don't think it's so much that one is destined to be a writer, for example. A person might write, but that is what she does, not what she is. And what you do often changes throughout life. Just as the coat I wore as a boy no longer fits me as a man, my life's path has evolving tasks. If I'm halfway awake, I'm cognizant of what I'm supposed to be doing in *this* moment. The quality of our life always can be known from different levels. It keeps shifting and changing. Instead of saying, I'm a baker, I think you have to say, I happen to bake. Our livelihood is a way of doing our purpose.

What are you organizing around?

"By taking an observer position every now and then, by watching myself, I can stand back from the mundane, and feel or intuit a deeper purpose behind what I may be doing at any one time. And it almost becomes a short-term purpose in itself to be more mindful of what's going on. It may take awhile to see the whole, like a puzzle.

"At times, I think to myself, 'Here's how I normally react to a situation. Do I want to create something new?' I think it's important to make sure you do at least three different things a day: eat something different, take a different route to work, and stay out of the rut. As long as I'm touched by life, and responding in the moment, and I stay in tune with what's important to me—like honesty, or integrity,

RULES OF THE ROAD
FOR LIVING YOUR LIFE PURPOSE

Keep these ideas in mind when you are feeling confused or need a little support in taking new steps. To evaluate your current thinking, check the box if you can say yes to each statement. If you don't agree, you might want to write out how you feel or what your experience has been.

- ☑ I believe that my attitudes and beliefs structure how my world appears to me.

- ❑ I am absolutely clear that I want to live in the flow of my purpose.

- ❑ I can honestly admit what is working in my life and what is not.

- ❑ I believe that my intuition is guiding me to fulfill my purpose.

- ☑ I will commit to taking small steps toward those things that have heart and meaning for me.

- ❑ I can let go of struggling for power and trying to control others.

- ❑ I remember to keep things simple.

- ☑ I believe that everyone has at least one natural talent that is necessary to the working of the universal flow.

- ❑ I believe that my world can change as I change my attitudes and beliefs, and that anything is possible.

- ❑ I attract people and events at the appropriate time.

- ❑ I always have a choice.

If you can honestly check off every box, your purpose has already emerged, or is very close to being revealed to you. If there are any statements you cannot check, begin to hold these ideas in your mind, and make an intention to have these insights be made more clear by direct experience. When in doubt or under stress, review these Rules of the Road.

or keeping my word—then I feel alive in that moment. I may not know my life purpose, but as long as I feel excited and connected, I feel I'm on track."

SYNCHRONICITY, INTUITION, AND UNCOMMON SENSE

Most of us know how to get what we want. But all too often, we don't know what we want! We are taught skills such as reading a map to get from here to there. We are shown how to read, how to write, and how to add. We are instilled with the idea that life is tough and resources are few. We are advised to look out for number one and win at all costs. Millions of dollars are spent on career counseling to help us analyze ourselves and go after the hottest jobs so that we can plug in somewhere and be as productive as possible. We are taught that to get from A to C, you have to go through B. We are taught to believe that life purpose is fulfilled by the work we do. Even though people tell us that it's best to do that which we love, we don't really think that is practical in today's job market. How can I make a living doing crossword puzzles? How can I make a living surfing? How can I make a living watching the sun set? Most of the time, we let common sense make our decisions and let it go at that.

Let's be clear that there is nothing wrong with common sense or logical thinking. Normally, we pride ourselves on "being in control" and "on top of things." Again, self-discipline, accomplishment, and mastery are all worthwhile goals. We must, and do, use our heads in making good decisions that bring us into alignment with our deeper values. But this book wishes to address the other side of life. The part of life that is a mystery and a great adventure. To do that, we must use different skills and take a different approach. We must take another look.

Long-held theories about the way the world is supposed to work are changing globally in all the sciences—in physics and engineering; in biology, chemistry, physiology, genetics, bioenergetics, and the other medical sciences; and in the behavioral sciences. Books such as *Leadership and the New Science* by Margaret J. Wheatley open our eyes to the invisible organizing force beneath our physical reality. "The space that is everywhere, from atoms to the sky, is more like [an invisible medium], filled with fields that exert influence and bring matter into form."[3] Field theorists postulate an organizational field that is built up by the combined knowledge of members of a species. After a critical mass of the species has learned a new behavior or skill, the new patterns seem to exist as a structuring field, making it easier for others in that species to learn that skill. Systems analysts are now finding that rather than trying to control a system, we need to increase our intuitions about how it works so that we can interact with it more harmoniously. Depth psychologists and medical intuitives speak of the archetypal energies that exist in the collective consciousness. These core energy patterns exist cross-culturally and live through us as the stories we live individually. We are beginning to see that order is an inherent part of a system. This order (purpose) organizes our lives by processing—through our beliefs, our cultural and individual conditioning—incoming information. We are encouraged to look, not so much for the cause and effect of the old Newtonian worldview, but for an emerging purpose in any event.

Wheatley and Kellner-Rogers write, "A self-organizing world is best understood by delving into its paradoxes. Life, free to create itself as it will, moves into particular forms, into defined patterns of being. Pathways and habits develop. . . . Who we are becomes an expression of who we decided to be." And, "The world asks that we focus less on how we can coerce something to make it conform to our designs and focus more on how we can engage with one another, how we can enter into the experience and then notice what comes forth. It asks that we participate more than plan."[4]

Organization wants to happen. Order is an inherent force within you. Joseph Campbell once said that the basic theme of all myths (the archetypal stories by which we live human lives) is that there is an invisible plane supporting the visible one. This book draws your attention to that invisible plane. Trust that your invisible purpose is prompting you to give it the space, the players, and the information that it needs to bloom. The time has come to probe the mystery of life—the mystery that astonishes us or pokes fun at us in "coincidences," or synchronicities. The mystery from which our intuition draws uncommon sense.

TWO ASSUMPTIONS THAT IMMEDIATELY CONNECT US TO OUR SOUL'S PURPOSE

There Is a Purpose in Everything That Happens

> Intuition is the creative, universal intention expressing through *you*.

When you take the perspective that everything that happens—or doesn't happen—in your life is *necessary* to the fulfillment of your life purpose, you begin to become more alert and tuned in to what you may have been oblivious to before. This one assumption gives you a sense that no matter what your external world looks like, you have the ability to learn, grow, and choose the next step based on what is given.

You don't have to wait for the lightning bolt of "Now I know what my purpose is" to strike you, as long as you see each moment as a creative opportunity to be who you are, to take a stand for what you value, and to send out an intention for what you desire to create next. Looking for the purpose in everything is one internal shift of perspective that will change your entire energy field. This open attitude literally raises the vibration of your energy field, and allows more synchronicities to open new doors. *Remember, your external world is a direct representation of your internal world.*

Messages arrive constantly, but we may gloss over them as merely ordinary encounters. For example, Jean, sixty-one, had just fallen in love with a younger man after twenty-four years of being single. Before that, she had lived with someone for ten years, but they separated without marrying. While she had always dreamed of getting married, she was afraid that this love was coming too late. She was afraid that maybe she was just imagining this special attraction with a new man. One evening, she attended a meditation session where she knew no one. Another woman took a seat several chairs away from her but, at the last minute, moved over to sit next to Jean. In the course of chatting together, this woman, who looked to be in her late fifties, told Jean that she was about to be married to a man she had met last year. The woman said meeting this man was very unexpected because she had totally given up ever getting married, since she had been single for over twenty-five years. They were very much in love. This is an example of a seemingly simple, but purposeful encounter that seems to bear directly on an internal question that we are currently

[handwritten marginal notes: "Life purpose won't strike in a moment"; "This is how ur purpose of ur life to supp is be who To show you are, reconcile yourself w/t enve. (Inner peace)"]

thinking about. This type of meaningful and unexpected event is what we call synchronicity. Synchronicity, as we will see throughout this book, is the magic that moves you forward.

Anything Is Possible

This second assumption, expressed in so many ways by various spiritual teachers, was once again brought to my attention by psychotherapist Colleen McGovern as I was writing this book. Truly believing that anything is possible cuts directly to the heart of our process. When Colleen and I were discussing that belief, I turned my attention inwardly for a moment, and thought, "Do I believe that anything is possible?" I have to say that I do believe that now. I have experienced some amazing turns of events, and I *do* believe that miracles can occur. As soon as I checked this belief inside myself and thought, "Yes, anything *is* possible," I felt a subtle movement in my solar plexus that seemed like a relaxation, or like a tiny door opening. Try it for yourself.

If you can't truly say that you believe in miracles yet, that's okay. But you can begin to ask (pray) to receive divine help to resolve any situations you would like to change. Ask that you begin to attract people who have experienced unusual synchronicities or miracles to help develop your faith. You will soon be amazed at what comes your way.

WHERE YOU FIT IN THE BIGGER PICTURE

Who You Are

According to a recent study by sociologist Paul H. Ray, there is an emerging new culture in the United States whose views and attitudes are increasingly shaping the mainstream. The people who make up this new point of view are largely female — 67 percent to 33 percent male — and interested in not only environmental issues, but deeper issues of ecological sustainability. They are highly interested in personal development, they enjoy working with new ideas, they like to travel, and they value foreign cultures. They are deeply concerned about health, whether it be personal, social, or planetary. They are interested in psychology, spirituality, and humanitarian issues. They are aware of the systemic problems facing the world, and understand that each person, seed, species, community, state, nation, continent, and weather pattern is inextricably interrelated and interconnected.

Largely middle-class, members of this culture are more apt, however, to leave the societal mold and strike out on their own to explore ideas in workshops and seminars. Instead of watching TV, they read and listen to the radio. Although they may have plenty of material comforts, they are less fixated on external consumerism and more interested in developing themselves or serving others.

How do you fit into this picture? If you resonate to the ideas presented above, you are part of this new influence, and it's very possible that any questions you have about your life purpose stem from an unconscious association with this new field of collective energy. I have come to believe, after meeting people all over the country and receiving many letters from around the world, that each of us is working with a group of souls who share similar purposes.

The new worldview is emerging all over the planet, and it is emerging or surfacing within many disciplines—predominantly in the rise of subtle energy healing, body work, acupuncture, naturopathy, hypnotherapy, regression therapy, nutrition therapy, spiritual psychology, and the increasing interest in what is now called the perennial philosophy. It is emerging scientifically out of quantum physics and mind-body research in medicine. It can be seen in the growing interest in bringing spirituality into business and leadership. In all these cases, the emphasis is shifting away from our previous belief that life is a predictable event that can be controlled if only we have the right facts, the right goals, and the determination to follow through.

The new culture realizes that problems must be approached, not with piecemeal remedies and superficial Band-Aids, but by using principles that favor systems thinking, holistic planning, cooperative relationship, and win-win objectives. The new view looks for the spiritual meaning in each occurrence, valuing the diversity of opinions, histories, and cultures. The new view notices that synchronicities open doors and provide solutions of a higher quality than could have been achieved by coercion and control.

Thus, individual life purpose is inextricably woven into the purpose of the whole.

Shifting Perspectives

The second half of the twentieth century, beginning with the volatile 1960s, ushered in a new era of questions about who we are, what impact we each have on the world, and what individual responsibility really means. We began to think of the consequences of unlimited growth and expansion. The time had come for systems-field thinking. In systems thinking, we must look at how every part of a system affects every other part, and what the individual contributes to the whole. When thinking in terms of systems, we might ask such questions as "How does using pesticides in Iowa affect weather in Borneo?" "What has to happen physically, mentally, emotionally, and spiritually for healing to take place?" "How do we nurture the richness of diversity and live in harmony?" In the 1960s, different segments of our culture began to wake up to where change needed to happen — in civil rights; in our assumptions about when to wage war; and in economic theory, especially with regard to discrepancies in the management and distribution of resources.

About this same time, a new catchphrase swept through the spiritual community. *We create our own reality.* Suddenly, the word was out, and the consciousness of a major group of people shifted direction — toward an internal focus instead of an external focus. As when we turned twenty-one, we suddenly realized we were responsible for ourselves and what we were attracting.

The idea that reality is the way we view the world — and that our perception of it *is* the world — took some getting used to. Sometimes people interpreted "creating their reality" in such a way as to promote guilt. For example, "I created my cancer, so I must not be spiritual enough" or "I created being hit by a car, so I must not be thinking positively." Taking this idea literally, as if all creation was a *conscious* decision, creates unnecessary confusion.

> "Most of us put a great deal of time into work, not only because we have to work so many hours to make a living, but because work is central to the soul's *opus*. We are crafting ourselves — individuating, to use the Jungian term. Work is fundamental to the *opus* because the whole point of life is the fabrication of the soul."
>
> *Thomas Moore*[5]

We must remember that there are many complex factors in any illness, accident, misfortune, or miracle. We can never know completely why things happen to us. Sometimes a soul may be born with a deep purpose to experience something very painful or limiting that can only be learned through a traumatic event or impoverished condition. Because we are born with free will, our soul does not program us to experience an accident at the corner of Elm and Howe at 4:14 P.M. on December 15, 1997. However, part of the purpose for this lifetime might be to learn to receive love from others. It is possible that this soul will experience great spiritual growth as he or she overcomes a physical or emotional challenge. What looks like a tragedy at the human level of understanding may be a transforming event in the overall development of a soul through many lifetimes. The point here is that there is no knowing at what level an event was "created" by us. A disease may have been created at the soul level, the karmic level, or it may be that because we drank too many martinis for thirty years our liver finally caved in because it was biologically overwhelmed. Instead of dismissing starving people because they created their karmic condition, we must, at all times, practice lovingkindness and compassion and give service where we can.

However, our beliefs about the nature of life *do* create our responses to what we perceive to be the world. Our perceptions, attitudes, and beliefs *are* what we see mirrored in the external, physical world. So when we say, "I create my own reality," what we mean is that we choose to paint the world a certain way and believe that that reality is truth.

We are born to be directors of energy. We are born to create. Some things we create without much consciousness. Some things we create very intentionally. Somewhere on this spectrum of creativity— whether it is at the soul, karmic, subconscious, or conscious level— we have in our lives exactly what we want to be there *at the moment*. That does not condemn us to be there forever. It is just what we have currently created with our level of awareness, the way we have focused our intention and desire, and the specific choices and actions we have taken.

Things happen. How we deal with them is up to us. Sometimes we have lots of choices. Sometimes it looks as if we have no choice. In reality, we always make some kind of conscious or unconscious choice about how to handle an event. History is rich with stories about people who have suffered the most extreme deprivations and trauma and demonstrated both ordinary and exceptional courage, compassion, and creativity.

How Are We to Live?

At the deepest level of consciousness, our collective question is: What are we here to do? We know there is something we should be doing. What is it? How can we all help accomplish this evolutionary task?

Because we live in a world where we divide things into hot or cold, good or bad, light or dark, right or wrong, our mind naturally separates everything into either/or or black and white concepts. Interestingly, the reality of life and the underlying universal laws are usually formed from a paradox—which means both/and rather than either/or. To be on the path of your life purpose is to learn to be comfortable with paradox.

The first basic paradox of our lives is that nothing is fixed; and yet nothing is random or accidental, either. We cocreate with our spiritual source. We have free will, and yet we are not in control. The second paradox is that when we set our intention for what we desire, we achieve it usually only after we have released our need to have it. This is the paradox of *intention* (personal desire and will) and *surrender* (letting God or the universe provide what is best for our highest good). You are both a finite earthly being, and an infinite soul of great spiritual dimension. You are both/and. You are the drop of water and the wave. You direct yourself, and you are directed.

Finding Your Place in the Universal Field
of Human Consciousness

Our greatest spiritual truth is that we are one with our creator. We exist within the universal field of consciousness, and can affect that field through our intention and desire. According to quantum physics, time and space are only conceptual models we use to be able to show up for lunch on time. Any intention we have is immediately received by the universal field of energy. Pioneering physicists such as Dr. David Bohm and J. S. Bell have brought us the understanding that everything in the universe is affected by everything else. In *Synchronicity, The Inner Path of Leadership*, author Joseph Jaworski translates the technical language of physics behind these ideas: "The simplest explanation of Bell's theorem is this: Imagine two paired particles in a two-particle system. If you make them fly apart or take them apart any distance—putting one particle in New York, say, and another in San Francisco, then, if you change the spin of one of these particles, the other particle will simultaneously change its own spin."[6]

Furthermore, research into the nature of light has shown us that light is both a particle—that is, a *piece* of the whole—*and* the wave—or the whole. In the same line of thinking, then, let's imagine that each of us is both a piece of humanity, and the whole of humanity. In the systems view, each and every one of us, from bushman to ballet dancer to vice president of marketing at General Electric are all linked together in a timeless moment with no separation from time or space, dancing in one divine interplay. Therefore, what we do for ourselves we do for everyone. Jeanne Achterberg, author and professor of psychology at the Saybrook Institute in San Francisco said in an article for the *Noetic Sciences Review,* "We live in a biochemical, neurophysiological, resonant quantum soup. If this is true, the responsibility that we have for our inner life is enormous, and extends far beyond one's own personal and spiritual development. Whatever our inner experience might be in terms of love and passion, hate and greed, abundance and longing, or any other human qualities, may well not be ours alone."[7]

Our personal question about our life's purpose may very well be the tip as well as the foundation of the collective iceberg—part of the much larger question of where do we go from here? If we consider these individual longings in the light of systems thinking, perhaps we can see them, not as isolated, narcissistic musings, but as equivalent to the DNA of our soul, the generative driver of evolution itself.

So we have our dilemma: I know that I am supposed to be doing something, but I don't know what it is. Let's take the first part of that sentence: *I know that I am supposed to be doing something.* We are born knowing that we have a purpose inside us. We are born knowing that there is work to be done. If we lack spiritual awareness, or grow up with people who program us to see the world as dog-eat-dog struggle and hard work—a competitive nightmare—then our purpose seems to be to beat the system. Our only goal is to take care of number one, stay out of trouble, get ours first, and be suspicious of anything we cannot eat, sell, see, or explain.

If we step outside of our conditioned mind-set for a moment—maybe we travel abroad or read a good novel or watch a sunset or adopt a child—we begin to think that there is something more interesting we could do with our time on earth. Or we might awaken at four o'clock every morning and face our unmet needs for belonging, for recognition, for a sense of achievement, and for the respect of our family and friends. We might come face-to-face with our thirst for knowledge, our desire to do something for others, and our need to understand our place in the world before we die. We might feel the tears of longing for the absolute necessity for love, beauty, music, and the silent grace of nature.

We would not have been born if we had not had an inherent purpose for living an earthly existence. Someone in one of my workshops said—and I don't know where she got this information—that for every birth, there are ten thousand souls who were vying for that opportunity. Think about it. You were the one who made the cut!

No matter how much we may drift across the landscape of our life, no matter how much we straggle through the days, we are not born as aimless souls. Nor are we born without compasses. We are not born without names, and we are not born without coordinates.

So in the middle of the night, at stoplights, or in the endless checkout lines of stores (sometimes our only times of reflection), we wonder, "What is my life's work?" our assumption is that there is some defined, measurable, and findable title, occupation, profession, livelihood, career, calling, service, talent, or identity that is hidden just beyond our reach. Its location usually feels *external* to us, as if someone in authority will someday ordain us. We mistakenly think it is only attainable by luck or incredible, superhuman worthiness. We believe that the attainment of our purpose will make us financially secure beyond all fear, guaranteeing respect from all who cross our paths. We assume that if we're hardworking and lucky, fame will validate our struggles. The lack of attainment, on the other hand, perhaps makes us feel worthless or invisible. When we're feeling down, we build a good case that if only we had been better nurtured and our talents understood and cultivated by our selfish or controlling parents, we, too could be popular like Jerry Seinfeld, or an outstanding writer or inventor, or someone like Mother Teresa who *really* made a difference in the world.

The point is that we so often externalize "purpose," and cast it as something invisible to us and unattainable, except in some golden future when we have sudden clarity about what it is, and our grant for the Ph.D. finally arrives. Until then, we brutalize ourselves for not being further along in our lives.

Our purpose, I believe, is not a thing, place, occupation, title, or even a talent. Our purpose is to be. Our purpose is *how* we live life, not what role we live. Our purpose is found each moment as we make choices to be who we really are.

YOU

you are a self-organizing system
in an invisible field of energy
organized by your purpose and a stream of continuous
    information

information is the nutrient of a self-organizing system

you read this book to know yourself
it is by knowing yourself that your purpose is revealed

living on purpose means you are
an opening through which God flows

purpose is about developing relationships
purpose is about bringing attention and intention
into the present moment
    moving ahead with new ideas
    giving and receiving support
    volunteering
    mentoring
    listening to the imagination and intuition
    communicating
    taking action based on inner direction and
    hints from the external
    being adaptable
    taking responsibility and ending the victim stance forever
    surrendering to the divine will and working with the lessons
    developing fluidity, tolerance, compassion, and
        the ability to love

CAROL ADRIENNE

People are sometimes troubled that perhaps seeking one's life purpose is a luxury only for the well-heeled who can "afford" to choose something artful, creative, or humanitarian. Many people actively complain that poor people don't have the luxury of thinking about life purpose or living a life in accord with a higher purpose or spiritual values. An Austrian industrialist once said to me in the lobby of a grand hotel in Istanbul, following a talk I had given about the importance of holding a positive vision for the future, "There's a real world out there. There are people starving. I don't think they are going to care about finding their life purpose or thinking about contributing to a larger world plan." He continued heatedly, "Those people in there [the audience] are just going to leave this beautiful hotel and go on spending money on themselves. They are not going to change." His comments, I knew, came from his own frustration and deep caring about how to inspire people to follow the dreams they were born to fulfill. When such a question arises, we must keep in mind two things. First, on a physical level, there is a hierarchy of needs that one must fulfill before the larger, philosophical questions are ready to be addressed. Second, on a spiritual level, a soul chooses the conditions that will best nurture it in this lifetime, so a person could be living any sort of life and it could still be very much on purpose.

The despair and frustration that we feel about the world and how much we might be able to affect it for the benefit of ourselves and others is real and necessary. Our despair keeps us in touch with the depth of our purpose, and the necessity to go on even in times of utter

> "Strange as it may seem, life becomes serene and enjoyable precisely when selfish pleasure and personal success are no longer the guiding goals."
> *Mihaly Csikszentmihalyi*[8]

darkness. Paradoxically, frustration and even hopelessness take us into the void, the place where we surrender, and let something larger than ourselves enter into our lives and take us where we need to go. Even when you are most on target, life can seem overwhelming and discouraging, and you can't help but ask, "Does anybody really care about this? Is anything I'm doing making any difference at all? What's the point?" This is but one part on the spiral path of purpose. We work hard to meet our goals, and when we do—or don't—we reach a point of needing to reassess and move on, again.

The Purpose of Life

According to reports from people who have had the experience of remembering what they feel are previous lifetimes, it seems that people take on an earth life for as many reasons as there are individuals. Some of the people said they came back to help others, and to grow spiritually themselves. Some said they came to acquire new experience as a supplement to what they had already done in other lives or to correct tendencies that were ingrained over several lifetimes. Some said they came to become more social after lifetimes of relative isolation or impoverishment. Others said they came to work out personal karmic relationships.

The following ideas are some of the common threads that we find when we try to conceptualize what the purpose of our life might be.

1. The purpose of each life is to cocreate the life we are given—to direct our living energy in ways that matter to us.
2. Each of us comes to earth with an inner guidance that directs us to people, places, and events that allow us to fulfill our purpose synchronistically.
3. Our purpose is unfolding constantly, although we may not be aware of it if we are fixated on a certain goal or timing.
4. The purpose of our life usually has something to do with learning how to love more fully, more deeply, more constantly, more unconditionally.
5. The purpose of our life may be to develop a characteristic such as faith, trust, courage, or forgiveness.
6. The purpose of our life may be to aid the spiritual development of another.
7. The purpose of our life may be with another soul with whom we have unfinished business.
8. The purpose of our life is found in activities where we lose track of time.
9. The purpose of our life is found where we are moved to open our hearts to that which we had previously been closed.
10. The purpose of our life is found as we go about our daily round. It is also found in moments of transcendence such as a spiritual awakening in the forest, a near-death experience, or after any accomplishment, large or small, that connects us to something greater than ourselves.

11. Our purpose in life is to be, as fully, as present, as authentically, as we can be.

MAKE A WORKING PURPOSE STATEMENT

Okay. We've been talking about what life purpose is and is not. Now let's get serious about you. We are going to begin by making a working purpose statement. Don't panic. Let this exercise be simple and fun. Follow the steps that follow, and let your intuition prompt your answers. You can always change your statement tomorrow if you find another, better way of expressing the essence of You. This simple process is intended to be a starter kit for framing a working life-purpose plan.

Why "working"?

You are an organizing field of energy with an inherent purpose. Your purpose *is* working, but if you don't *feel* it's working, then this process will help increase your awareness of how you contribute to the world. With any increase in awareness, our lives begin to take on more meaning and movement. Use the working purpose statement on page 46.

Step One
I LOVE TO . . . Write down several activities that you <u>love</u> to do.

Look for things that are *absolutely easy* for you to do—things that you may not have received any training to do, but you are just "good at." The following suggestions are given to help you get started, but your activities might not be listed.

ACTIVITIES

I LOVE TO . . .

talk	listen	teach	write	sew	tinker
garden	repair	analyze	drive	sail	walk
run	mentor	paint	read	beautify	win
surf	collect	persuade	explore	feed	cook
record	problem-solve	negotiate	heal	advise	reveal
edit	critique	direct	produce	campaign	inspire
advocate	renovate	guide	dance	stare out the window	

WORKING PURPOSE STATEMENT

Answer the following questions as quickly as you can, without thinking too much about each one. Let the answers flow without judgment. After answering all or most of the questions, make a short, imaginative statement that seems to capture the essence of what you are all about. If your statement makes you laugh, cry, or smile, you are on the right track. When you write your statement, make sure each word is *exactly* the word you want, and if it doesn't seem quite right, keep searching for the word that lifts your spirit.

Use this as your working purpose until you find a better one!

RECOGNIZING MYSELF

When I was a child, I wanted to be ⎯⎯⎯⎯⎯⎯⎯⎯⎯⎯

When I was a child, I always loved to ⎯⎯⎯⎯⎯⎯⎯⎯

The activities I love now are (see box on page 45) ⎯⎯⎯⎯

⎯⎯⎯⎯⎯⎯⎯⎯⎯⎯⎯⎯⎯⎯⎯⎯⎯⎯⎯⎯⎯⎯

My best qualities are (see box on page 47) ⎯⎯⎯⎯⎯⎯

⎯⎯⎯⎯⎯⎯⎯⎯⎯⎯⎯⎯⎯⎯⎯⎯⎯⎯⎯⎯⎯⎯

The qualities I would like to develop and express are (see box on page 47) ⎯⎯⎯⎯⎯⎯⎯⎯⎯⎯⎯⎯⎯⎯⎯⎯⎯⎯⎯

⎯⎯⎯⎯⎯⎯⎯⎯⎯⎯⎯⎯⎯⎯⎯⎯⎯⎯⎯⎯⎯⎯

I shine when ⎯⎯⎯⎯⎯⎯⎯⎯⎯⎯⎯⎯⎯⎯⎯⎯⎯

I excel at ⎯⎯⎯⎯⎯⎯⎯⎯⎯⎯⎯⎯⎯⎯⎯⎯⎯⎯⎯

I am most myself when ⎯⎯⎯⎯⎯⎯⎯⎯⎯⎯⎯⎯⎯

What I do effortlessly is ⎯⎯⎯⎯⎯⎯⎯⎯⎯⎯⎯⎯⎯

I keep being drawn to ⎯⎯⎯⎯⎯⎯⎯⎯⎯⎯⎯⎯⎯

PUTTING IT ALL TOGETHER— MY WORKING PURPOSE STATEMENT

I seem to be "in the business" of:

Step Two
I AM . . . Write down a few top qualities that you love about yourself, or that others have seen in you.

Do not be shy or modest about seeing your best qualities. Don't be limited by this list.

I AM

humorous	enthusiastic	comforting	determined	intelligent	gentle
kind	courageous	direct	inspiring	supportive	optimistic
visionary	compassionate	flexible	entertaining	knowledgeable	practical
open	generous	strong	energetic	calm	adventurous
persuasive	patient	insightful	spontaneous	quick-thinking	original

---

Step Three
I WOULD LIKE TO . . . Write down the qualities that you would like to possess.

I WOULD LIKE TO HAVE MORE

humility	generosity	compassion	capacity to love	kindness
courage	faith	integrity	leadership	service
creativity	research	inventions	tolerance	fairness

ability to make people laugh
ability to bring peace
artistic or musical ability
capacity to heal
capacity to rise to an occasion
positive impact on the environment or human rights
ability to present complex material simply
snazzy elegance
fabulous dancing
common sense
uncommon sense

Step Four

Putting it together. Take your elements from Steps One, Two, and Three and write them together on one page.

Your goal is to combine those elements into one statement, by distilling the essence of yourself into one short, snappy, imaginative purpose statement. Take your time with how you combine your elements. *To be a truly effective working purpose, this sentence must carry an emotional charge to it that either brings tears to your eyes or makes you laugh with delight!*

Example 1

Victoria, a mother and job searcher, wrote for Step One: "*I love to beautify surroundings*—whether it is my home, someone else's home, doing beauty make-overs, or weeding out closets. I just love to do these things."

For Step Two she wrote: "I am *enthusiastic* and *determined* when I want to accomplish something. For Step Three she wrote: "I would like to be recognized for *my ability to make life a little more beautiful and worth living.*"

She combined these elements into the following purpose statement and read it aloud. "I am the Queen of Beauty and Joy." She couldn't help adding the rhyming "Oh, boy!" because her purpose statement so clearly and simply captured the essence of what she wanted to express.

Example 2

Chuck, a newspaper reporter, wrote for Step One: "*I love to sail.*" But, he asked himself: "How could that be part of my purpose in life?" For Step Two he wrote: "I am *intelligent* and *patient.* For Step Three he wrote: "I am recognized for *my ability to present complex material simply.*" When combining his elements he came up with this purpose:

"I *sail through life,* allowing the current to take me where I need to go so that I can *disseminate knowledge* to the four winds." Commenting on his purpose statement, he said, "I love the idea of sailing through life because I like to feel I'm on the move and using my instincts to set my direction!"

Example 3

Arlene, a hypnotherapist, said, "I love to *read, explore ideas, write, edit, guide, heal,* and *beautify.* I'm *visionary, creative, compassionate, insightful,* and *intelligent.* I'd like to be recognized for my *ability to help people grow.* After reflection, she suddenly wrote: "My purpose is *to know and be known.*"

Example 4

Wendy, a mother of three who is looking for a career, wrote: "I love *to talk and listen.* I am *gentle, kind,* and *comforting.* I'd like to be recognized for *my service to others.*

Unsure about her purpose, Wendy was asked, "What do you do first thing in the morning after you get the kids off to school?" "Turn on my computer and start talking on the chat lines!" She laughed without hesitation. She finally wrote: "My purpose is to turn myself on by *connecting to people.*"

Example 5

Bill, a currently unemployed software technician, wrote: "I love to *discover, construct, edit, integrate, refurbish, innovate,* and *reflect* on my discoveries. I'm *humorous, patient, insightful, generous,* and *adventurous.*" At first, he came up with: "My purpose is to *lead others* to *laugh, love,* and *live.*" He then changed it to: "My purpose is to *laugh, love,* and *live.*" And then, remembering his passion for sailing, he wrote: "My purpose is to be Bill the Pirate!"

LET YOUR PURPOSE SHOW YOU THE WAY

Be clear about your intention to express what you love to do, and to be led to ways to play the role you are uniquely equipped to do. Read your statement each morning and evening, and when you are having trouble making decisions, read your statement and let its essence trigger off within you the decision that is most in alignment with it. Finding ways to use your talents puts the adventure back into the game of life. The surest way to know that you are fulfilling your purpose is simple. Are you feeling joy? Are you feeling deep commitment? Are you being the real you? Do you enjoy an activity whether or not you get paid for it?

VISUALIZING PRACTICE

The more you can actually experience the feeling of using a talent, the more you will attract opportunities for its expression. In addition to reading your working purpose-statement each day, try this short, easy imagination practice:

Think of one thing you love and do well. Close your eyes and remember the last time you did it. Really bring that positive feeling into your body through your imagination. Do this every day for three weeks. As soon as you are able to easily reconnect to that wonderful experience, you will begin to have requests for this talent or you will receive money for it.

VISUAL REINFORCEMENT

Collect a stack of old magazines that show pictures of people doing things that resonate with your own purpose — pictures showing travel, humanitarian activities, leadership, sports, healing, interior design, fashion, spiritual or social life. Tear out pictures that represent your goals and dreams. Paste or tape those pictures to construction paper or cardboard, or use a folder or binder to keep your collection for easy perusing. Scatter pictures of yourself in among the magazine pictures to reinforce the message to your subconscious. Anytime a scene or an object or an event happens that looks like something in your binder, note it down. Take action when opportunities present themselves. Trust that your purpose is working through you. The more you become aware of the manifestation of your dreams and thoughts, the deeper is your connection to your purpose.

STRENGTHENING THE CHARACTER
REVEALS LIFE PURPOSE

Naturopathic healer Brendan Feeley of Washington, D.C., set a goal
of living an external ordinary life, but also had the desire to grow in
a spiritual direction. That desire seems to have taken him exactly
where his purpose lay. Notice how Brendan's first priority, gaining
stability in the external world, allowed him the freedom for the unfolding of his spiritual vocation.

Learning to See Yourself

"I began my full-time practice in natural medicine, homeopathy, and
Vedic astrology four years ago," Brendan told me. "However, I've
been intensely interested in these fields since the mid-1970s. I've been
able to turn my curiosity and hobby into a full-time career.

"Growing up in the west of Ireland, I always had a strong interest
in spiritual life. I rejected Catholicism at the age of sixteen because
I couldn't seem to find answers that made any sense. At the age of
eighteen, I started reading the Vedic philosophies of India.

"I was totally dedicated to meditation for the next fifteen years.
During those years, I explored a lot of healing methods, became interested in astrology, Jung, and archetypal psychology. At the same
time, I was studying to get my M.A. in engineering in Dublin. Even
though I worked in engineering, I was more interested in people, and
their psyche and soul. I really believe that the only reason I chose
engineering was to keep my feet on the ground.

"Initially, I was very confused about relationships and marriage and
just living in the world. I couldn't find any purpose in anything. After
eight years of meditating, I was even more confused about relationships. At that time, my experience of spirituality and meditation
seemed outside of the mundane life—too exalted. I gradually discovered for myself that the path in the world is the path to God. Living
an ordinary life is the path to self-discovery.

"Around 1981 to 82, I had a terrible **"We think that ordinary life**
spiritual crisis. I asked myself, from the **is not good enough for us."**
bottom of my soul, what was the pur-
pose of life? I was a pretty typical male, living the archetype of the
puer [the *puer eternus* is the mythological, forever-young Peter Pan

type], thinking I was above and beyond it all. We think that ordinary life is not good enough for us. We end up with no capacity to make commitments, no capacity for stability in relationships. Our career is only about making things happen in the world, about always looking good, or always knowing what is the latest and greatest in books, films, technology, in everything.

"Of course, we begin by living out our cultural expectations. Christianity, by its nature, has a masculine, patriarchal philosophy. The archetypal masculine spirit always wants to reach for the heights — it's a myth of ascension. I started to understand how I was living my life in unconscious response to the collective energy. It was like unraveling the impact of culture on my own psyche so that I could begin to see myself alone.

"That's when I had my breakdown. I spent a number of years feeling adrift and confused. I did not try to control this chaotic time. I allowed it to teach me, and I desired to learn whatever lessons it brought. I knew that it was my process of individuation.

"During this period of not knowing what to do, I began to see the confusion as a good thing — as positive. I began to feel more empowered by living with not knowing than by a false certainty which I had had before. I made a decision to put myself in some situation where I could cultivate stability."

"I was afraid of becoming depressed or letting my emotions get me down. I felt it didn't matter what I did, as long as I could cultivate stability. I had had too much desire for change before that and was continually dissatisfied. I felt I had to face that dissatisfaction. I took a job with a large corporation and stayed there for about nine years.

"After some years had passed, I finally felt that I had entered my path in the world. I felt I was using the world to see my own self. I was able to go *into* boredom, dissatisfaction, irritability, disappointment, and contemplate the meaning behind those states of mind. I took the position that there was value in every experience. All the complexities and relationships in my life — with my bosses and co-workers — the one purpose behind everything was for me to see myself. I got to see how I interacted, my assumptions, and my interpretations of life. As far as I was concerned, the world was God talking to me through everyday life. The world was my way of having a conversation with God in the theater of the soul."

"The ritual was very simple. I just told myself to see through my everyday experiences. Just to take a look at what's going on. There is a beautiful metaphor in a story by poet Robert Bly. The great German poet Rilke had an ambitious young student who came to him and said, 'I want to be a great poet. What do I do? What do I do?' Rilke told him, 'Go to the zoo. Keep looking at the animals until you see them.'

"So the idea is that you keep going to the zoo and you keep looking until you see. What you see is yourself—your own nonsense, your own assumptions, your own false self. The world is a mirror for that false self. As far as I'm concerned, until we see the beauty in every ordinary experience, in the ordinary gifts of life, we see nothing. The secret of life is in seeing every tiny experience as a gift. And in that gift there is beauty and there is pain. Just because there is pain doesn't mean there is any less beauty.

"My faith in life grew and grew and grew the more determined I became just to live an ordinary life. I began to think about the people in the west of Ireland where I grew up. There was something they had that I wanted to get connected to again. The people there were just ordinary men and women with no illusion or expectations about reality or culture. These people scarely had enough money to live on, but their stories and their community life were incredible. So rich!

"That life, however, isn't enough for what I need now. I think, in truth, I'd get bored there now. I think in the United States there is a passion to be philosophical. It is more of a psychological life, and it has a mythological impact. Before I was in the grip of something (the *puer*) that wanted to go higher and away from the ordinary. In Vedic astrology, there is a concept of a planet that is referred to as a *graha*. A *graha* is something that grips a human being. We know that the planets are archetypal patterns, so we are all in the grip of something, and we have to wake up and see through this.

"What I love about American culture is that there is so much interest in archetypal ideas and the life of the soul and psyche. I think there is more capacity here to move and to wonder and to change into new things.

"When I was thirteen, I had a serious liver ailment. My mother went to a local woman who had the ability to heal jaundice. She gave my mother an herb, and I was cured within a week. The doctor had told me it would take a year to get better, and he had no medication for my condition. This event left an indelible memory. From that moment on, I had an insatiable appetite to study herbs. Even in high school, I was told that I should study medicine, but it was never even a consideration. I think I instinctively knew that medicine wouldn't allow me to do what I was really interested in.

"I couldn't set a goal for my career because I didn't know what my goal was. So, instead, I set a goal to look into ordinary things with a symbolic mind so that I could see the meaning *for me* in those events. And for this work, I believed I would have to have stability. Therefore, it didn't seem to matter too much what the job was. *Once I set the goal to work on myself, my career automatically happened for me* [emphasis added]. My hobby in astrology and natural healing became my career.

"I'm amazed I've ended up doing this!" Brendan laughed. "I didn't have any goals to end up here. I only knew I wanted to work with people in some capacity, and that desire along with my interest in healing evolved into my present practice. Even while I was holding down my full-time job, I was always totally dedicated to my hobbies.

"However, just because I'm on track with my purpose in life doesn't mean that I'm ecstatic every day. I'm happy that I'm not in that addiction to an exalted state. My life is very ordinary and very satisfying. I married four years ago, and I'm now a father. I enjoy my work. But my focus is very much on strengthening my capacity for being conscious of myself in everyday life.

"It is the symbolic path. Life is a symbolic process. One thing leads to another."

Brendan's sense of fulfillment seems to have less to do with any specific career or job description, and more to do with expressing the life inside of him in each moment. We need not think we are off the track—lost in space—if we cannot call ourselves special, rich, or famous. The work we are born to do, if we are dedicated to staying "awake" during our lifetime, will be birthed through us.

Our job is to know that there is an indwelling purpose that will always look very different from what we had thought we were up to. Our purpose is in our blind spots, and our confusions, and in our pathologies. It is the force behind our passions. Our entire attracting field of purpose organizes the incoming data of our reality and allows us to make the choice that is us.

TALKING TO YOURSELF

How would you describe yourself without referring to what you do for a living?

Who has made a difference in your life? What were their most notable characteristics?

INVENTORY OF LIFE SATISFACTION
Your Life Wheel
How Well Do You Get Around?

DIRECTIONS: The eight sections in the wheel represent balance. Seeing the center of the wheel as zero and the outer edge as 10, rank your level of satisfaction with each area of your life by drawing a line, creating a new outer edge (see example). The new perimeter of the circle represents the Life Wheel. Imagine how bumpy the ride might be if this were a real wheel!

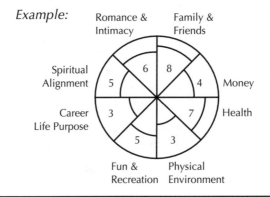

Example:

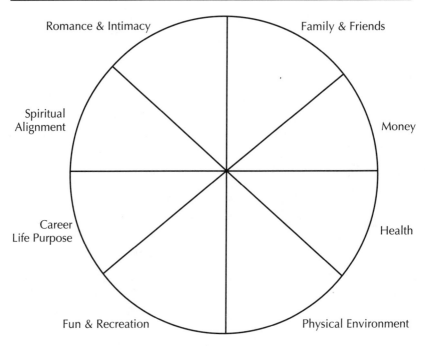

CHAPTER 3

Taking a Stand Moves You into Place

❦

A true vision takes on a life of its own.

GREG ANDERSON[1]

FLOW OR CONTROL?

As we learn to go with the flow of synchronicity and intuition, another paradox presents itself. How do we hold the idea of going with the flow and also set a course that is in alignment with our purpose?

A key element in learning to set our direction and follow what life presents is knowing and trusting ourselves. How do we do that? Usually when we are presented with a crossroads and are required to make a decision—enrolling in college or joining the Navy or choosing one job over another—we give an inordinate amount of attention to *figuring* out what is the best course of action. We tend to stay in our heads. We gather information, and get others' opinions. When we are on a spiritual path, we also learn to listen to our heart and choose to do what is heartfelt.

Making decisions intuitively requires that we become attuned to our energy body. I have found that one of the best questions to ask myself when trying to make a decision is "Does this decision make me feel more open and expanded, or does it make me feel slightly shut down or contracted?" If you are not used to tuning in to your feelings like this, it may take some practice. Begin to ask this question in ordinary situations, and start practicing becoming more aware of the minute fluctuations of your energy field.

In this chapter, we begin to explore the idea that our life purpose — and our power — is revealed in where we draw a line — where we take a stand — what we choose. Not only do we listen for the wee small voice, but we also speak our truth. That truth is the first step in our individuation process toward becoming who we were meant to be. We have to show up in life, and be on our own side. We have to be willing to say, "This is who I am," and then look for the support that follows.

In order to live your purpose, you must be able to say, "This is how I choose to live." Living purposefully comes from giving your word — to yourself — and keeping it. If you truly want to know your life's work, you will find your answer in that to which you commit your spirit. Only after you have kept your promises to yourself can you be effective in a larger sphere.

One of the students in my life purpose class, Bill Voelker, called to ask if he could meet with me individually to discuss how to get on track with his life's work. Over tea, I asked Bill what he felt was his "problem" at the moment. He promptly answered, "I feel out of balance." I asked him what being out of balance felt like. What did he feel he had too little *of*?

> "Given that we're here, given that there is this life and it is as it is—how can we live in it? How can I live in it in a way that maximizes, that fulfills the capacity for wakefulness, love, freedom, liberation of the human heart?"
> Jack Kornfield [2]

"I feel that I'm out of balance by spending too much time on things that aren't going anywhere, and almost no time on *something that feels like it's just lying there waiting for me to do* [emphasis added]. My question," said Bill, "is, 'How do I get the wheels in motion? What is the guiding force or idea that will help me keep on track toward doing my life purpose?'" He stopped for breath, and added that he had heard Lynne Twist, author and board member for the Institute of Noetic Sciences (IONS), speak at an IONS meeting, and had asked her these same questions. She had replied, "Take a stand. You cannot be everything you might be if you are always keeping your options open." Bill said that this advice really resonated with him. He realized that he needed to take a stand on something that engaged his interest one hundred percent, and go for that.

As Bill and I talked, the synergistic energy began to flow and we both began to see some main principles emerge from our own life experiences and his questions.

Most of the principles outlined below have become clear to me over the past few years. In my own life, I seem to move ahead by getting an intuition that is so clear it is almost like the readout on the front of a postage stamp machine that says, "This machine sells postage stamps. Deposit the amount shown and pull the lever under your selection."

Most of us have inner struggles about what to do, and conflicting voices that pull us back and forth among fear and confusion and clarity. Why? Because we are continually required to grow beyond the boundaries we have inherited and established. To live a fulfilling life — or just to keep from withering — we must have both stability and growth. The voice of stability wants to stay in the familiar. The voice of growth urges us to venture into the unknown. There is a timetable somewhere deep inside each one of us that says we *must* take the next step. We can either let someone else call the shots, or we can make our decisions based on who we are as individuals. So, of course, we have two voices. One voice says, like the cartoon character, Popeye, "I yam what I yam." An-

In early 1968, California Rural Legal Assistance lawyer Maurice 'Mo' Jourdane was given the challenge, 'If you really want to help the *campesino*, get rid of *el cortito*—the short-handled hoe.'

"*El cortito,* 'the short one,' was a hoe that was only twenty-four inches long, forcing the farm workers who used it to bend and stoop all day long—a position that often led to lifelong, debilitating back injuries. . . . Within weeks of experiencing firsthand the pain *el cortito* caused, he and other CRLA attorneys began a seven-year battle to outlaw the most insidious tool ever used by California agriculture.

"For Cesar Chavez, who played a pivotal role in the long drama, there were few greater moments than when *el cortito* was finally banished from California's fields in 1975. In his youth, Chavez knew the hoe well, having used it to thin countless rows of lettuce and to weed sugar-beet fields along the Sacramento River. Later he would say he never looked at a head of lettuce in a market without thinking of how laborers had suffered for it from seed to harvest."
        Susan Ferriss and
        Ricardo Sandoval[3]

other one—the combined voice of our "authorities" such as our family, our social circle, our employers—says, "Who do you think you are? Get back in line. Sit down and be quiet. Play it safe. We know best." These unquestioned beliefs will be part and parcel of how you allow new opportunities into your life. At any time, but particularly when things are not going well and you are discouraged, see if you can identify a *root belief* that you have just been thinking about without even knowing it. Throughout this book, I encourage you to stop, look, and listen to the thoughts that arise in you. *Anytime* you feel stuck, listen to what you are thinking. Those thoughts are perhaps more responsible for your outward dilemma than any external obstacle.

CHOOSING

Stefani, a single woman in her mid-thirties, recently learned what it means to take a stand. She had taken one of my Pathfinders classes two years ago, and had called to talk to me about her recent upheavals.

She had had a very responsible, and stressful, management position in a medical technology company. After working there two years and doing a good job, Stefani was called into her boss's office on a Friday afternoon. She had no idea what the conference would be about. "Without any preamble whatsoever, my boss said, 'Stefani, we are relocating you to Chicago. Your job here is being eliminated. I want you to pack your main items and be ready to leave on Monday morning.' I just stared at her in disbelief when she said, 'Chicago. Monday morning. Go.'

"I was so stunned, all I could say was 'No, I don't think I want to move to Chicago.' I faltered a bit right there, and I think she thought she had an advantage over me. That's when she said really nastily, 'Stefani, you don't understand. You don't have a choice. Your job here is being eliminated.'

"I looked at her for a moment or two, and I remembered from our old Pathfinders group that we *always* have a choice in life. I looked her in the eye, and I said, 'I *do* have a choice, Mona. I am choosing to leave this company.' She dropped her jaw—and get this—she said, 'But, Stefani, what about your credit cards? How are you going to pay your credit cards?' That's when I got up and walked out."

Over the next few weeks, I kept in touch with Stefani, and followed her progress. In the beginning, taking a stand had energized and empowered her. She wisely gave herself time to relax, walk, read, swim, and think about what kind of job she wanted next. In fact, during this period, several other employees from her old company called her for advice about their own transfers. She kept telling them that they needed to really think about giving up their homes and moving their families for a company that had so little regard for their employees' lives.

However, after about three weeks of personal renewal, Stefani hit a period of panic and self-doubt—afraid that she was going to use up all her savings and have to take any job out of desperation. She and I did some work on getting clear about her true intention—her real values about the kind of company she wanted to put her energy into. She began to focus on herself as a *resource* that was valuable to others. She carefully asked questions and screened for companies that seemed to be in alignment with her values.

She quickly found herself inundated with offers from all directions and from several different fields. "My reaction was that it was almost too much. I had people calling every day with an offer. I almost became addicted to the interview process because it always came out so positively that it made me feel good! I began to be concerned that I had taken the idea of intention too far!

"I believe that what happened was that I had turned a corner about seeing who I was and wanting the company to fit for me—not trying to be who they wanted me to be at all costs. For example, when an interviewer would ask me how I handled stress, I'd say, 'Very well. What's stressful about this job?' Or someone would ask me, 'What are your weaknesses?' and I'd say, 'I don't have any. What are the weaknesses of this company?' Maybe I was being too self-confident, but people were responding so positively to me!

"Finally, I chose a job with a medical software company. I initially liked their social responsibility, their core values, their numerous awards for excellent service. In addition, I was being heavily pressured by friends and family to go for 'this great opportunity in the Silicon Valley.' 'The Silicon Valley! You'll never starve for a job!' they all told me.

"I decided to take the position even though it meant a two-hour commute each way. It also meant leaving my health club, my walking path, and relocating my home. After two weeks of intense training in programming and software analysis, I came to the conclusion that this was not something I wanted to do. I told them that, regretfully, I would have to leave. I had to face the fact that I was going against my grain—in interest as well as lifestyle.

"I quit without knowing if any of the other jobs were still open. However, I called back my second choice, Clorox, and they took me with open arms.

> " 'The Silicon Valley! You'll never starve for a job!' they all told me."

"That night, I had a dream in which I was showing up for my first day of work after five months. I went into a small office. I was greeted by two friendly ladies. I began to work, but had the feeling I was in the wrong place. I proceeded to work for a couple of hours when I realized it was about ten A.M. Suddenly, it dawned on me, 'I'm at the wrong job!' In the confusion of all the job offers, I had shown up at the wrong place. Then I remembered that I was supposed to have gone to Clorox. I called Clorox, explained what I had done, and they said, 'Come on over. We are waiting for you.' This dream really affirmed that I had finally made the right choice—at least for now!

"I feel this job is not the end-all. It's going to facilitate a greater goal for me, which is now to go back to school. Even more important is to be able to get my health back, which I could not do if I am in the car for four hours a day."

SIX PRINCIPLES FOR ALIGNING WITH YOUR LIFE MISSION

In our discussion, Bill and I came up with the following ideas that seemed to be the core of living one's life purpose—not by controlling events and rigidly trying to implement a five-year plan—but by using intuition, taking advantage of surprising synchronicities, taking action, and using uncommon sense—that is not simply accepting other people's opinions.

Principle 1—Act on passion. Notice what your passions are. Do more of that. Take a stand for who you think you are—at least for now. If you think you have no passions, look again. What do you do that you enjoy so much you lose track of time? What kind of work would you call "too good to be true"? What do you do even if you don't get paid for it? Within these activities are the seeds of your passion.

Principle 2 — Be discerning. Let your *passion* command your spirit without harming anyone else or your reneging on responsibilities that are truly yours. Use discernment. Stop doing things where you are just putting in time.

Principle 3 — Listen. Follow through on persistent intuitive messages.

Principle 4 — Commit. Do whatever it takes to put you in motion toward doing what your intuition is telling you.

Principle 5 — Stay open. Let synchronicities confirm that you are on the right path, even if their meaning is not crystal clear.

Principle 6 — Learn trust. Trust the process.

YOUR QUESTIONS ARE IMPORTANT
TO THE WHOLE

We are at a time in history when our question about our purpose in life, far from being a luxury, may be one of the most practical and valuable questions to ask. It may, indeed, be the central individual question of this era. It may be the question that ultimately leads us to continuing the human experiment on planet Earth. Individually, we know that it's time to take a stand. Why?

Each of us is part of a larger movement. There is a reason each of us chose to be born at this time in history. When we take the view that we were born by choice — not chance — and that we have free will and can choose who we wish to be at every moment, we lift ourselves out of the tendency to see ourselves as a victim of past circumstances.

We are not alone. Studies in the new sciences show that we are linked by our intention, thoughts, desires, and actions to a world much greater than we had thought existed. We find that doors will open to us when we commit to a course of action and follow the purposeful coincidences that move us forward.

SEVEN POINTS TO REMEMBER
WHEN TAKING A STAND

1. Anything is possible. Life is much more mysterious than we used to believe in our old paradigm, in which we thought that if we did A and B we would always get C. But anything is possible. The future is not inevitably determined by our past. What you have done up till now need not limit where you are going. You were meant to be here, and your individual life purpose is part of an unfolding mystery of human evolution.

2. You cocreate your world with universal intelligence and collective wisdom. Our everyday reality is an outgrowth of our attitudes, beliefs, language patterns, choices, and actions. This means that our purpose is *within* us. We were born with an inherent driving force that wants us to succeed, wants us to fulfill the mission. We are spiritual beings temporarily living an earthly life, and we are always connected to the universal source of all life. We have guardian angels, old friends, and groups of souls in the spiritual dimension who help us remember who we are and what we came to do. The more we ask for support—and we must ask—the more amazing coincidences begin to happen. Many times we achieve our aims effortlessly by letting the universe handle the details.

3. What you experience as the world—material reality—is but one aspect of a whole system of energy fields. Our physical reality is accessible through our physical senses. More complex, and equally "real," worlds exist in other dimensions—accessible through our non-physical capacities. Grasping the idea that each of us is part of the whole energy field, and that the wisdom of this field is available to us through intuition and intention, will change our notion of who we are and how we might evolve.

4. You are always connected to this invisible world. We get glimpses of the spiritual side of our existence through dreams, intuitions, flashes of insight, miracles, divine intervention, energetic healings, or psychic revelations.

5. You can make a difference in the quality of life. As part of a unified field of energy, our individual life purpose is necessary and fits into the whole purpose.

6. Doing what matters is spirituality—integrity—in action. We automatically raise the level of spirituality on the planet when we choose to act with integrity even when the cost to ourselves may be very high, and when we choose to operate out of love rather than fear. When our goal is to give love, no matter in what situation, we are already fulfilling our life purpose.

7. *Fulfilling your life purpose contributes to the whole field, and adds your weight to the critical mass.* Whether or not you can identify your life purpose, you always have the opportunity to give and receive love, and add light to any situation.

Taking a Stand

One day I called Kwong-roshi, the abbot of Sonoma Mountain Zen Center in Santa Rosa, California. I wanted to find out how he knew, if he knew, that he was destined to be a master Zen teacher. A few years ago, he was ordained in the Soto lineage of the great teacher Shunryu Suzuki-roshi. I had met Kwong-roshi and his wife, Laura, in 1975–76 as a student of Zen practice as part of my curriculum in graduate school.

I wondered, when I left a message at the Zen center, if he would remember me. A few days later, I received his cheery hello, and an appointment for an interview. Uncharacteristically for me, I scheduled nothing else that day, knowing that I must in some way prepare to make that journey back up the mountain. Unbelievably, twenty-one years had passed since my class with him.

The day of my visit was bitter cold and gray. Along the way, I noticed that not much had changed as my car began to climb into the heart of Sonoma Mountain, not a tall mountain, a hill, really, but with a beauty all its own. I watched for omens, and saw a herd of six deer tussling in front of a huge barn. There were circling hawks, two egrets, and two swans. My favorite part of this trip is passing through the one-lane narrows of a tiny, but majestic grove of redwoods. Suddenly, one's world becomes *within* — dark, sheltered, and silent. There in the narrows, the road ahead is invisible.

I parked my car in the lot in front of the garden. Everything looked the same except that someone had placed about twenty different-sized Buddhas around the redwood tree to the right of the office. In a moment of spiritual materialism, I was tempted to go and buy three or four of them.

Taking off my shoes, I entered the small all-purpose room, where lunch was just concluding. The first person I saw was Roshi in a gray-green sweater, pants, and a thick wool scarf. Not recognizing me at first, he suddenly broke into a smile and we embraced. His wife, Laura, was seated, talking to students. I noticed that she had the short, grown-in hair of a newly ordained Zen nun.

I was asked to sit in meditation before seeing Roshi, and I entered the spacious barn-turned-zendo, remembering that my friend, O. B. Wetzell, had donated his services in remodeling this innately superb structure into an exquisite spiritual temple. Directly in front of the door was a fifteen-foot wooden statute of Buddha. I sat on the far side, selecting a round, black cushion, and faced the wall, as is the custom in sitting zazen. I sat there in my winter coat, loving the cold, loving the silence, and loving the wooden walls—the whole embracing spiritual presence.

Roshi called me into his *dokusan* room, with its rustic, subtle beauties, the altar full of simple objects—a newly carved wooden box from a German student, a photograph of Suzuki-roshi, candles, incense— perfect in every way. There was no distance between us.

> "Nothing can get done abruptly. The real changes are slow and invisible. For example, it seems to me that the attraction the West has felt toward Buddhism for some years now is tied in with two particular notions, which have nothing spectacular about them, but which are very deeply felt. The first is *ahimsa*, nonviolence, which is gradually becoming an established force. The second is the notion of *interdependence*, which has been a part of Buddhist thought from time immemorial."
> His Holiness the Dalai Lama[4]

The last time I had sat in this room, in 1976, I had met a very different man. I had just finished sitting in meditation for three days. At the end of a three-day *sesshin* (continuous practice of meditation), the student meets the master one-on-one in what is called *dokusan*. After three days of sitting with yourself, with all your demons, itches and aches, and your helpless, angry, whining, deeply sad and disillusioned self, you meet a set of fathomless eyes, and are face-to-face with the depths of your being. It's only fifteen minutes or so, but you don't leave the same person you were when you entered.

I was glad that Roshi was giving me an informal meeting. He began in midstream by telling me about the amazing experiences he had in 1993 when he and Laura were invited to go to Poland to teach Zen. "There was such a thirst there for religion and sex," he said, quietly recalling those days. "The first time we went, we had Suzuki-roshi's book translated and it sold ten thousand copies. The year after that, I couldn't go because I was sick. So I told them to go ahead and do it for me. They were afraid. There were difficulties. People were fighting about the procedures. On the first evening, the students were to do a circumambulation [walking meditation], and they had forgotten to bring flashlights. But the fireflies came instead. That was a sign to them that everything was going to be okay. This was a good thing to do, and the energy grew from that. I was happy because they were empowered. This is a happy thing for a teacher, when people do it for themselves."

I asked him if he had any sense of why he went to Poland from this quiet, out-of-the-way enclave on Sonoma Mountain.

"Oh, yes. When I was about eight or nine, I saw many war movies. The pictures of Auschwitz just stayed with me. I felt helpless, and I couldn't do anything. Even in college, I felt the emotion and tried to shut it out. As I got to be an adult, I thought I had gotten over it. A little over ten years ago, we were doing a joint *sesshin* with the Zen center in Los Angeles, and about two in the morning I got a phone call direct from Poland to my room. It was a mistake, a wrong number. But it turned out to be a sign. That same year, 1986, I was invited to go to an ecumenical session in Poland.

"It was one of the most overwhelming experiences I had ever had. It was winter and bitter cold. The Communists were very much in power. But just at a drop of a hat, four hundred people would come to hear the talk. I was invited by a Korean Zen master. We sat in the basement of a Catholic church with no heat. People would ask questions. Even seven- or eight-year-old boys would get up and ask a dharma question. It was intense. Just the effort they made to walk us to the airport or to give us what they had was so great. These were just regular people, not particularly spiritual people. There were shopkeepers and housewives—prostitutes and just all kinds of people. Here, we would never have had that kind of opportunity to meet anyone like that. They have so little material things.

"So then, they asked if I was coming over to acquire a *sangha* [spiritual community]. I said no, I didn't think so, but I still wound up with nine people. Someone said in English that most of them were alcoholics. So I worked with them. That was the beginning. People come at the drop of a hat.

"In 1995, I would have one hundred fifty *dokusans*. It was so in-

tense. All these people at breakfast, lunch, and dinner, asking questions—in Polish! In 1993, there was the first Western Buddhist
conference with the Dalai Lama in Dharamsala. He went to Poland
that year, and he remembered me. We had a wonderful meeting. We
were going to these horrible places like Auschwitz and offering incense and flowers, and giving talks.

"One outstanding part was meeting some of the last survivors of
the camps and the people from the Solidarity party. One highlight
was when we were in the furnaces of Auschwitz. It so happened that
I was the only one who had incense. I gave mine to His Holiness,
but there was no place to put the incense so it would stand up. I
said, 'I think you have to lay it down.' It was symbolic because the
people couldn't stand up there, either."

We were silent a moment. I could not imagine a more archetypal
event of a lifetime than what he had described: standing in the fur-
nace of Auschwitz handing the Dalai Lama a stick of incense.

"We went to one place where over twenty thousand people were
shot by a firing squad. It so happened that I had flowers, and I was
going to place them there, but His Holiness didn't have any flowers,
so I ended up handing them to him. That moment of handing the
flowers to His Holiness felt like an eternity. I saw the videotape later,
and that moment just looked like a normal action—handing over the
flowers—but it felt like an eternity while it was happening."

We talked more, and then I asked, What about his own journey?
What did he want to be when he was a little boy? How did he get
to where he was today? What had been drawing him to pursue his
lifework? What did he think was the purpose in the activity of being
a roshi?

"I think my early physical weakness drew me. And a kind of helplessness. Also the identity of the human spirit, and how it can go up
instead of being crushed. That's how I kept my direction. I was in a
car accident in 1957 where I almost died. I had just gotten married.
I had fallen asleep at the wheel." I thought it was interesting that he
started waking up to his life by falling asleep at the wheel—especially
since the practice of Zen is rooted in mindfulness and not staying
asleep! I said this to him, and he laughed merrily, the way only Zen
priests do, as if you have just shared something you thought was
brilliant that was obvious to them aeons ago.

"My mother always made us work. I was always working, so the accident was the first time I had been able to stop. This was the time of the beat era. There was no Zen teacher at that time. I met Suzuki-roshi because I had read about him in a Japanese-American newspaper article written by his first student, Bill McNeil. I was a mailman then, and I remember reading the article before I delivered the newspaper. Bill had asked Roshi why, if he believed in liberation, did he have a bird in a cage. Suzuki-roshi walked over to the cage, opened it, and the bird flew out the window. I was so impressed by that. I didn't go to him directly. My ego was very strong.

"I first met Suzuki-roshi," Kwong-roshi recalled, "when I went to the converted church where he practiced. He came in one door and I came in another, but I didn't bother to turn my head to see who he was. He was just walking. Just walking up to the altar, and he just moved some flowers on the altar. He didn't look up. I looked at him and thought, 'This is really square,' and I left. That was our first meeting.

"On the way home, I found a big, abandoned picture of the Buddha. It was pretty big, and I couldn't get it into my closet, so I stuck it in the hallway. I think that picture brought me back to the temple. It's in the community house now."

What hooked him enough to keep going back to meditate and practice Zen? It isn't easy to keep meditating at five in the morning and five in the evening.

"What can I say? I just knew I should do this. This is what I wanted to do. Of course, it was Suzuki-roshi. I'd never met anyone like that. He changed my life."

Did he ever think that he would become the successor to Suzuki-roshi, the ninety-first teacher in the lineage?

"No. There were no monks or nuns there then. It was just the love I had for him. It was the first time someone had really seen me, and not judged me. He saw me. Of course, I was very frightened of him, and I just wanted to be a good

> "I believe happiness and joy are the purpose of life. If we know that the future will be very dark or painful, then we lose our determination to live. Therefore, life is something based on hope. . . . An innate quality among sentient beings, particularly among human beings, is the urge or strong feeling to encounter or experience happiness and discard suffering or pain. Therefore, the whole basis of human life is the experience of different levels of happiness. Achieving or experiencing happiness is the purpose of life."
> *His Holiness the Dalai Lama*[5]

student. He saw that I was very tense, and he knew my father was a Chinese doctor, so he said, 'Do you think your father would approve of your drinking a glass of wine at night so you could relax?' Very gentle. Very gentle."

We discussed the meaning of his spiritual name Zen San Jakusho, which literally translated means Calming, Gleaming Zen Mountain. He pointed to a picture of Suzuki-roshi's father and teacher, explaining that Suzuki-roshi is the eighty-ninth master in the Soto lineage of teachings.

"When we bought this property, I noticed that the telephone poles along Sonoma Mountain Road are numbered, and number eighty-nine is exactly in front of our property. Perfect. I knew this was un-doubtedly the place. Also our nonprofit organization number is ninety-one. Because of the timing of my ordination, I am ninety-first in the lineage. Other people may not think anything of these coin-cidences, but these are signs for me."

I returned to my original question about what led him to keep going down this path.

"One thing was Laura [his wife]. We had agreed we didn't want to get stuck in the conventional world. One of us would work, and then the other would be off, and then we would switch. We were also in the McCarthy era. I was kicked out of school because I had a beard. It was very scary. After the car accident, I had gone back to my classes with a goatee, and the teachers said I couldn't do that. The beard represented something to them. On principle, I had to leave. I chose to leave even though I had wanted to be an art teacher, and I was making A's and B's and it was my last semester.

"Oddly enough," he continued, "a couple of years ago, I got on a plane late at night coming back from Paris, and they put me up in first-class because they had overbooked my seat. I happened to be seated next to an Army officer, who had been participating in a World War Two memorial ceremony in Paris. To make a long story short, it turned out that he had later become a politician, and he knew exactly how to expunge my name from the blacklist. This meant that from 1957 to 1993, this issue was finished. I was free!"

I was struck once again by how standing up for what we believe in so often puts us exactly on the path that we are meant to walk. For Roshi, standing up in art school for the right to wear a goatee caused him to leave the conditioned path that he had chosen, and to start down the unknown path to his true purpose.

Roshi smiled and began to draw the two Buddhist peace symbols, which were the original swastikas from which the angled German swastika was adapted. The Buddhists draw them straight, one with a clockwise direction and one with a counterclockwise direction. "The clockwise one means to go *with* the stream. In Zen we say, 'Go with the stream,' but sometimes you have to go *against* the stream. Then you feel very lonely, but that seems to be part of the package. Loneliness."

TALKING TO YOURSELF

What have you been passionate about in the past?
If you could have anything you wanted, what would that be?
What aspects of your life or career are you really committed to?
How could you make a difference in the quality of your life?
What would you like to change in the world?
What would it take for you to be living in total integrity?

CHAPTER 4

Anything Is Possible

∽

Again and again the sacred texts tell us that our life's purpose is to understand and develop the power of our spirit, power that is vital to our mental and physical well-being.

CAROLINE MYSS[1]

OPENING THE CHANNEL

The concept that life is a field of possibilities is so important that we will explore it more deeply in this chapter. If anything is possible, you *could* have the answers about your life that you seek by the end of this day. Similarly, if anything is possible, and *your past does not define your future,* you might dare to enlarge your dreams.

Anything is possible is an affirmation of the unlimited creative power of the universe. Belief in this idea creates an open channel, allowing whatever is yours to have to come to you. Your indwelling life purpose, beliefs, intentions, desires, and fears shape this creative potential into the people, places, ideas, things, and events that flow to you. The belief that anything is possible seems to me to be the most efficient belief working in my life.

Although many religions teach some version of the idea that God works in mysterious ways and faith can move mountains, we often limit ourselves through social conditioning and a taken-for-granted belief in a mechanistic, cause-and-effect world. In order to make a shift in the way you view reality, it is necessary to consciously intend to let yourself be guided by intelligence of a higher order than whatever limiting beliefs you have so far learned in reaction to fear. Consciously holding the belief that anything is possible is a good way to begin attracting clarity about your life purpose. As your personal experience of synchronicity grows, and as you begin to meet others of like mind, your belief that anything is possible will sink deeper and deeper into your psychic structure.

In this chapter, you will meet three people who have accomplished their dreams—so far. Each of them has stopped to ask, "What is important to me?" Each has seen an opening, an opportunity, and taken the risk of going for what they felt was waiting to be expressed from within. Colleen McGovern is a neurolinguistic practitioner (NLP) and consultant in Belvedere, California. Helen Johnson is the founder and director of the Re-Entry Program on the campus of the University of California at Berkeley. Kermit Heartsong, thirty-six, is the founder and president of Word Origin, Inc., a game company he developed in order to help families play and learn together.

These people, no different from you or me, worked on the principle that anything can happen, and that limitation exists only in the boundaries we set in our thinking. As a child, we believed that an old broomstick could be a horse or a witch's broom or the staff of a warrior. Our natural imagination is flexible, open, and endlessly creative. Our imagination is the royal road of manifestation. Over time, fear and the need to be accepted tend to put shackles on our creativity.

What feelings arise in you when you consider the statement, "Anything is possible?" If you can, take some time to write down your feelings about this principle. Write out any objections, arguments, "proofs" to the contrary. Anything is possible is another way to say, "I trust that my needs will be taken care of." "I trust that my purpose is organizing my life." If this idea is hard for you to accept, ask yourself, "Where did I get my skepticism?" "Who or what has a greater authority over me than this idea that anything is possible?"

Anything is possible recognizes the truth of limitless universal intelligence and the field of pure potentiality. We live in a world of possibilities. And we are connected to it all.

FOLLOWING UNCOMMON SENSE

Some people say that metaphysical ideas don't work if you don't believe in them. Metaphysical principles themselves teach that the basis of change must first come from a change of inner thoughts—beliefs. However, miracles are known to happen to those of little faith! I heard a story recently about a woman in her seventies who had planned to go on a trip to Europe with her grown son. They were going to visit certain sites so that the son could study and make architectural drawings. Two weeks before the trip, the mother was diagnosed with bone cancer and was told she had only a few weeks to live. Her doctors ordered her to cancel her trip.

> "Our nonphysical assistance comes from ranges of nonphysical Light that are higher in frequency than our own. The intelligences that assist and guide us . . . are of a higher rank in creation than we, and therefore, can provide us with a quality of guidance and assistance that we cannot give to each other."
>
> *Gary Zukav*[2]

Refusing to change her plans, she and her son went on the trip. They went to all the places on their itinerary, although her health steadily deteriorated and walking became increasingly difficult. One day, the two of them went to a church in Italy where the son sketched for several hours while the woman sat inside on a pew, resting comfortably while he worked. Afterward, as she walked out to the car, they realized that she was walking without a limp. Three weeks later, back home, the woman appeared to be in excellent health. Her doctors could find no sign of the cancer. It turned out that the church in which she sat was well-known for its healing energies, although she and her son had had absolutely no knowledge of this while there. Only later had they found out this information. In this case, the woman was healed with no *conscious* belief in the healing properties of the church, but she, no doubt, carried within her psyche the possibility that life was more mysterious than it might appear.

It usually pays much greater dividends to invest in faith rather than in worry.

Giving Up the Form

I had met Colleen McGovern through mutual friends. They had related several tales about her ability, while traveling abroad, to be in the right place at the right time or to meet the *only* person in town who spoke English and who could provide the exact piece of information needed at the time. More recently, she had announced her engagement to her fiancé, David, which seemed a romance fit for a novel. Wealthy, handsome, a spiritual seeker himself, and ten years younger than she, David proposed on a trip to Hawaii, arranging for Colleen's engagement ring to be delivered to her on the head of a dolphin!

Although modest and unassuming about these events, Colleen admits that through much work at self-understanding over the last several years, she has begun to see the results of identifying and rethinking limiting beliefs. With a strong spiritual base, she has come to believe that *anything* is possible.

"In the 1980s, I worked for Fortune One Hundred companies. That life was absolutely a reflection of what I believed. I was constantly on the road selling products, living out of a Day-Timer and a suitcase. I had two beliefs that kept me working hard. The first was that I *had* to do this kind of work simply because I was so good at it. On the outside, I looked like a very accomplished, organized employee, but the truth was, I was continually exhausted.

"The second belief was that 'I have to take care of myself.' This fierce belief in total self-sufficiency meant that I lived a very separate-from-God type of life. This independence belief came from early childhood, because it was often so painful to become involved with my mom. Whatever I received from her usually had such a high price. This pattern of keeping to myself was so strong, I didn't let anybody in for years."

Colleen's strengths of being organized and persevering, which rewarded her with success in the business world, also served her well as she began to pursue a spiritual path of learning about herself. For several years, she read, meditated, studied, and took a variety of classes, which opened her to universal truths and principles. Her biggest breakthrough, she said, was the realization that her internal perceptions about what was or was not possible absolutely defined or limited what she could attract in the external world.

Eventually, she changed careers and started her consulting practice. Instead of re-creating a workaholic schedule with the new career, she decided (set an intention) she wanted to have time to explore other interests such as gardening, cooking, and painting. With absolute conviction that what she needs will always show up, her appointment book for the following week is filled by Monday morning. She does no advertising now, and comfortably supports herself by working three days a week.

> "It's not about positional power; it's not about accomplishments; it's ultimately not even about what we do. Leadership is about creating a domain in which human beings continually deepen their understanding of reality and become more capable of participating in the unfolding of the world. Ultimately, leadership is about creating new realities."
>
> *Peter Senge*[3]

"In working with people on these principles, I am able to see them manifest amazing changes, time and again, as they find and change the beliefs they have been living by since childhood.

"The two most important points that I see are: One, anything is possible, and two, even though a situation appears one way, there is *always a solution within the specific situation* that may not be obvious on the surface. Whenever I am facing a conflict inside myself or an obstacle, I automatically ask myself, 'What am I believing that is limiting this experience?'

"A couple of years ago when I wanted to begin to work three days a week, I, of course, confronted the old paradigm that said I had to work full-time to make enough money to live on. In my old days in the corporations, I started out believing I had to work even more than full-time because I wasn't married. When I started to do individual consulting, I confronted the collective belief that it is difficult to survive in private practice.

"I now work only three days a week and fully support myself—well. My work is, literally, effortless. I don't do any marketing, but I do provide very good service to people. I believe that part of my purpose is to be doing other things besides my practice, so that belief seems to pave the way for those other things to fall into place, too.

"My fiancé says I'm like a laser beam. On Monday, I wake up and I think about the kind of week I want. For me, I feel more secure if I have my appointments set up ahead of time so I don't have worry about it. I look at the holes in my schedule and intend for people to call in for appointments. They do. It is so amazing. I believe that when you are living your own truth—when you are in the integrity of your own path—the universe supports it. I'm not taking all the credit for this phenomenon, because I know that I work with God's energy. I don't know if this is true, but I know that I believe it. It works for me. I believe when one believes in possibility, it allows all this possibility to show up.

"To me, the idea of lack is the unawareness of the infinite capability of the universe. For example, if you feel a lack of right livelihood, you must have a belief that stops you from experiencing your true purpose. That limiting belief would be different for everyone, based on many different factors. One person might believe, 'Everybody else has the talent to have the perfect career but me.' Or another one might think, 'Some people have all the luck.' Or, 'If only I had had a better education, I would be successful.'

"I now believe that the mechanism for achieving the desire is inherent in the desire. For example, if we have a desire, let's say, to be a musician, it is the universe's desire to express music through us. It's a thought form that is intended to be fulfilled through us. For example, I knew that when I was having so much trouble finding love, something was amiss. A couple of years ago, I stopped asking for love to show up in the form of a boyfriend. Instead, I asked myself, what would a boyfriend bring to my life? What do I really want by asking for a boyfriend? What is the real importance of having a boyfriend? When I went deeper into my motivations, I found that what I really wanted was the feeling of making a contribution while sharing this activity with someone. I had been asking for a boyfriend, but what I really wanted was to be working with someone else and have that bring me joy and service.

"So I started doing things I liked that were of service. I did some volunteer work. I did some work with a friend. I helped some teenagers out of some tight spots. I looked for different ways to have the root experience I was seeking. I just kept building these experiences.

"I met David when he and I were working together on a project with a shaman. We worked hand in hand as a team. It was an exquisite experience. Out of that work together, we fell in love. So, for me, I concentrated on the desire of the ultimate feeling outcome, and stopped asking for the form, which was the idea of the boyfriend. If I had written down a list of characteristics that I wanted in a man, I would only have gotten a quarter of what I actually found in David. I instead focused on the feelings I wanted to experience. What showed up was a man well beyond my dreams. I think we do ourselves a disservice by trying to do the work of the creative force that produced oceans and trees. If something can produce that, it can certainly fulfill my intention to contribute to the world better than I could imagine."

WRITING YOUR OWN JOB DESCRIPTION

In the small lobby of the Re-Entry Program on the campus of the University of California at Berkeley, these words of George Eliot are painted on a column that holds up the building: IT'S NEVER TOO LATE TO BE WHAT YOU MIGHT HAVE BEEN. The Re-Entry Program offers a variety of services to help people who have returned to college after a hiatus. Unlike younger students who go immediately into college and have a definite social identity and are used to the rigors of academia, returning older students are often unsure of both their social standing and their academic abilities. They may have jobs, families, and many responsibilities to juggle. Returning students often feel isolated and uncertain about measuring up, and, as a group, have their own special concerns and needs.

I interviewed Helen K. Johnson, a pillar in her own right—as the founder and campus coordinator of the program—in her cozy office. Unassuming in manner, Helen has a very calm, grounded presence. Her story is a classic example of the adage, Find a need and fill it. I asked her to tell me her story of what it was like to leave a luxurious home in fashionable Burlingame at the age of fifty and return to school in order to pursue a purpose that was by no means clear at the time. What are the pitfalls of making so radical a change? I wanted to know. What are the fears people have about making a decision to return to school after they have been "out in the world" for some time? She immediately warmed to the topic.

Going Back to School
"The first is money. People are worried about how they are going to finance school—go to school, work, live, take care of their family and all the issues around the money aspect. Secondly, everyone has some fears that their brain may not work well enough!" She laughed knowingly.

"Other fears are changing the status quo. People think, 'If I leave what I have now, maybe I won't find anything better even if I go back to school.' Or they may be afraid to go because they had problems learning in high school or feel insecure about their ability to write.

"Most of all, people are leaving their comfort zone, and they have to leave whatever status they have in their current job. Suddenly, they are listening to the professor, where in their job, people listened to them. They may have left a good job with no sense that going to school will lead to anything. And, of course, they face all the questions and opinions from their families or relationships." Helen had all of these same questions when she decided that she had to leave her comfortable suburban life and develop herself—or else.

A native of Scotland, Helen emigrated to the United States at age nineteen. She married and had children. "In 1957, pregnant women were never seen in an office. It simply wasn't done." But after thirteen years of staying home, she became active in her community. "I was always told I was clever. Friends kept telling me that I should go to the university, but I just did not have the confidence to do that."

Lack of confidence is a crucial point as we feel the call to make changes in our lifestyle. People may be giving us messages about our next step, and yet if we lack the confidence to take action, we cannot take advantage of those messages. I asked Helen what she suggests that people do to build up their self-confidence.

"I think it's important to look around for people who are role models. Who else has done it? I think it is absolutely essential to take small steps. For me, that was starting at the community college level. And, instead of imagining the whole process, I just told myself, 'I'm only taking one semester.' I didn't think about the whole four-year plan. It was too overwhelming. Just commit to one semester, without feeling your whole life has to change.

"It's also important not to feel that you are burning any bridges. Make it as easy on yourself as you can. You also need to realize that you will probably feel uncomfortable for a while, and that is normal. You're changing, and if you were always in your comfort zone, you'd never be forced to do anything different than what you are doing.

"You have to be willing to learn all over again. We all have to be able to keep learning if we are going to live to be eighty or ninety. If you give up a job where everybody listened to you, you have to be willing to let that drop. It may chip away at your self-confidence, but if you see that you are really taking charge of your life, and are willing to do whatever it takes, you start to regain that confidence you had before, but in a new way. You will learn and grow, and then reach a plateau and maybe feel stagnant—that's normal.

"Reentry students bring so many new dimensions to education. They bring a whole life perspective to the classwork. If you can see yourself as part of the process, then you can see your contribution along the way. This helps you feel connected to what you are doing even when you don't know where it is leading.

"A big part of our reentry program is simply getting people together to share their common feelings, so they can see they are not alone or isolated. This makes such a big difference. For those people who have not yet made the step, we have orientation meetings so they can meet others just like themselves, and all our staff are reentry students."

I asked Helen to tell us her own experience of leaving her settled family life to become a student, and eventually to found this much-needed service.

"I went to community college and got my A.A., and frankly, got lots of attention for my writing skills. When I got to the university, I started getting feedback like 'trite' written across the top of my English papers! It was a real test for me. But I kept at it, and had no idea how I would fare. School was a transformation for me. I discovered a whole intellectual side I did not know was there. I wound up getting straight A's and graduating Phi Beta Kappa. At the time, I didn't even know what that was! I was so naive that I thought you had to get invited to go to graduate school, and didn't know you had to apply. As it turned out, four professors *did* ask me to join the English program.

"Just as I was entering graduate school in 1981, I also entered menopause. At first I thought I had had a stroke. I was getting lots of hot flashes, and suffered terrible memory loss. I was under such stress because of being in graduate school and separating from my husband and leaving my affluent life in Burlingame. But I knew if I didn't do it, I would die. That's how important it was to me.

"There was nothing written about menopause then, and frankly, I was terrified about the insomnia and the memory loss and the fact that my brain was just not working the way it had been. I couldn't think, and nothing seemed normal anymore. But I knew that I had to go on with my intellectual development, and I think that really helped me enormously in keeping my brain from atrophying. Evidence does show that if you keep giving yourself challenges, the dendrites in the brain don't curl up and die. But finally, I gave in and took estrogen.

"There came a time when I had to get paid work, which I found, psychologically, very different than doing volunteer work at which I was very adept. I had so many fears about getting a job that I entered short-term therapy. Part of the therapy was to draw pictures about my fears. I drew a huge barbed-wire fence across the page, and drew my head with eyes looking over the fence. It seemed pretty grim to me, but the therapist said, 'Oh no, look. Your head is over the fence and you can see your way!' "

> Lack of confidence is a crucial point as we feel the call to make changes in our lifestyle. People may be giving us messages about our next step, and yet if we lack the confidence to take action, we cannot take advantage of those messages.

What were the worst fears about going back to work? I asked.

"Oh, I was so afraid of my memory loss, that I was not as sharp in my thinking anymore. I was fifty years old at the time. I was afraid I wouldn't measure up. I was afraid I couldn't take the routine of working nine to five. I was afraid of being evaluated and found lacking. But even with all these concerns, I knew I had my education, and I was not going to give up.

"Again people told me I should teach at community colleges, but I didn't have the confidence for that. So I took a baby step. I interned at the Women's Center. It didn't seem so much like the *workplace*. I thought they would be kind to me. It was the same thinking as when I emigrated to the United States from Scotland when friends said, 'Why are you going?' I said, 'I'm only going for six months.' That made it seem easier to handle.

> "When we are stuck on a problem, what keeps us from acting for change is either a lack of information, or that we have been wounded in our sense of personal power on an issue, or that there is no system in place that enables us to move the issue forward. [By asking strategic questions] I open up a door for . . . people to move beyond their grief, guilt, and powerlessness . . . to active dreaming and creating of their own contributions."
> *Fran Peavey*[4]

"When I got to the Women's Center, there was this stack of memos from women who had called in about wanting to go back to school. There was nothing, no counseling in place for them, and I just kind of sat there. Women would come in and I could see their anxiety. I thought, 'They are just like me.' This was a gift. I thought the university needed to provide for this, because these women are coming from complex lives, they are not living in dorms, they are not in sororities. *But this problem was invisible to the administration.* They could not see this population as distinct in its needs.

"I began to talk to all the different departments, like financial aid and registration and housing and was very naive about the territorial politics.

"I came to realize and finally *know* that working with reentry students was what I wanted to do. My internship was not renewed, and I was not on good terms with the director of the Women's Center. But I managed to get a little office and I painted it and just decided this was what I was doing. I got a grant the first year, and within two years, the Re-Entry Program became part of the official administration of the university. I am doing all the things I love — mediation, counseling, advocacy — using interpersonal skills I didn't even know I had. I wrote my own job description, and I feel I have the perfect job for me. I still feel that passion about what I am doing, and I have a sense of meaning every day. It gives me pleasure, and it's good for the university and it's good for the students."

Is There a Need Near You?

Helen tells us that the problems and issues of reentry students as a group were not being addressed by the university administration because those problems were *invisible* to them. The identity of this group only gained prominence because of Helen's courage and ability to see a need that was waiting to be addressed. In doing so, she found her purpose. Is there a situation in your work or community that is invisible because no one is taking the time to identify it?

DOING THE DREAM

How many times have you had a creative flash about a product, and thought to yourself, "Wow, this is such a good idea. Somebody should sell this thing." Perhaps you doodled your idea on a piece of paper, and maybe even talked to someone about how much it would cost to build or get off the ground. But eventually, your paper with the doodle gets misplaced, or you throw it away thinking, "Who am I kidding? I don't have time to deal with this. Probably wouldn't work, anyway. Besides I don't have any start-up money."

Kermit Heartsong, founder and president of Word Origin, Inc., thinks differently. A thirty-six-year-old black San Francisco entrepreneur, this man followed his heart all the way to the top, with an idea that was born out of a shocking experience. His story intrigues me because it is a classic example of how synchronicity, perseverance, and following one's deepest values puts you on a road you could never have imagined walking. I'll let him tell his story.

All Work and All Play

"Words and language were always important to my mother. As a result, she read *everything* to my brother and me. I would go to bed with a book and a flashlight, and then when I had to turn off the flashlight, I'd read by my brother's night-light.

"When I went to college, I didn't know what I wanted to be, so I went along with some of my friends and studied engineering. I graduated from UC-Davis, but I had no interest in becoming an engineer. It wasn't me. I also realized at that time that my vocabulary had slumped during college because I hadn't taken many literature courses. I tried reading the dictionary, and using some vocabulary card packs. It was all so boring. I started thinking how people could learn better, learn while they're engaged in a game, having fun.

"During this time, I was doing odd jobs. I was working in a latch-key program for inner-city kids. Some of these kids had never been to the beach, so we'd take them out to the beach or to professional offices to show them different things. One day, I started playing a word game with some ten-year-olds. They were pantomiming the action words when a thirteen-year-old walked in. I wanted to include him, and asked him to spell 'ladder.' He thought for a second and began to spell it with an 's,' " Heartsong recalled.

"I thought, 'Uh-oh, something is wrong here.' I wrote out a word and called him over. I asked him to read the word 'house' and he said, 'Ladder.' He had, by the way, made it to the eighth grade. You hear about illiteracy all the time, but until it slaps you in the face, you can't know how devastating it is. He couldn't sound out basic words like 'sit.' I was so concerned that I wanted to talk to his parents. This boy's parents were very suspicious, and they wouldn't let me help him.

> "Make the decision to serve wherever you go and to whomever you see. As long as you are serving, you will be receiving. The more you serve, the more confidence you will gain in the miraculous effects of this principle of life. And as you enjoy the reciprocity, your ability to serve will also increase."
> Greg Anderson[5]

"It's interesting because in this neighborhood there were so-called gifted children, and in each case, their parents took the time to read to them, to play games with them, to engage in some kind of activity that kept their brains active. When you see the faces of these little kids whose parents read to them, you see how much they love reading, too. So these two instances—of the suspicious, uninvolved parents and the involved parents—said to me, hey, there has to be an element to engage the parents if the kids are going to learn.

"The key is to reach these kids at a young age, so that they are hungry for learning. My games are about bringing families together. I have one game called Articulation—the Family Version, and it's designed on two levels so both children and parents can play in the same game, but the parents won't be bored.

I asked Kermit what kept him going in the early days of getting his idea, his vision, off the ground.

"Call it being hard-headed and naive! The game industry is a very hard industry. In the beginning, I had one piece of binder paper with my basic ideas on it. Over the next couple of months, that piece of paper grew to thirteen pieces of paper, describing in detail all the things I wanted the game to do. I started talking to everyone I could find in the game business. I bugged the people at Trivial Pursuit and Pictionary for six months till they brought me in. I asked them nuts-and-bolts questions like, How much does it cost to manufacture games? How can I get distribution? Will I make a profit with the first run? After I got my information, I decided this was a great thing to do.

"Family and friends had initially given me money for the business, but the first big break came when I was playing basketball, and I ruptured my Achilles tendon. There were three orthopedic surgeons who put me back together, and, of course, I tell them what I'm doing.

They all love words. So after I got out of the hospital, they all came over to my house, and we talked and all three of them helped my company get started. Without them, I couldn't have gotten started. Several other synchronicities, like being led to the right buyers, kept happening often enough that it made me think I was on the right path.

"The biggest thing happened last year. Things were moving along okay, but it was all piecemeal. I hadn't had any big growth spurt; I didn't have money for promotion, or marketing people. I had no office. In 1995, it is make or break time. If I don't get funded at this point, it will all have been for nothing. A friend of mine tells me about this group of socially responsible investors called the Investor's Circle. She thought my games were a fantastic idea, and she told me that I had to have these people see my proposal. So I send in my three-page proposal. I wait. I call again, and I send them one of my catalogs because the three-pager was sort of bland by itself. Another week passes. It's July, and time is running out if I'm going to get a presentation together for the gift show. Three weeks before the show, they call me in. You have to understand that *thousands* of people send in three-page proposals, and they only select ten. I'm number ten. They tell me to prepare a ten-minute presentation, and they said don't bring more than twenty business plans because you'll never go through that many.

"I practice, and practice my speech. This is it. I can't emphasize this enough. This is either going to make or break the business. If it doesn't work, it's over for me. I fly to Atlanta. I make the mistake of sitting in the room while the other nine people are making their presentations. I am sweating profusely, and thinking, 'Oh my God. This is it.' There are a hundred people in the audience—the Gettys, the Mellons, the McKays—all these people who have made big money.

"But then I started to relax, and I prayed. It was like something came over me. So now it's my turn. I walk up calmly, and ask for a moving micro-

> **"But then I started to relax, and I prayed. It was like something came over me."**

phone. I step away from the podium and I begin to engage the audience. I just began to talk. I just told the story. From that point on it's just magic. They laugh. They clap. They feel what I am feeling.

I gave them both the personal side and what we're trying to do as a company.

"Afterward, each of us set up our booths and in five minutes I was out of the twenty business plans they said we'd never go through. At lunch I was at this huge round table, and everybody was asking me questions. I couldn't eat a bite.

"Shortly thereafter, I got twelve investors and that turned it all around. I think back now, and that was only a little over a year ago.

"When I first started my business, I tell people, I was living in a room so small that I would wake up in the morning in bed and put my feet on the floor, and my hands would be at the computer. Now I have seven people working here and eighty outside marketing reps and thirty-seven products."

STAYING ON PURPOSE
• *Every* situation has a purpose.
• Doing what you love aligns you with the flow of synchronicity.
• You attract what you focus upon.
• Universal intelligence is perfect and operates effortlessly.
• You always have a choice.
• Set your intention and ask for support.
• Let the universe handle the details.
• Trust the process.
• Your life is part of the larger world plan.

And what does he think about his purpose, his path?

"This is a path I'm on right now." He paused to reflect a moment, and said, "I remember that when I was in high school I had a dream. I had the idea for an inner-city boarding school that would teach kids not only the basics, but more. Teach them languages, art, music. When I worked with kids in the latchkey program, it was tough to spend time with them, and then know they were going back to abusive environments. I want to get to them when they're young. I want to excite them to learn. I want to let them know somebody cares about them. The fact that we are cutting funds to education is mind-boggling to me. We need to give kids art and music and broaden them instead of narrow them down. This may sound crazy, but I think I'll probably wind up working with children someday."

TALKING TO YOURSELF

What innovative ideas have you had that excited you?
What happened to them?
What touched you about:
Colleen McGovern's story?
Helen Johnson's story?
Kermit Heartsong's story?

Reread these stories in six months or a year. See if anything about these stories touches you in a new way, and notice how your thinking has evolved.

CHAPTER 5

The Magnetic Force Field
of Your Life Purpose

༻∞༺

In a sense it is like thinking of the things you want as being on a string that is infinitely long, but is nevertheless attached to you in some invisible way. It is only a matter of trusting that you can bring that string to you and that whatever is supposed to come to your life will be there when you have developed the capacity to receive it. But the trick is, you cannot receive it or even come close to manifesting it if you have an absence of trust in yourself as an extension of God.

WAYNE DYER[1]

ESTABLISHING A FIELD
OF POSITIVE ATTRACTING FORCE

Have you ever had the experience of being away on a long trip and calling home for messages? Do you ever have the feeling that somehow you have a "life" that is waiting for you back at your home location, even though "you" are away on a trip that somehow isn't as real as what you left behind?

Let's imagine a visual image of your "life" as an energetic field. This energetic field attracts to you people, opportunities, and events. Within that field is a central point of purpose around which incoming energy is organized. Affecting and modifying that central point of purpose are energetic subfields of beliefs, attitudes, past experiences, expectations, unresolved emotional states, and other unconscious material. At all times, we emit a certain energy pattern based on our physical, emotional, and spiritual states. The model of a magnetic force field is intended to suggest that we not only radiate out energy from a centralized self-organizing, indwelling purpose, but that energetic field also attracts in, or magnetizes to itself, those people and things that will help fulfill that purpose. It would seem that our energetic field also must necessarily filter all incoming information through our beliefs, expectations, past traumas, and experience. We will only utilize information that we pay attention to consciously, and store information that we have not been able to pay attention to. Since our goal is to work symbolically and energetically on our perceptual field in order to help us begin to see our deeper mission in life, let's play a little bit with this rather simplified model in order to become aware of the interrelated energy fields of our life.

How energized are you at this moment? On a scale of one to ten, if ten is "I feel terrific!" how do you feel *right now*? If you feel fairly content and awake—let's say you give yourself a rating of six or seven—then take a moment to affirm to yourself, "Even as I read these words, my life is beginning to shift in ways that attracts opportunities to fulfill my purpose." If your energy level is in the two or three range, try to remember, "Anything is possible." Obviously, some days we feel we can take on the world, and others we just want to hide out.

Whenever you feel discouraged or depressed, begin to think of every tiny thing in your life for which you are grateful. When you focus on being grateful for such things as the roof over your head (if you have one), your comfortable bed, hot water, the smiles of your children, the tree next door, the ability to move freely—whatever you focus on with true appreciation and gratitude—you are generating a higher frequency of energy. By living and taking action in a higher frequency (which is also a deeper and richer frequency), you are more aligned with your purpose.

> "You participate in this form of data bank exchange, so to speak, with all the souls that you are close to, and, to some extent, with all the souls that touch your life. As you shift your data bank content and the information that you send to a soul, it is processed through his or her own system. It is at that level that the cause and effect of your intentions, the way that you choose to shape your energy, influences others."
> *Gary Zukav* [2]

Since each of us exists within the universal field of intelligence, then it would seem that *the more people reading this book and other material of a similar nature, the easier it is going to be for you to align with your soul's purpose.*

Intuitive trainer and author Penney Peirce once told me, "I try to remember that I am surrounded by a friendly, cooperative etheric

---

THE MAGNETIC FORCE FIELD
OF YOUR LIFE PURPOSE

Attracts Opportunities Based on Your *Beliefs* About

- Your Strengths
- Your Weaknesses
- What You Love
- What You Think Is *Necessary*
- The Nature of Life
- Right and Wrong
- Your Level of Creativity
- Your Conscious Intentions
- Your Unconscious Motivations
- Your Level of Optimism
- Responsibilities and Loyalties
- Significant Achievements and Proud Moments
- Success/Failure/Rewards

- How You Measure Up
- Your Ability to Find Meaning in Events
- Your Ability to Stay in the Present
- Your Ability to Be Yourself Around Others
- Your Ability to Trust Your Process
- Your Ability to Laugh at Yourself
- Your Ability to Handle Fear
- Your Ability to Surrender
- Your Ability to See Purpose/ Messages in Obstacles

---

field. I call it the field of the Knower. For example, the other day I needed a little story of someone healing themselves by their intuition for an article I was writing. I called all my friends but nobody was home. As soon as I reaffirmed that the field was with me, and that I didn't need the story to come from other people, I immediately remembered a story of my own. Getting what you need from the field of universal energy is as instantaneous as you allow it to be."

WHAT MAKES UP
YOUR MAGNETIC FIELD OF PURPOSE?

Describe your own magnetic force field by filling in the answers in the pages that follow. Answer as honestly as you can even if you find you frequently choose the option of "Weak" or "Depends" for some of the questions. These answers help bring any fears, apathy, or blockages to your attention, not so you can judge yourself as inadequate, but so that you can begin to concentrate positive energy in those areas. There are no right or wrong answers. There are no problems to be overcome; simply bring your attention to any area with the desire for it to be strengthened or released.

My strengths are_____

_____

My ability to see the purpose in obstacles is

Very Strong   Strong   Average   Weak   Depends

Generally, I believe my ability to take emotional risks is

Very Strong   Strong   Average   Weak   Depends

Generally, my ability to take financial risks is

Very Strong   Strong   Average   Weak   Depends

Generally, my ability to speak my truth on controversial subjects is

Very Strong   Strong   Average   Weak   Depends

My ability to laugh at myself is

Exceptional   Fabulous   Great   Okay   Depends

I *believe* I am creative

Absolutely   Very much so   Somewhat   Not Very   Depends

My level of optimism is

Very, Very High   High   Moderate   Low   Depends

My ability to find meaning in events is

Very High   High   Moderate   Low   Depends

My ability to surrender (let go of control) is

Very High   High   Moderate   Low   Depends

In my life and family, I am responsible for_____

_____

I am loyal to_____

_____

I trust myself to make good
decisions   Absolutely   Most of the Time
                                   Sometimes   Maybe   Depends

I tend to judge myself harshly when_____

_____

Fears block my progress   Constantly Often Occasionally
                                   Hardly Ever

My top three fears are:
    1. Fear of Death 2. Fear of Public Speaking 3. Fear of Making a
    Mistake 4. Fear of Being Ridiculed 5. Fear of Meeting New People
    6. Fear of Looking Dumb 7. Fear of Being Trapped 8. Fear of Being
    Invisible 9. Fear of Being Alone 10. Fear of Not Belonging
    Anywhere 11. Fear of Poverty 12. Fear of Illness and Pain 13. Fear
    of Authority 14. Fear of Making the Wrong Decision
    15. Fear of_____

The significant events that have molded me are_____

_____

_____

The achievements I am proudest of are_____

_____

_____

The activities I love are_____

_____

I would describe myself as_____

_____

My current intention is to_____

_____

I stay focused in the present best when_____

_____

I would love to attract_____

_____

YOUR MAGNETIC FIELD LOSES POWER THROUGH THOUGHTS, LANGUAGE, AND ACTIONS THAT ARE ROOTED IN

- Negative self-judgment
- An inordinate need for control
- Blaming others for your situations
- Pessimism
- Desire for or acts of revenge
- Unexamined commitments
- Societal beliefs
- False loyalties
- Regrets over failures
- Resentments about injustices
- Hatred
- Fear

Thoughts

- You lose creative power when you think from any of the above energy-draining processes.
- To stop the loss of power, train yourself to notice when your thoughts are rooted in any of these energy states. Suspend that thought. Let it go. Visualize detaching from it. Remember it is only as real as the energy you give it.
- Ask yourself, "Do I really want to continue this kind of thinking? Why?"

Language

- Begin to listen to the language you use in conversation with others. The unconscious stores as Truth everything you say or even joke about.

Actions

- To regain energy, practice forgiving yourself and others in any problematic situation. Forgive and make an intention to move on.
- Watch any tendency to keep bringing these patterns back into conversation.

FIND OUT TO WHAT OR TO WHOM YOU GIVE YOUR POWER (ENERGY)

Part of your purpose in life is to master the use of creative human energy. When you are in the spiritual dimension, you have no physical body to manage or physical energy to manipulate. Once you are born, you are able to create form by working with physical energy. Some of us are so eager to achieve, to make our mark, to express ourselves, that we work nonstop. Do you burn the candle at both ends? Do you work marathon hours and then become a slug? How do you handle your physical life vehicle (your body!)? Do you keep fit or binge on physical sensuality? Some souls incarnate with the specific desire to feel and touch everything in life, reveling in the sensuous experience of earthly life.

If you believe that your mental attitudes create your worldview, and are responsible for helping to attract your life purpose, then you may find it helpful to see just how much of your energy goes into positive attraction and how much goes into negative attraction. These negative mental attitudes arise because you unconsciously feel separated or isolated from your spiritual source. When people feel separated, they try to make things work by concentrating only on their own willpower and trying to control everything. When you remember to align yourself with your own nature and your life purpose, you naturally are in touch with your natural power. When you align yourself with even a single value, like compassion, trust, self-respect, or following through on synchronicities—life becomes more meaningful, often more fun, more hopeful, and you feel resourceful. Your purpose is God's purpose, and the creator desires that you fulfill your purpose.

The following exercise, inspired by the work of Caroline Myss's tape series—*Energy Anatomy*—is offered to help you imagine where you may be losing creative energy.

Imagine that you have one hundred percent creative energy when you wake up, plenty to spend in creating and attracting the life you want to live. Are you really functioning on all your cylinders? Maybe not. Most of us spend a considerable amount of time stewing or fretting, worrying, resenting, regretting, and generally jamming our internal circuits. Even though we desire success, we send out worry thought-forms that will only return to us *negative results*. However, we do have a chance to clean up our act if we know what that act is. More often than not, our thoughts are the source of what we consider to be external problems. According to such observers of the human condition as physicist David Bohm, the root of our problems lies in the very nature of our completely unrecognized, unexamined, fragmentary thinking.

POWER-LOSS ANALYSIS

Read the statements below, and make an intuitive estimate of what percentage of your creative energy you spend on any of these categories. To make this work, you have to be very honest with yourself. Imagine your percentages in increments of thirty minutes, one hour, two hours, etc. *per day*. Just allow your intuition to offer up a percentage number. Trust that it's accurate! Add up your percentages when you're done.

If you want to identify your power loss visually, do a mind-mapping picture of your energy field with lines to all the people and situations to which you are currently losing energy.

POWER-LOSS ANALYSIS

Without spending more than a minute or two on each one, answer the following questions. Use your best estimate of how much energy you spend nonconstructively.

Who and what do you blame for any negative situation?_____

In what way do you feel pressure to achieve to please your family or any other group?_____

What percentage of your energy goes to pleasing your family?_____%
How much energy do you spend being pessimistic?_____%
How much energy do you spend thinking about revenge?_____%
How much energy do you spend trying to *please* your boss?_____%
How much energy do you spend in negative self-judgment each day?
_____%

How much energy do you spend in regrets over failures?_____%
I resent (who or what)_____
How much energy do you spend in resentments?_____%
I hate_____
How much energy do you send to your enemies?_____%
I try to control (who? what?)_____
How much energy do I spend in trying to control others?_____%
How much energy do I spend worrying each day?_____%
Total daily creative energy spent in areas that *will return negativity
directly to you*_____%

In the following stories, you will meet three people who have found a sense of purpose in the different stages of their lives. Each has experienced a deep call that necessitated them to keep moving forward on their path—in the face of much uncertainty. As you read, notice how their fields of energy have drawn them into a life of purpose and fulfillment. Boona cheema, a native of India, now directs a multimillion-dollar social agency in Berkeley, California. Jerry Horovitz has woven an impressive tapestry of interests, skills, and careers into his own publishing company. Laura Kwong, the vivacious wife of Zen Master Kwong-roshi, teaches and models the practice of Zen Buddhism in a spiritual community.

BOONA CHEEMA

The guiding principles by which boona cheema's (she prefers her name spelled in small letters) family lived were "faith, service, and purpose." One of her father's favorite sayings was "In whatever it is that we do, it's important that the casualties be as few as possible." Listening to the events that shaped her life, I was struck by the obvious purposefulness behind the early experiences of this deeply spiritual and focused woman.

Boona cheema is the executive director of BOSS, a nonprofit agency based in Berkeley, California. A better description would be that she is an unstoppable force of integrity, intelligence with wisdom, good humor, and compassion. Born in India on the day the bomb was dropped on Hiroshima, she came to the United States in 1971 as a penniless immigrant. She wound up receiving emergency services from the newly established Berkeley Oakland Support Services, and before long signed on as a street counselor, becoming its director in 1979. Since that time she has built BOSS (now called Building Opportunities for Self-Sufficiency) into an agency with an annual budget of over $6.5 million and a staff of one hundred, which provides a variety of housing, economic development, community building, and community services options for people in poverty. Her journey is a good example of how necessity combined with vision and a desire to serve in one individual can make a tangible difference in the lives of many. I wanted to learn how her calling had unfolded. We did a very brief time line of the significant events that kept her moving into her purpose. Her time line is quite striking in its seeming purposefulness.

Living the Family Creed of "Faith, Service, and Purpose"

"I see homelessness as class warfare," boona told me. "I see the urban poor in America as having very similar issues as refugees when it seems they have no connection to their community. The homelessness and uprootedness feels very similar to my own early years of being uprooted in the partition of India in 1947.

"There are great role models of strength and spirit everywhere in people who are living impoverished lives—even in people who seem to be making the wrong choices—selling their bodies or using drugs. Their choices do not mean that they have given up their spiritual center. In the United States, we are not ready to recognize this, and so we judge them to be impoverished in their souls. My life has taught me that I can lose all my material possessions tomorrow, but I cannot lose who I am."

Boona outlined some of the events and lessons that gave her the experience of the mystery and spirit of life:

August 6, 1945: Birth. The day Hiroshima was bombed. One of her life themes is always the war within the human spirit, she said.

The partition of India in 1947: Became a refugee along with three generations of her family. A deep feeling of helplessness at being disempowered by an external force—in this case, a political action.

Sent to Catholic school at age eight: Family's intent to give their female child a good education. Learned to live within rigid conditions, and to question authority in a skillful, nonthreatening way.

Visited the Golden Temple of the Sikhs at age nine. This religion, repressed by both Islam and Hinduism, taught her the message of universality. She was impressed with their creed that whoever comes in need to the temple will be fed and sheltered.

Met the Dalai Lama at age thirteen: She was with her father who was helping to settle Tibetan refugees when she met the Dalai Lama, who touched her head. "Even though I was too young to really know who this man was, I continue to feel this as a blessing of great proportion."

Worked as a journalist: Developed critical thinking and broadened her view of the world.

Studied improvisation and acting in India: By playing both male and female roles, she balanced her inner masculine and feminine.

Marriage and emigration to United States: Learned what it's like to be hungry and not know if she is going to be able to make a new life.

Birth of her son: "So this is what love feels like!" Her heart opened. From that moment, she was no longer afraid of war, death, or poverty. She also awakened to the need to conserve the environment for future generations.

Attended divinity school: She took action on an inner need to add discipline and formal learning to her naturally intuitive nature, so as to be even more effective in life.

Involvement with drugs: Finding herself challenged by something bigger than she was, boona learned she could not get to sacred places by shortcuts. Humbled by the experience, she realized how powerful is the force that holds the universe together.

Met and married second husband: First relationship where each completely accepted the other, and each enhanced the other's path. She felt even more freedom than before.

Conscious choice about community and work: "It's easier for me to be with people who are struggling to get to a better place in their lives.

"You can go to all the workshops you want and read all the books on spirituality, but it's all self, self, self, until you begin to help make the world a little better place for everyone. When I meet someone I look for their assets and strengths, how beautiful they are. Talk about what strength it takes to sleep on the sidewalk every night in thirty-degree weather! We have to develop the ability to see what's on the inside, not just the smelly clothes. We have to be able to connect to the anger, the self-doubt, the fear—wherever a person is standing. I've worked single-mindedly on trying not to judge others. When I feel racism or fear, I recognize it and work on seeing beyond it. The culture is very isolating, and we need to reach out and cross the boundaries."

I asked her how she handles the overwhelming task of serving the needs of so many. "I am very single-minded. I get clear about the reasons why I am doing something, whether it's raising money or setting the budget. I am convinced that one person's journey can make a big difference in the lives of the children and elders that he or she encounters. I don't hold on to a lot of stuff emotionally. I don't create a lot of systems. If I had to give myself a title, it would be a warrior—in the good sense—

> "Between these two poles, it seems to me, we seek to become complete: between shedding our self-consciousness and taking on a new awareness, between the awesome fears that shrink us and the capacity for love that enlarges us beyond measure, between the need for vigilance in the face of danger and the trust that allows us to sleep."
> *Kathleen Norris*[3]

rather than a bureaucrat! My weapons are my mind, soul, and spirit. This is not easy work, and I don't waste energy getting entangled in other people's issues and conflicts. I feel very purposeful. I want to lend my strength and courage equally to others who may have strengths and courage of a different kind. I'm going to continue to confirm, touch, grow, and change with whatever is in front of me. I can say, 'Yes, today is a good day. I'm not going to participate in adding any casualties to the world.' "

THE FLOW OF DIVERSITY

Jerry Horovitz is the sole proprietor of a small publishing house, Amber Lotus, which publishes greeting cards, calendars, and journals. The themes of all the work touch on the beauty of nature, the art of ethnic cultures, and visionary art. I had met Jerry some years before, and had known him then as an urban planner and design consultant who played basketball and practiced Buddhism. At that time, he was adding a fêng shui component to his practice. Even though I didn't know Jerry well, three things stood out very clearly in his nature: He exuded integrity and commitment, he practiced his spiritual principles, and he seemed to be pursuing some core question in each of several career moves. I wanted to know what had motivated him in these diverse directions.

Right Livelihood

"I want to avoid spending so much time doing what's urgent that I never get to what's important," Jerry said about his new venture. "I see this business as a marriage of art, commerce, and service, which has always been my goal. Part of my work involves making the artistic decisions that will also be good for business. An even bigger part of the business is the relationship end of it. I want the process to be as artistic as the product. It would be hypocritical to be an artistic company, and be a Neanderthal in my business dealings, or just have a cookie-cutter process. When you are really working from honesty and thoughtfulness and true concern, it shows in the finished product and in the relationships you have with customers, vendors, employees, everybody. I don't want to be in business if it's not going to be artistic and caring.

"The other day," he continued, "I had a small order for calendars from someone in Berkeley. Since I was already going in that direction, I called and offered to drop them off at her house. I think she was a little flabbergasted to be getting them hand-delivered from me! When I dropped them off, we got to chatting, and it turned out she came up with the idea of introducing my work to a good resource. Now, I hadn't had any expectations beyond giving her the calendars. But networking relationships grow best, I think, out of honest and caring service. I believe strongly in what goes around comes around. I have no idea if this company will make money, but I think if I operate with these values, it will work.

"I also think that the timing is right for me to go into business. I'm forty-seven years old. I've traveled to over fifty countries. I've had a lot of fun and dabbled in many things. It feels like the right time to really get involved in something I can grow with, and my range of skills is well suited for this type of business.

"At the same time," Jerry continued, "some people might think this is a crazy time to get involved with the publishing business. We can see that the big chains are swallowing the small players. Am I crazy? Will I figure out a way for it to work? I frankly don't know. But somehow I have trust that there is something here for me."

Jerry's attitude shows three very important beliefs that are necessary for staying in alignment with our soul's purpose: (1) He has a strong intention about his work ethic that satisfies his head and heart—and checkbook; (2) he sees beyond the conventional thinking ("the big chains are taking over"); (3) he trusts himself to know what will be required of him for success, and he trusts that something deeper is supporting his efforts. Had synchronicities been significant? I asked Jerry.

"Absolutely. I met my distributor synchronistically. I was intending to interview a certain distributor at the American Book Association in Chicago, when I accidentally ran into someone whom I already knew. He instantly saw how we could work together to both our advantages in the market. He immediately saw the larger picture, which is always something I highly value in people. I feel very fortunate that we came together at the moment that we did."

Since Jerry has had a great deal of varied career experiences, I was curious to know what he had wanted to be when he was a little boy. Was there any sign of the type of life that he would live as a man?

"I remember when I was about eight years old, I looked into *Parade* magazine. I saw an article about planning the future. I thought, that's what I want to do! Plan the future. Of course, my parents wanted me to be a doctor or a lawyer, but I always kept this interest in the future. After I graduated from college, I became an associate in a city planning firm. From that experience, I got my first big realization, and that was that I wanted to work for myself. In order to do that, I needed a master's degree, so that took me back to school. There I made a second realization. Where the other students were going the pragmatic route, wanting to get jobs in an agency, I was more interested in the people aspect of the work. For example, what happens to the *people* who get displaced in engineering projects? With that viewpoint, I was able to get work as a social environmental planner. That started me on the way.

"My next realization came when I found out that you can't really plan the future! You can have all the great plans in the world, but it comes down to the fact that political and economic considerations determine the outcome of all the plans. So I was disillusioned and left that field. At that time, I was also doing a lot of political organizing and writing. A lot of the changes in my life have come about because of following my own needs either for personal development or because I wanted to stay in integrity as much as possible.

"At this point, I was burned out doing reports and studies that weren't ever enacted and which were too removed from people's real needs. I wanted to give direct help. So I went to get a certificate in massage work. That was rewarding for a while, but again I soon faced a similar kind of disillusionment. Giving direct service didn't seem fulfilling enough to me. I'm interested in consciousness and action, more than form.

"Right after I had decided that body work was not engaging me fully, I got the opportunity to be a facility developer for the Children's Council. This was great because it was a chance to use all my experience so far—the planning, the community organizing, and the people skills—with the aim of building more child care and family centers. I could be of service for a good cause. In each case, whether it was the massage or the planning or the activist work, I was always working to transform people's awareness or consciousness. Even though my career path seems wildly divergent, I think the thread that connects it all is my interest in the development of consciousness.

> "Each of us bears what I call an entelechy. Entelechy is Greek, meaning 'seeding, coding, dynamic propulsion.' It's the entelechy of the acorn to become an oak tree, the entelechy of a baby to be a grown-up in the world. The entelechy of you or me is to be—god only knows what! Sometimes, we get glimpses of entelechy. Part of our purpose is to track into the entelechy of maturation."
> Jean Houston[4]

"I used to worry, 'What is the meaning of life? What should I be doing with my life?' Now I see that maybe you don't even really know why you're doing something or what the meaning is. It's just something you're doing. If you can be relatively comfortable, and there is something of value in it, maybe that's enough. Maybe you don't see the purpose until later. If you looked at all my jobs, you would think I don't know what I'm doing. But, there is a thread there, and it keeps coming up in each thing. Most of the time our work is probably a reflection of what we are working on inside ourselves. When you see someone involved fanatically in politics or maybe being a devotee of a guru, something is being worked out in their *personal* story.

"Maybe we have to back off from dwelling on whether we are achieving some theoretical life purpose. Maybe we just do what is in front of us and do that well, and do it with an open heart. Do the best you can with what you're connected to at that moment. That's your life purpose for that moment. Don't try to find some absolute best thing. Go in the side door or the back door, and maybe you'll find what your life purpose is. I like that old adage, If you have lemons, make lemonade. Go with what you have, and don't take yourself too seriously. Maybe you don't know the purpose of what you're doing right now, and maybe it's an intermediary step, but you'll meet someone there. You don't want to stay in a dead end, either, but you have to assume that there is a purpose for that moment."

Going Away and Coming Home

Finally, Jerry's story has one other element that I have found in many people who feel they are living their life purpose. That is the element of having gone somewhere else and come home with a new perspective. Perhaps each of us must, at some point in our lives, reenact the archetypal hero's journey by setting out for faraway places. A big part of the process of discovering ourselves is our also seeing and touching the life experiences of other human beings around the world. That process is driven by the archetypal urge within us to see a fuller picture, to incorporate the knowledge of other societies and to experience "tribal" realities. We must leave the known path, and strike out for the unknown. In that journey, we come to different conclusions about where we fit in than we can ever do if we remain sheltered within the unexamined belief system into which we are born. I asked Jerry to tell me if, or how, his travels had helped him see his own place in life.

"My travels have absolutely influenced my own sense of my path. In 1983, I decided to take four months off and go to Asia and visit nine different countries. The high point was trekking the Himalayas where Tibetan Buddhists live. I found in their lives and villages a certain inner strength and solidity. They have nothing. They own nothing. They live on land too desolate to grow crops. And yet they seemed to be the happiest people I had ever met. I wanted to know what was inside them that gave them that joy.

"When I came back to the United States, I started studying Tibetan Buddhism, and that study has directly placed me in a position that allowed this new business to come into my life. I didn't know when I decided to travel in Asia that it would lead to my being a publisher. Sometimes things don't seem as if there is a deeper purpose, but I think that if there is a strong drive to do something, unless it's a base instinct, follow it. You have to follow where your dream is, even if it doesn't seem directly related to your life purpose or career. So with the publishing business, I may have found a way to have a greater impact than all the other jobs or careers I've had so far. And this may not be the end, either. I just feel fortunate that I've had the opportunity to keep homing in on what interests me at that moment."

SOUL MATES

Laura Kwong, Kwong-roshi's wife and soul companion of forty years, spoke with me about her own spiritual path. Her hair was starting to grow out since being shaved for her ordination as a Zen nun the month before. I had known Laura twenty-five years ago when she was interning for a therapist's license. I knew she was the mother of four grown boys. She reminded me that early in life, she had studied tap dancing.

Vivacious, with a strong presence, she told me, "I resisted becoming ordained as a nun for years. It took me years just to recognize what the longing was that I had always felt.

Zen Teacher, Tap Dancer

> "I've seen that people are nourished by compassion and great freedom, just as plants in the garden are nourished by sunshine and rain and fertilizing and proper seeds."
> Jack Kornfield[5]

"The night before the special ceremony where I had to shave my head, I didn't want to do it. I thought, 'Oh, I'll be so ugly.' But I took the scissors and began to cut. It triggered my memory of my wedding day where my mother made me cut my long hair. I remember that when I was with him [Roshi], it wasn't just getting married. It was like I had found my soul mate. We were like that. Now I am ordained, and finally I have accepted him as a spiritual teacher. But we are still having the best time. The other night, I put on my makeup and my beaded dress and we went out to the Sheraton Palace Hotel and we danced. Both parts are me. The person I was early in life—the dancer who loved makeup and social life—was on the outside. The other one—the spiritual one—was always on the inside. Now the spiritual one is on the outside—and the other one—the dancer—is on the inside. And it's all unfolding by itself in uncanny ways I can't even begin to understand. For example, my first dance teacher just became a Buddhist!

"My teaching is more visible now. But if I had known about this path, I probably would never have gone for formal practice. But now, I have enough life experience and spiritual discipline that for me zazen practice is very important and valuable. It's about sanity and clarity. There is something true and naked about it. I couldn't run away from that. It's like appreciating water, and it's refreshing, and then you want more. It's when you appreciate water, you don't have to have soda or anything else.

"When I was little, dancing was always there, with an inner desire for something like goodness. I was very aware that the world was in such suffering, and maybe I was in dance because I was the one who entertained everybody and could make everyone feel better. Because the inside is very in touch with how people hurt. I was aware of that as a child, but couldn't articulate it.

"In my practice, I am not too serious. I am very enthusiastic about it! The joy seems to come each day as I get closer to my true self and the true universe. It's very exciting, but what is so exciting about it? I will probably struggle with that till I die. That is my question.

"When people ask me about trying to find their lifework, I remind them that they need to know their true self, and of course our method is to do zazen. By meditating, they become accessible to themselves, in a very naked, direct way. Actually, this information is always with us. But we don't know where it is. It's very important to practice and spend time with yourself. You are the one who has all the information. We are just providing the setup for it all to happen. We provide the theater and the rituals called Zen practice! We have to open to subtle knowledge. We have to hear the heart beat. Feel the wind. Hear the knowledge arising out of us in the moment, not in the future. Where you stand in the moment is where it's unfolding. Even if you don't know what your life purpose is, being mindful of the present moment is your purpose."

TALKING TO YOURSELF

Purposeful points on your path. Jot down your own rites of passage in a simple time line from birth to now. What were the defining events in your own life? What do you think was the purpose of each event—i.e., what did the event teach you? how did it move you? how did it change you?

After constructing your time line, ask yourself:

> *How did my parents and early environment specifically shape me?*
> *Supposing these souls (my parents) were chosen by me, why would I have picked them?*
> *As great souls who accepted their contract to be present in my life, what did my parents convey at the highest spiritual level by their language, thoughts, and actions?*

What Is in Your World Picture Right Now?

Draw a picture of the most important things in your life right now. Don't worry about your skill in drawing. Use stick figures and symbols to indicate:

> *Everything you consider precious and valuable to your well-being.*
> *Those things you would like to attract into your life.* Put a big heart around those things you desire.
> *Those things you want to release.* Put wings around those things you want to let go of.
> *Your values: Look at each thing you have drawn, and underneath the image write a word for* the value *it represents to you.*

Your picture now represents a map of your values. *By consciously aligning yourself with your values, you are directly in touch with how to live your purpose.*

For example, Sarah had drawn a grove of trees, a home with smoke curling out of the chimney, her computer, her cat, and her car, and four people in her family seated around a table. She wanted to attract in a trip to Brazil, a big writing assignment, and more money. She wanted to release her frustration with her brother, her addiction to chocolate, and her tendency to be self-critical. Below is how she gave a value to each of her visual symbols.

SARAH'S VALUES

Symbol	Value
Grove of trees	Closeness to nature, solitude
Family seated around table	Feeling loved and supported
Cat	Unconditional love
Home with fireplace	Stability
Car	Mobility
Computer	Creativity

CHAPTER 6

Synchronicities Unfold Your Purpose

⌒∞⌒

We could make our lives so much more interesting, and develop so many new capacities, if we sought to work with the unknowns of emergence, rather than try and plan surprise out of our lives.

MARGARET J. WHEATLEY AND MYRON KELLNER-ROGERS[1]

WHAT IS SYNCHRONICITY?

A synchronicity is an apparently chance encounter that nevertheless seems cosmically orchestrated. If we are to align ourselves to our purpose, it will be necessary to recognize and open ourselves to these catalyzing events.

Synchronicities are forces that come together in time and space, providing just what is needed. The occurrence strikes the participants as special, unexpected, or unexplainable by normal cause-and-effect rationales. The effect of a synchronicity on the psyche is to trigger an awareness that maybe a greater—or even a divine—purpose is at work. Synchronicities seem to be external answers to an internal psychic state. For example, perhaps we need some particular information, and unexpectedly we run into someone who provides us with exactly what we needed. Synchronicities are a moment in time when we are united with people or information in a way that cannot be described by a linear explanation. They cause us to stop and think. Another name for them is Providence.

The term *synchronicity* was first used by Swiss psychologist Carl Jung, who began to see "coincidental" occurrences as perhaps a phenomenon of a different world order. Until recently, our explanation of the material world was based only on logic and understood in terms of cause and effect. For the past five hundred years, the scientific method looked for linear paths between a cause and its predictable result. This is what we call "proof." Proof is the ability to show why or how something happened, and to re-create that occurrence at will. Causality satisfies our mental need to explain life. Causality gives us certainty.

Things have changed. Cause and effect only partially explains our physical world, as quantum theorists have found. We are not as bounded by time and space as we thought. For example, scientists have separated molecular particles, and then changed the spin on one of the particles, and the related particle instantly changes *no matter how far apart they are.* The interrelatedness of the particles was maintained without being affected by time or distance. It seems that all things exist within one interconnected field of energy.

According to depth psychologist Marie-Louise Von Franz:

> "But serendipity was at work again in [Joseph] Campbell's life, or 'synchronicity' as Carl Jung was now calling it, the meaningful coincidences that not only seem to happen without our intention but ultimately reveal themselves to make perfect sense in terms of our inner needs and the quality of the times. Indeed it was a friend of Carl Jung's whom the invisible helpers sent Campbell's way in 1941. The meeting would evolve into a mingling of destinies that would profoundly affect not only the life but the entire corpus of work left by each man."
> *Stephen and Robin Larsen*[2]

Synchronistic thinking, the classic way of thinking in China, is thinking in fields, so to speak. In Chinese philosophy such thinking has been developed and differentiated much more than in any other civilization; there the question is not why has this come about, or what factor caused this effect, but what likes to happen together in a meaningful way in the same moment?[3]

In our normal way of doing things, our first thought is to attack a problem straight on. For example, if we are out of work, we enter into a logical process of finding another one. We get our resume updated, we make copies of it, and we send it out to twenty companies. We are called for an interview; if we like the company and they like us, and we start our new job. Our lives have changed—we have a new place to go every day, new people to interact with, new duties and a new career track. Nothing seems unusual in our job-seeking (cause) and job-finding (effect). We are able to understand this rational line of activity, and it makes perfect sense. We feel in charge. Or we can follow the synchronicities that open up a way of doing business we could never have planned. This is how Jill Coleman moved her career-counseling business to Portugal without ever making a conscious plan to do so.

Jill Coleman called me out of the blue as I was writing this chapter. She is a successful executive recruiter, and has her own seminar business geared to helping people find their lifework. I decided to include her story since it shows a combination of synchronicity, intuition, and intention. Jill's intuition led her to the right place to reconnect with an old relationship after fifteen years. Once there, her intention and determination to see this synchronicity through provided her with an entirely new life—one she never dreamed would happen.

Love and Business

"In July of 1996, an old girlfriend and her husband called me to work for a high-tech company in Europe," Jill told me. "They place human resource consultants all over the country, and were making their first international placement. I talked to them on Tuesday and within a week I was on a plane to Europe. I spent two months recruiting for a company in Brussels and Amsterdam. I was not interested in a long-term recruiting job, so I told them I had to leave by the end of August, even though they were paying me more money than I had ever made before.

"At the end of August, two girlfriends and I decided to go on vacation. I wanted to go to a beach area near Greece, but one friend firmly insisted that we go to Portugal. For me, Portugal was 'been there, done that.' I had spent a lot of time there in my twenties, but since she kept insisting, I decided to go after all. We rented a villa there in the Algarve.

"Fifteen years ago, I had traveled through Portugal and wound up having a relationship with a Portuguese man named Fernando. I had commuted between San Francisco and Faro for two years. I studied Berlitz Portuguese and made just enough money to keep going back. The last time I had seen him was in 1986.

"Since my friends and I were living only five miles from Faro, I decided to get in touch with Fernando.

"I figured he would be married and have a houseful of kids. It was hard to reach him in the beginning. But my compulsive side said, 'I am going to find this guy.' I became very focused on reaching him. I went back to the café where I had first met Fernando, and the man who owned the café remembered me. He said he would try to arrange a meeting.

"Well, to make a long story short, we got together, and it turned out he was not married. There was an immediate chemistry between us again. I am now in the process of moving my business there. I had literally resisted going to Portugal on vacation, but it seems like the hand of fate stepped in!"

> "The theme of the Grail romance is that the land, the country, the whole territory of concern has been laid waste. It is called a wasteland. And what is the nature of the wasteland? It is a land where everybody is living an inauthentic life, doing as other people do, doing as you're told, with no courage for your own life. That is the wasteland. And that is what T. S. Eliot meant in his poem *The Waste Land.*"
>
> Joseph Campbell[4]

BEING IN THE FLOW EVEN WHEN STALLED

What if your car doesn't start one day, and because you have to walk instead, you wind up meeting someone who changes your life? Father John Rossner, an Episcopal priest and professor of religion at Concordia University in Montreal, was twenty-four years old and had just finished school at Brown University, where he had specialized in ancient history and classical languages. He tells this story.

"I had a little red MG in England, and I had brought it back to the U.S. after active duty there. One Sunday, another graduate student asked me to drive him to a church outside Providence for Sunday Mass. For the first time since I had the car, it wouldn't start. So I suggested that we walk to St. Stephen's Church on the campus nearby. It happened that the preacher that day was the Very Reverend Edward S. White, Dean of Nashotah House in Wisconsin.

> "When this new type of commitment starts to operate, there is a flow around us. Things just seem to happen. We begin to see that with very small movements, at just the right time and place, all sorts of consequent actions are brought into being. We develop what artists refer to as an 'economy of means,' where, rather than getting things done through effort and brute force, we start to operate very subtly. A flow of meaning begins to operate around us, as if we were part of a larger conversation."
>
> Peter Senge[5]

"As I was leaving the church after Mass, the dean was at the door greeting parishioners. As I shook his hand, I casually remarked, 'Oh, you're the dean of one of our seminaries. I have often thought I would like to go to seminary one day.' At that point, the dean grabbed my arm and pulled me to one side, saying, 'Wait right here, young man. I want to talk to you after people leave.' In a few minutes, we resumed our conversation and I told him about my recent graduate studies, whereupon he asked, 'Can you teach ancient Greek?' and I told him I had been tutoring it. Then he said, 'Good. My professor of New Testament studies has told me I had to find someone to teach Greek. I'll offer you room, board, and free tuition for three years if you will come to Nashotah House to do your divinity degree and teach for us at the same time.' I accepted, and that experience changed my life.

"After lunch, I went again to the parking lot behind the graduate residence to check out the MG. I was going to have it towed, but it started up right away!"

Dr. Rossner's example shows a high-powered synchronicity that can cause a major shift in life direction — not unlike being touched by the wing of a guardian angel and being directed to look down a new path.

LEVELS OF MEANING IN SYNCHRONICITIES

What about less clear occurrences such as thinking about someone who then calls on the phone? What does one make of running into an old friend at the supermarket? So what if your college roommate from Taiwan calls when you are about to embark on a trip to Taiwan?

As in everything in life, there are hierarchies of importance, levels of meaning on a continuum. Just as a message from your newfound love is of a higher emotional priority to you than a message saying that your recycling pickup date has been changed, I believe that synchronicities must be evaluated in this same light. Sometimes when a friend calls just after we noticed her name in our address book as we were looking up someone else, she may have a message for us. That happened to me a few weeks ago. During that time, one of the questions on my mind had been what to write about for a monthly column. One morning, I happened to be looking through my address book, and for some reason Cori Kenicer's name came to my attention just for a tiny moment. I briefly thought, "Hmm, haven't heard from Cori in a while [I actually hadn't talked to her for about nine or ten months]." About an hour later, she called me. That struck me as very peculiar as she and I are not in the habit of chatting, and so I told her my brief thought about her. As it turned out, Cori was, once again, the perfect person for me to interview for my column. Cori happens to be one of the people I study from time to time because synchronicities have played such an outstanding part in her transition from real estate agent to travel writer. We will hear more about her story in the next chapter.

WORKING WITH SYNCHRONICITIES

I suggest that when you experience any kind of odd "coincidence," try becoming still for a moment. Let your mind wander slightly, as if you were "relaxing" your intuitive faculty and letting it roam about to bring you what you need to know. Ask yourself any of the following questions: (1) What have I just been thinking about? (2) What is my connection to this person? (3) Does this person have anything to tell me about any of my current questions or interests? (4) What does this coincidence seem to suggest? Does it seem to be a yes or a no answer to any question I have even subtly been asking? (5) Do I feel energized? Does this feel like a go-ahead signal? (6) Do I feel a draw to see this person again? (7) What seemed to be taking place as we met?

I have noticed that oftentimes the most important information in an interchange seems to come at the very end of the conversation—almost as an offhand remark. Something is wanting to be said. If there is any hesitation about your parting with a person, don't be too quick to move on. If something is nagging you at the back of your mind, watch where your energy gets stronger in the conversation. Consciously see the other person in a good light. Notice their smile, their eyes, their earnestness, and send them positive energy. If you feel inspired to mention a project or question you are currently working on, do so.

When you receive a call, take a moment to remind yourself that maybe he or she has a message for you, even if you think the call is a disruption. Even if they don't have a literal message, their call may cause you to think or look in a direction you had previously overlooked. Remember, your field of energy is attracting to you the people, places, and events that will help you find and fulfill your purpose for the current time.

You never know where your next inspiration is coming from! I received a call one day from someone I barely know, but had been avoiding because I feel he drains my energy. I was in the middle of the chapter on the shadow side of life purpose. As this person began telling me about some of his personal problems, it triggered off a very fruitful chain of thinking.

AS TIME GOES BY

By the same token, if you are trying to get through to someone and fail to do so on several attempts, you may want to reconsider that their input is not needed at this time, or that someone else may be a better source or contact.

Trust your process. Years may go by before the next major synchronicity pops open the next door. Dr. Rossner related a further development on his first synchronicity.

"I spent three years at Nashotah House. In February of the year during which I was to graduate and be ordained in June, I happened to come out of a classroom just at the very moment when Father John Bruce, the professor of Old Testament studies, was coming out of his classroom into the cloister. We walked together to the refectory. On the way, I saw a little man in clerical dress in the distance. He was wearing a tall fur hat, which was unusual in Wisconsin at that time. I asked Father Bruce if he knew who the man was. He said, 'Oh, that's Father Hertzler. He's the rector of a large parish in Montreal. He's here looking for a part-time curate who might be interested in doing further graduate studies at McGill University and working part-time.' I said, 'That's the kind of thing I'd be interested in,' although I hadn't really started thinking about it yet. Father Bruce said, 'He's staying at the dean's house,' and he took me over there. It was the same Dean Edward S. White who had found me by synchronicity at St. Stephen's Church on the Brown University campus, and had hired me to teach at Nashotah House! Father Bruce explained that I was interested in Father Hertzler's offer of a part-time position as a curate in Montreal with further studies at McGill, and he said, 'Wonderful. You'd be perfect.' At that moment, Father Hertzler walked up to the door. We spoke and he offered me the job. Of course, I accepted it.

"If I had not come to Montreal then, I would never have been offered a job teaching at Sir George Williams/Concordia University there four years later. And if this had not happened, I would never have met my wife Marilyn, and we would never have founded the International Institute of Integral Human Sciences (IIIHS) in 1975. Today the IIIHS is a nongovernmental organization affiliated with the United Nations, which has touched and influenced people's lives in many continents throughout the world."

The next three people you are about to meet all share one thing—passion. That passion and a sense of purpose—for music, service, challenge, and adventure—seems to have brought to them exactly the circumstances that would allow them to succeed. For musician Steve Cooper, his lifelong passions have attracted into his life everything that he has needed to feel he is fulfilling his dreams. These synchronicities happen for him in small ways as well as in life-transforming ways, as you will see. For healer Mary Lee Banks, early circumstances gave her all the ingredients to manifest her life purpose. For Leyla Bentley, life has been one grand challenge after another, allowing her to thrive *and* to make a difference in outrageously different cultures and circumstances. As you read, you may sense the freedom of spirit that each has achieved by hard work and dedication to their passion.

I had interviewed Steve Cooper, a musician and leader of two bands, the Steve Cooper Orchestra, and the Dixie Patrol, for *The Celestine Prophecy: An Experiential Guide* back in 1994. A year and a half had passed when Steve called me again. I felt there must be a reason behind the question that he was ostensibly calling about. Sure enough, Steve was just about to have the most meaningful event of his life. "Call me in a week," he said mysteriously, "and I'll be able to tell you all about it." I waited, and on the appointed day, I called. I asked him to start at the beginning.

Following the Melody

"I feel my life purpose is to be a musician in all the aspects of performing, teaching, and arranging. I have done everything I wanted to do in life, and it's all happened by the most bizarre coincidences. Because of all the synchronicities, I became interested in metaphysics about ten or fifteen years ago. Now I think that I subtly affect other people and open their eyes to synchronicity by telling them the stories that happen to me.

"I have literally manifested everything I ever wanted. I think there might be two ways of looking at how these things came to be. First, it could be that I had a strong enough intention that I attracted these events into my life, or it could be that I was getting a strong image of the future happenings in my mind's eye and somehow knew this would happen. For example, maybe I met exactly the type of woman I wanted because I knew that she was going to come into my life. I don't know."

I knew that Steve had an uncanny knack of tuning in to (no pun intended) exactly the information he needed in the moment. I remember one of the stories he told me earlier. One day, he said, he was delivering a box of music tapes to a musician at a country club. Having forgotten which direction to turn to get to the club, he was sitting at a railroad crossing wondering which way to go. At that moment, over his car radio there came a commercial for the country club and the announcer said, "Don't forget, turn left at the railroad tracks!"

"A couple of months ago," Steve continued, "somebody called me and left a message. I had forgotten who it was, and was going to listen to the message again on the answering machine, but thought, 'Wait a minute!' I suddenly remembered that a television show I had been waiting to see for about two weeks was just about to start. The subject was about taking dogs to nursing homes, which is something I am very interested in. Within sixty seconds of the show's opening, there on the television was the person who had called me. He was on the show talking about taking dogs into nursing homes! I had no idea he was involved with any of this. He had just called me to leave a message saying that he was available to play in my band.

"Another time, I was attending an electronics show in Las Vegas. I was in a little room watching a presentation film demonstrating high-definition TV. It was really boring, and I started thinking about the biggest band job I had for next year, and how we would be replacing the band that had played the year before. I had never heard them or seen this band and was wondering what kind of bass player they had had. Just then the film I was watching showed a concert by *this same band,* and they panned right up to the face of the bass player. I was able to see everything they do. That was so eerie, that I was sweating for half an hour afterwards.

"What I did this week, though, was the biggest thing of my life, and it just happened to me. This was like my whole life purpose. I could never have imagined this would happen. If I had dreamed this event, I would never have expected it to happen in real life. Not only did it happen, but everyone I encountered treated me like a king."

Steve recounted how in childhood, he was an avid fan of a bigband leader whom we'll call Mr. X. He listened religiously to him on radio and television. This person so influenced him that Steve taught himself several instruments at an early age, and became adept at figuring out the arrangements of the music of big bands just from listening to the records.

"Well, I got a call recently from the conservators of Mr. X's musical library. They invited me to come look at it. When I got there, they let me copy by hand whatever I wanted. I couldn't believe this. Every one of his arrangements was on a shelf in alphabetical order, and they let me copy everything I wanted. It was like a dream for me. There were ten thousand arrangements and I knew exactly what I wanted. It was like having access to anything you ever wanted to know. I can't believe it happened. Not only that but I met several people who knew him, and saw scrapbooks with pictures of friends of mine who used to play with him. I even saw a picture of the concert I had gone to with my mother, and the spot where we sat! The ultimate was seeing one picture with Red Nichols [a band leader whose every piece he collected] and Mr. X. It was beyond belief.

"When I was young, my parents had insisted I become a teacher. They said, 'Otherwise you'll be a music bum, and you will spend your whole life sitting on the floor listening to records.' I *do* sit on the floor and listen to records, and people pay me money to do this! I have more work than I can handle. I tried to get away from music, but it just kept coming back."

In the last ten years, through these amazing, ongoing synchronicities, Steve has either met, played with, or been given access to the musical libraries and arrangements of his most influential musical mentors—Red Nichols, Jimmy Palmer, Bob Crosby, and Mr. X.

"I have worked very, very hard, but it's been good because it has taught me the value of hard work. It showed me I could do anything. I still teach part-time because I have some wonderful students and they need the teaching. But I've done everything that I never would have believed I could do—played with the top society bands in Chicago, played on the *Oprah Winfrey Show*, the *Mary Tyler Moore Show*. Two years ago, I got to play first trumpet for Steve Allen, who was another one of my heroes. One of the songs I played with him was 'Moonglow,' which reminds me of the whole story of my life. I was standing there playing and I had tears in my eyes. Everything I wanted has turned out, but it is always later than you want it, and you have to pay your dues. I had to practice, and it's taken a lifetime to accomplish, but it happened little by little."

"I SUDDENLY REALIZED MY MISSION"

I am always interested in how people start businesses—and keep them functioning successfully. Particularly intriguing is someone like Mary Lee Banks, who comes up with an original product that is not in the mainstream thinking. Mary Lee is the founder of Earth Tribe, a company that sells organic essential oils for healing. She started out in her basement and has developed a strong mid-sized company based on network marketing.

Gathering the Tribe
"When I was young, I wanted to be a witch or a witch doctor. I loved the idea of witches like Disney's, who could bring a cat named Thomasina back to life. Witches seemed like a wonderful thing. My great-grandmother and my grandmother were always doing herbal concoctions from the garden. Mother said I was a witch doctor be-

cause I was always bringing in sick birds. I grew up in Walker, Minnesota, near Leech Lake Indian Reservation. It is a tourist area. There were nine hundred residents, but in summer there would be ten thousand people up there. We lived on the same land as where my ancestors had lived. There was no crime in our community. It was a rural, country life, but a little more sophisticated because of the constant influx of tourists. On my father's side, my great-grandmother was Ojibwa.

"I thought everybody grew up like I did, having medicines from the earth. When someone got sick, my mother or grandmother would pull up a root or boil some mushrooms. I was so surprised when I saw friends with pill bottles and pink, heart-shaped soaps. My grandmother made all our soaps. As I got older, I realized that people bought things like this in stores. Now I'm very proud of my family background. I still use my grandmother's recipes.

"When I went to college, I wanted to make my living in health. I soon got discouraged about medicine or about being a doctor. I wanted to design my own degree in holistic medicine, but my professors told me I'd never be able to make a practice in the holistic field.

"Not long after this setback, I was making breakfast, and a friend turned on the oven, but didn't light the pilot. I went over to light the stove, and blew up the kitchen. I had second-degree burns all over my upper body and face. The doctors at the University of Michigan hospital said I would probably be scarred for life. They told me not to go near the sun, and that I would age faster than normal. I was determined to prove them wrong.

"I went back home and began to use the essential oil of lavender. This was fifteen years ago, when essential oils were unheard of. After a few weeks, I went back to the doctors. They couldn't believe it. I had healed without scarring.

"I was intrigued by what had happened to me, but I found it impossible to study these methods in the States. No one knew what I was talking about. Fortunately for my life's work, I had a Swedish dentist as a boyfriend, and he went to work for a Swedish pharmaceutical company. I went with him. We lived in Athens, London, and Stockholm. What was wonderful was that I was able to formally study clinical aroma therapy in Europe, where it was becoming mainstream, especially in Britain. I studied with some of the people now considered masters. I also worked for a European pharmaceutical company, and got a view of pharmaceuticals from their point of view, which differs from the FDA here.

"When I came back to the States, I started bringing in my own oils and making my own products. At first, I had no intention of doing this as a business. My strength was in making the potions. I gave them to friends, and one friend set up a seminar for me at the Beverly Hills Hotel. It turned out that there were some beauty editors there, which was great good luck. They wrote several stories about the oils. I began to get several celebrity clients, such as Sigourney Weaver. Around this time, I was pregnant with my twins.

> "Family guides watch over family destiny. They monitor the life path of each individual and that of the family as a group. They rescue unwary children, especially under-fives and teenagers who wander into the track of disaster. They also take stock of the accumulated karma that family members have come together to work out."
> Leah Maggie Garfield
> and Jack Grant[6]

"*Woman's Day* magazine wrote an article, and they mentioned my address. I didn't know what month the article was coming out. I was busy with the babies who were about two or three months by this time. One day, I went to my mailbox, and it was overflowing with envelopes. There was a note that said, 'Please come to the desk for more mail!' There was a whole box of more envelopes—all inquiries about the piece on aroma therapy. My husband was actually the one who said, 'You should probably start doing this as a business. A lot of people need your help.'

"So there were three events that were responsible for my starting this business. First was the burn accident and healing. The second was the birth of my twin boys, which made me want to work from home. I also wanted to give oils to women so they could have a great pregnancy. The third was when the envelopes showed up. My husband said, 'If you just sit in your room, no one will hear your message.' That's when the light bulb went off. It was an epiphany. I suddenly clearly realized that my mission was to bring this message out to people, and give them the benefit of these little life-enhancing oils from nature.

"Now every day the testimonials and letters are just incredible. I was standing at the bank with tears running down my face while I was reading a letter from a woman who had been suicidal after a car accident. She was allergic and couldn't take any drugs. She wrote that she took Calming [one of the essential oil blends from Earth Tribe] and it changed her life. Sometimes the effects of these oils are dramatic and irrefutable. Because of them, my life has been changed.

"I believe that if you follow your heart, doors will open where you don't even know there are doors. This is so important for women. If you make money your only goal or object, it gets in the way, almost like a wall. If you don't think about the money, but keep your eyes on what you love, on what helps people, then everything else seems effortless.

"Where my heart really lies is in changing the lives of the next generation. I really think aroma therapy is one of the most important rediscoveries of our time. These methods of healing reconnect us with nature, and by doing so, we are healing centuries of disconnection from nature. Using them brings parents and children closer together. Applying oils promotes touch and more of a healing bond. I think essential oils are bringing feminine strength to the forefront, healing centuries of disregarding the natural wisdom of women and women as healers."

Mary Lee has found purpose and meaning by bringing forward the gifts of her heritage. Her story is also a good example of how one person's decisions affect many others—perhaps future generations. Her commitment to her own path can even be seen in the context of a larger movement toward wholeness and a return to earthly roots.

Switching for a moment to a favorite anecdote, Mary Lee said with a smile in her voice, "You know Cleopatra was the greatest aroma therapist of all time. She seduced two of the most powerful men in the world, Julius Caesar and Mark Antony. She would scent the sails of her vessel before crossing the Mediterranean. The Romans would know of her arrival before they could see her. It was her calling card. In the beginning, when she was trying to have an audience with Julius Caesar, he wouldn't see her. So she had herself rolled up naked in a carpet, and scented it with oil. Guards carried in the carpet and rolled her out, and the story goes she and the emperor spent the next three days in the royal chamber. She conquered half the known world without any bloodshed! She did it with essential oils.

"I think women bring intuition, instincts, love, and humanity to private enterprise, and we give a lot back to the community. Instead of just looking at numbers and quotas, we make our decisions from our heart and our soul. I believe that is where major life decisions should come from."

OUT OF CALIFORNIA TO AFRICA

I had gone to Sacramento to teach a workshop. Leyla Bentley had seen the announcement of it, and called to invite me to stay overnight after the workshop. She now lives in East Nicolaus, population 270, about twenty miles north of Sacramento, California.

I had first met Leyla in 1989 when she was the top membership saleswoman for the San Francisco Chamber of Commerce. We had become friends, and two years ago I got a letter from her in Botswana. She had joined the Peace Corps and was living in Africa. I was extremely curious to know how she had made this transition.

Leyla is fifty, attractive, and vivacious. Her tanned face is almost never without a wide smile, and a twinkle in the eye. What impresses me about her is that she will take a chance on doing something completely new to her, jump in with both feet, and somehow always manage to win an award or accomplish the near-impossible, even while claiming that she only did what was in front of her.

Adventure Woman
"When I joined the Chamber in 1984, I had never been in sales before," she began. "I'd always been a manager and coordinator of medical offices. At that time, the Chamber was in a semishambles. I was going to be working on commission only. I never really thought about how scary that might be. I just went to work enrolling people. My boss was quite amazed. He told me he'd never seen anything like it in his working life. Very soon I was making more than anyone else. The only person making more than me was the CEO.

"I enrolled all kinds of people—not just traditional businesses. I thought everyone should be in the Chamber, so I got massage therapists, transactional analysts, psychics, anyone."

I had to laugh. I'll never forget the first time I showed up at the Chamber for the orientation meeting for new members. Leyla greeted me, although she had not been my initial contact. I remember her smiling broadly and shaking my hand, saying, "Oh, I'm so glad you're a numerologist! We need you in here." Leyla's support had meant a lot to me.

"Why do you think you were so successful?" I asked.

"Well, I really focused on educating people on how the Chamber could help them in their particular business," she replied. "I invited them to events that were pertinent to them, and sometimes I got them invitations to meet people that they wouldn't have met without my pushing it a little bit. I never followed the rules too much!" She burst out with a laugh. "I also like being on top. No question. But what people liked about me was that I was so enthusiastic. They told me that they felt that I really listened to their business problems, and sincerely tried to bring new possibilities to them. I guess I got *passionate* about *their* business, and ultimately it helped me with my own business — of selling."

"So this was a whole new field for you. What had you done before that?" I asked idly.

"Oh, brother. You wouldn't believe how I fell into the previous job, either. Talk about your synchronicities. I had gone to my dentist who knew I was looking for a new job. My dentist mentioned my name to a friend of his, Dr. Richard Walden, who needed an assistant. He was an internal medicine specialist and an educator to other doctors. He came to my house, interviewed me, and said he needed an assistant for his clinic in Mount Shasta, California. He didn't tell me his clinic wasn't built yet!

"He was doing preventive medicine, which was a new idea in 1972. Here I was twenty-six years old, and he says, 'By

> "So I said, 'Okay. I can do that.' "
> *Leyla Bentley*

the way, I'm leaving for China in a couple of days. I don't have an office set up in Mount Shasta yet. I have a piece of land, and I've ordered a modular office to be delivered while I'm gone.' He needed an asphalt parking lot, a water well dug, water and sewer lines put in, permits from the planning commission, and he wanted to notify all the doctors who would refer to him so that they could start sending people. He wanted appointments set up with patients, so that when he returned from China he could start seeing people the same day. So I said, 'Okay. I can do that.'

"In addition to getting the physical structure in place, I hired office staff and lab and X-ray technicians. I set up all the equipment, and set up his books. The day he arrived home, he walked in and started seeing patients."

"How did you do all that?" I asked, astonished.

"I must have been insane. No, honestly, I just thought, 'Well, that's what he wants, so go do it.' After that he taught me how to draw blood and do EKGs, urine analyses, and blood analyses. I even saved two lives because of finding certain cells in the blood samples. I can't remember what they were now."

"But you weren't a nurse." It was as much a question as a statement.

"No. In fact, I decided I wanted to get a bachelor's degree and an RN degree at Chico State University. I knew if I worked at the student health clinic, I would be able to get a degree for free. I had no idea there was a year-long waiting list for those jobs, and I applied and got a part-time job. It was perfect because it allowed me to go to school without tuition.

"I was assigned to Dr. Stephen Cowdrey, the medical director at the clinic. He was considered the hardest doctor to work for, very difficult, and his turnover of nurses was high. But he and I got along great. One day, he called me in and said, 'I don't want you to get bored.' I had always done more than my job required anyway, but I was surprised that he was taking an interest in me. Dr. Cowdrey was doing research on cancer screening for virgins. Believe it or not, women couldn't get pap smears in those days unless they had had sex or children. Doctors didn't think virgins were at risk for cancer, and Dr. Cowdrey wanted to test that theory, because he didn't believe it. So he taught me how to do pap smears and breast self-exams, and I wrote a marketing brochure for the student population to let them know about the service. Two afternoons a week, I saw patients who had never had intercourse.

"One day, the doctor called me in and he said. 'You know, you have a one hundred percent collection rate on your specimens [all the slides of the specimens were clear and usable every time]. How do you do that?' The average collection rate for the rest of the staff was eighty-two percent, and some of the doctors' averages were even lower."

"So how *did* you do it." I am always looking for the keys that make people excel.

"Well, I just loved what I was doing. I was very slow and careful not to hurt the patients. I always explained what I was doing to them. I focused on the patient, asking them about themselves, and listened to everything they said. I thought the work was really important for women, and I explained this was a special program that could help change state policy. I guess they felt 'enrolled' and important. That study was published, by the way, and it showed that virgins were just as much at risk as nonvirgins, and screening could save their lives."

As Leyla talked, I could see something in her method—both with the new members of the Chamber, and the patients that she saw. She had a knack for starting up a flow of energy between herself and others. She was able to raise the energy vibration, and created a special bond that affected all aspects of the work she was doing—even up to the specimen collection rate. Everything worked better because she was fully engaged and enjoying what she was doing. It affected everybody and everything.

"The Peace Corps was something I had always wanted to do. A few years ago, my life was in another transition. I had just become a bank vice president following my years at the Chamber. I knew everybody by then, and they wanted me to introduce the bank to all my contacts. I had the big office. I had just pulled in a two-million-dollar deal, but I wasn't happy working there. Then my aunt died and that threw me for a loop. I quit the bank job without knowing what I was going to do next, and basically took off from working for two years. I did some consulting and enrolled in the Rudolf Steiner school for teachers, and applied for the Peace Corps. Soon after that, they called me and offered me a position in the Eastern bloc of countries— Estonia, Latvia, Poland, and so on. But I didn't feel called to go to these countries, so I turned it down. I hoped it wouldn't hurt my chances for another post, since they have about twelve thousand applicants for two thousand jobs.

"I waited nine months and took a job launching a twenty-seven-city tour for a dance company. In the meantime, the Peace Corps called back and offered me Yemen or Botswana. I went to the library and read about Botswana and the issues there, and I knew that's where I wanted to go. I had six months to prepare, which allowed me to finish with the dance company. The timing was perfect.

"I bought a big container and I stored all my stuff in it. I had no debt, and I was free to go. There is no pay with the Peace Corps, but they give you housing and a food allowance. I was really ready to get out of this materialistic culture. I was sent to Kanye, Botswana, where I got my training working with the Bushman tribe, the Basarwa, who are one of the oldest tribes, going back forty thousand years. The indigenous people were easy to get along with. It was the Peace Corps volunteers that turned out to be the challenge. Two weeks into the training, I contracted malaria, and might have died if it hadn't been for the native people taking care of me. My roommate did nothing to help me, but finally the grandmother of one of the children came and put compresses on me. They got the truck of the chief's nephew and the *whole family* went with me to the hospital and stayed with me in the hospital for the entire next day.

"I was eventually assigned to the northern region with the Regional Industrial Office to develop training programs in business management for small-scale manufacturing companies. I was supposed to monitor the financial assistance program for start-up companies. These companies did carpentry, dressmaking, textiles, and metal and leather work. For the first six months, I was the only white person out of seventy people, and the only female in such a position.

"For the first six months, I couldn't get anything done. They didn't accept me and would sabotage everything I did — not give me phone messages, everything. A Nigerian friend told me, 'The most important thing to them is character. They will test you and watch your behavior.' I had come there to take charge, and that wasn't working at all. Finally, I gave up and went to my boss and apologized for all the things that he had said were insubordinations. I told him I had been wrong, and that he was the boss, and that I wanted to start over. That was the day everything shifted. He was a very lovely, very spiritual man. Everything was forgiven and he held no grudge.

"My task was to start building a program for developing small businesses. You can keep yourself busy doing what the Peace Corps gives you to do. But if you want to make a difference, you really have to go it alone. I was committed to not getting a grant to fund the program. I wanted it to be self-supported by local people. What came out of it was a continuing education course for small-business people. The challenge was that people only had about a seventh-grade education and minimal English. The sporadic course that they had already started was not working well. There was little follow-through or attendance, even though they were paying people to attend.

"I set up a course that was broken down into simple modules of planning, stock control, marketing, bookkeeping, and so on. Along with that, I identified a critical lack of information flow between the people and the administration. I wanted to change all that. I believed it would be intrinsically worthwhile to people to attend these classes. The administration did not believe my idea would work, but I figured I could get at least ten to fifteen people to come.

"On the first day of class, eighty-one people showed up from all parts of the country—some from five hours away. I really had to think on my feet! After that, we averaged fifty-five to sixty-five people every week. They all received certificates of achievement in business management from the University of Botswana. This was a big deal for those people with seventh-grade educations. I kept telling them they were pioneers, and reinforcing that their dedication was helping everybody in the country.

"Out of that was born community trade fairs, and an international trade show. We also started a Botswana fashion show and started a business for women that is still in operation.

"For me, the biggest thing was the joy of accomplishing something. It was intrinsically satisfying work. Learning came naturally."

TALKING TO YOURSELF

What stood out for you in the stories in this chapter?
How would you write your own story in terms of taking risks?
What synchronicities have you had lately? What would you guess was their message? In what way did they move you or touch you?
What new challenge has been brought to you lately?
What new skills would you like to learn?

PART TWO

TECHNIQUES

CHAPTER 7

Intention and Nonattachment

C∞⊃

When we are in this state of being where we are open to life and all its possibilities, willing to take the next step as it is presented to us, then we meet the most remarkable people who are important contributors to our life. This occurs in part through the meeting of our eyes; it's as if our souls instantly connect, so that we become part of a life together at that moment.

JOSEPH JAWORSKI[1]

INTENTION PRACTICE

An amazing and amusing synchronicity happened one day as I was writing this chapter. I received a call from Giorgio Cerquetti, an Italian writer and self-styled free spirit. "I used to call myself a yogi," he said, "but I now prefer to say free spirit." We had met last year, and he had called me to catch up and chat about some projects. Giorgio travels extensively interviewing people from all walks of the spiritual path, and has just finished a book on his personal experiences and research in the field of reincarnation. He is also the founder of a food distribution project that aids the homeless called Vegetarian International. Having just returned from a benefit in Atlanta, he was traveling in America for a few weeks to interview people working in the metaphysical field.

He and his friend Tara DeMarco arrived at my house for a visit at about two-thirty in the afternoon. We were talking of various matters when he mentioned, in an offhand way, his method for increasing synchronicities in his life. Since I had just begun to write this chapter on intention, that was just the kind of information I was looking for.

I turned on the tape recorder and began to take notes. By this time, he was sitting on the floor, yogi-style, and telling me:

"What I do each morning is to say, 'Today I want to meet good people.' By that I mean," he explained carefully, "that I want to meet people compatible with my path and with whom I can exchange information or messages about where to go next. I ask the universe to send them to me, and I will meet them. When I tell others about this method, I suggest that it's also a good idea to tape-record your own voice saying this, and then listen to that recording. At night, before I go to sleep, I say, 'I send my good energy to all the people I have met, who are thinking of me, who have crossed my path in any way.' Or I'll say, 'I wish all the people I have met good health, good fortune, and a good life.' In this way I send out positive energy. If a person's face comes into my mind in my meditation—perhaps someone I do not like—I will say specifically, using their name, 'I love you, John, and I forgive you.' This allows me to go to sleep with no anger, no jealousy. I clear myself each night.

"I promise that if you do this for three weeks, your life will change! You must do it for three weeks because that is the amount of time it takes to change the blood in your body. You want these thoughts to saturate your cells." He stared into my eyes intently when he said this.

In five minutes, my phone rang, in what turned out to be perfect timing. Earlier that morning, I had received two urgent messages from Mateo Madoni, whom I had met in Montreal last year. Mateo, a successful businessman who owns six restaurants and a martial arts studio in Montreal, is intensely interested in metaphysics and books such as *The Celestine Prophecy.* We had had dinner together, and he had poured out numerous synchronicities that had changed his life.

Today, oddly enough, my answering service had uncharacteristically faxed me his messages without my calling in for them. I had tried to call Mateo earlier, but was told he would return in three hours. As it turned out, when he returned my call, it was precisely when Giorgio—whom I had no idea would be visiting me today—was in my office.

Mateo began hurriedly, "Carol, I am so glad to speak to you. I must tell you that since I saw you last, the most amazing things have been happening. All kinds of phenomena. I have just returned from Hawaii, and I went to meet some friends of James and Salle Redfield

[James Redfield, of course, is the author of *The Celestine Prophecy*] in Sedona. I have written a manuscript about my experiences, and the people who have read it are very excited about it."

I raised my eyebrows at Giorgio and Tara. "May I put you on speaker phone?" I asked Mateo, who quickly agreed.

He told us about a few synchronistic and transforming meetings with certain people in Sedona, and obviously had more to convey, so urgent was his tone.

After a few minutes, Giorgio broke into the conversation, introducing himself, and urging Mateo to continue to tell us specifically what occurrences there had been. We spoke of these things for a few minutes—they involved his meeting a healer somewhere outside Sedona, which had further engendered some other unusual events. Mateo told us that he was returning to Sedona on the next Wednesday, and would be staying in a certain lodging. Giorgio knew the person who ran that place, and had already been planning to leave San Francisco for Sedona on Thursday next week. He had told me earlier that he wanted to go there, but didn't know anybody there, but was trusting that he would meet whom he needed to meet! Mateo, who is half Italian himself, quickly invited Giorgio to accompany him on some of the adventures that appeared to be waiting for both of them.

It was truly an inspired moment, particularly given that Giorgio had just finished telling me his meditation for establishing an intention to meet compatible people. All of us traded phone numbers like crazy, and hung up laughing.

INTENTIONS—CONSCIOUS AND UNCONSCIOUS

Intention is that activity of the mind, energized by the passion of the heart, that wills something to happen. It is the wish or purpose behind the initiation of an action. Usually, we define intention as something we consciously decide upon and choose with a desire for its fulfillment. Most of the time, our problem is that we don't know what to focus on! As we begin to become more aware of our intrapsychic process—that is, how we talk to ourselves and how we listen to our intuition—we start to notice where we habitually put our attention. Knowing where we put our attention is like knowing where we spend our money.

> **THE FRAME**
>
> "The most important thing in art is *The Frame*. For painting: literally; for other arts: figuratively—because, without this humble appliance, you can't know where *The Art* stops and *The Real World* begins. You have to put a 'box' around it because otherwise, *what is that shit on the wall?*"
>
> Frank Zappa [2]

Like anything else in life, any one desire or intention is interrelated to other psychic energy states within us. For example, John, age twenty, has the intention to find his life purpose. He knows that he has always been good in drawing and the graphic arts, likes to cook, and likes to read about psychology and philosophy. However, John's father thinks art and cooking are fit only for women. Moreover, when John mentions that he's somewhat interested in the field of psychotherapy, his mother derides the idea as too depressing and tells him there are already too many therapists trying to make a living. At that point, if John is more invested in what his parents think, and unwilling to go against their advice, his intention to know his life purpose is weakened by fear of displeasing others. In this state of psychic dependence, he might only halfheartedly pursue his dreams, or even fail to notice relevant information along these lines. At this point in his development, John's intention is undermined to the extent that he has not individuated from his parents' sphere of influence.

What Do You *Want* to Have?

Each day you have questions about one direction or another. You might be asking yourself, "Should I go to law school at night or go back home and run my father's produce business?" Going back and forth about the pros and cons, you probably bring up your question to your friends, saying, "I don't know what to do. I'm really confused."

Over the years, I have learned to look at the questions in life in a little different way. Now when I hear people ask "What should I do?" I suggest they reframe the question, and ask, "What is it that I *want?*" Instead of focusing on the confusion generated by having two choices (or more), bring your focus back to what you would *like to have*—in terms of the *ultimate feeling* you want to experience—surrendering your need to know exactly how that can be achieved at this time. Instead of getting stuck on the specific questions, try to imagine the kind of feeling state that you would most like to have. Look at your questions and try to find the underlying result that you are really striving to have. For example, with the earlier question about whether to go to law school or run the family business, what is the result the person most wants to have? Let's imagine that no matter where this person is working, she wants to feel she has made the right choice. She wants to feel excited about her work, and that she is using her talents to the fullest. She would then write these feelings out into a statement as if she had already achieved these goals. For example, "I am working in exactly the right place to use all my talents to the fullest, and I am working with people I have fun with. I make a wonderful living."

Passion, Belief, Affirmation

There are three important points to remember here. First, your statement about the ultimate result or feeling you want *must* generate some excitement within you. You should feel a real rush of energy knowing that you are achieving these goals. Second, you must be able to believe that *you* can have such great good fortune! Just remember, anything is possible, and let the universe handle rearranging the furniture for you. And third, be sure to affirm this statement in the morning, and a couple more times during the day. Before you go to sleep, ask that your dreams give you information about how to achieve your desired result. Be very specific in asking your dreams to answer your question, and write down everything you can remember in the morning. Take this information seriously, and keep asking for more details during your sleep time.

Using these methods to open your energy field will stimulate many new ideas, and your clarity will increase. Pay attention to how synchronicities also bring more information or the right contacts. Soon your path to this result will unfold in ways you would never have been able to anticipate beforehand.

> **LET'S *ALL* BE COMPOSERS!**
>
> **"Just Follow These Simple Instructions:**
>
> 1. **Declare your *intention* to create a 'composition.'**
> 2. ***Start* a piece at *some time.***
> 3. **Cause *something to happen over a period of time* (it doesn't matter what happens in your 'time hole'—we have critics to tell us whether it's any good or not, so we won't worry about that part).**
> 4. ***End the piece at some time* (or keep it going, telling the audience it is a 'work in progress').**
> 5. **Get a part-time job so you can continue to do stuff like this."**
> *Frank Zappa*[3]

What Are You Organizing Around?

> "We tinker ourselves into existence by unobserved interactions with the players who present themselves to us."
> Margaret J. Wheatley and Myron Kellner-Rogers[4]

Life is messy. Don't expect to go in a straight line from your current feeling of confusion to a sense of fulfillment and clarity about your purpose. We are constantly organizing new information through experimentation and trial-and-error. It's important not to see intention as such a concretizing force that your purpose can only be realized in a certain form. Be willing to let failures be just as important as successes, in that they give you further information about yourself and the world. We can be more creative when we focus our attention in the moment, rather than insisting on a preconceived form. In many cases, the path takes us to a choice we had, at first, not even considered or known about. When we polarize a question—that is, when we give ourselves only two options (law school or family business)—we somehow jam the energy circuits and slow down our progress. When we shift our intention to something broader and related to our *feelings*, it seems to unlock the energy field.

Purpose Is Seen in What We Pay Attention To

We don't have to struggle to create our purpose. Order and purpose are an inherent component of our life energy system. We organize ourselves around what we pay attention to. Intention is both a driving and a navigating force through which we attract an outcome.

How Open Are You?

We are connected to each other. We shape each other's experiences, behavior, and understanding each time we interact. Without much conscious thought, we are always *intending* something. Our intention may be to make a good impression, to look like we're trustworthy, to be friendly, to look menacing, to be happy, or to do the right thing. As you move about your life, you continually organize yourself in relationship to the world—to others.

It is usually through our various relationships that we experience a sense of our life purpose. If relationships are so important, then it might be useful to ask yourself, "How open am I to others?" "Do I *take in* what people say to me, or do I rush ahead with my own comments without really listening? Do I really listen with my intuition, letting a message become clear?" "How much trust do I have in others?"

What Kind of Intentions Do You Have with Various People?

Begin to notice your inner motivation when speaking with different people, such as your boss, your assistant, your children, your spouse, your parents, your colleagues. Are you suspicious or aloof with others? Are you overaccommodating? Are you willing to initiate contact? How competitive do you feel with others? Do you feel you must control any conversation?

State Your Intention to Fulfill Your Purpose

A strong intention to do what you love together with the willingness to be shown divine will— that is the foundation for a fulfilling life. Staying true to what you love allows you to pick up on pertinent messages and to avoid being overly influenced by the *opinions* of others. You will be able to *flow* with synchronicities, rather than feeling confused about how they might be relevant to your path. Living with intention *and* the ability to surrender to an even higher order increases your ability to withstand long periods where nothing seems to be happening.

What Makes Sense

Your intentions grow out of what you have seen, experienced, or *dreamed toward.* How do you know what information to pay attention to? As a self-organizing system, you will only pay attention to what makes sense to you, and which somehow relates to your deeper purpose. Research shows that most of what we see is something we have already learned. Trust your inner selection process instead of continuing to give energy to confusion, fear, and overcontrol.

In the following story, travel writer Cori Kenicer shares her experience of how synchronicity provides the exact information she needs whenever she is on assignment. Her story is a good example of the attracting power of an internal organizing field that is *on purpose.*

FROM REAL ESTATE AGENT TO TRAVEL WRITER

Cori Kenicer had been in the real estate business for many years before she began to seriously consider changing careers. Her dream was to be a travel writer. As that dream began to take shape in her mind as a real possibility, two things happened. The first event was being unexpectedly introduced at a business reception to a French-woman, who, upon hearing about her interest in writing, asked Cori to write an article on her business. Even though this seemed to be pointing Cori in the direction of her writing aspirations, she hesitated for a few weeks, not knowing who might buy such a story.

One day a couple of months later, while going on her daily walk, Cori happened to notice a new travel magazine, and had the intuition that that magazine might be receptive to an article on the French-woman's business. Because of Cori's inexperience with the customary procedures for submitting ideas to editors, she faxed her proposal directly to an editor at the magazine, instead of taking the more ac-cepted route of sending a query letter. As it turned out, the editor was very receptive to the idea and gave her the assignment to write the article. From that moment, Cori's professional life took off via one synchronicity after another. Her work quickly progressed to a focus on writing about the world of golf, and she is inundated with more work than she can handle. So far she has been on assignment several times to the Moroccan palace of a shah, to major golf tour-naments, and resorts all over the world.

Being on Assignment
"I have begun to take notes on all the events that happen so effort-lessly," Cori told me. "I've had literally dozens of synchronistic events, but there were two recent incidents that show how things flow in when I have an assignment to do for a magazine. It seems that when-ever I have an assignment, all of a sudden, everything crystallizes around that destination. Contacts, resources, and precise information just come into my life.

"The first incident happened when my editor asked me to do a story on golf in Monterey, California. It so happened that around that same time, I was interviewed on TV with some golf pros—one of whom was the head golf pro at a major resort in Monterey. He was a terrific contact for the story. Then my plan was to call the resorts one by one, and set up a visit. But just then, an invitation arrived in the mail inviting me to look at some of the resorts. Resorts will sometimes invite established writers to come and look at any changes and improvements they make, even if there is no assignment. And last, there happened to be a spread in the *San Francisco Chronicle* about current hot spots in Carmel and Monterey for dining and entertainment — so again all my resources were right there! It was amazing."

Another incident involved an assignment for writing an article on California golf courses from A to Z. Cori had synchronistically found all the information she needed except for one item. She was lacking one entry for the letter "X," and was mulling over how to find a golf course related to the letter X.

"All I could think of was 'X marks the spot,' " she said. "But what did that mean? I couldn't figure it out. Why does this run through my mind? I was driving down the freeway, and a car pulled out in front of me with a bumper sticker that says, 'Come and See the Mystery Spot in Santa Cruz.' Then I thought, 'The mystery spot — that's a visitor attraction in Santa Cruz, which has one of the finest public golf courses in the country — Pasa Tiempo, designed by Aleister McKinley. That showed me that Pasa Tiempo must be the golf course — it was the spot. So that gave me all twenty-six entries from A to Z."[5]

Here we see how Cori's subconscious message, "X marks the spot," kept her open, so that when she saw the bumper sticker with the word mystery *spot*, her subconscious gave her the "Aha!"

SURRENDER

Put your intention out there. Then let it go. Surrender is the crucial part of finding life purpose. Surrender can happen voluntarily or involuntarily. You will be able to surrender voluntarily once you can set a goal or an intention but not be attached to when or how it shows up. For example, you may say, "I want to design gardens, and I'd like to do it professionally." Once you have made your declaration, then it is your job to do whatever footwork you can to start the ball rolling in the direction you want to go. As you pursue work or training as a garden designer, you must follow through on ideas that occur to you ("I should call my cousin who's a contractor — he knows a lot of people with new homes"). Also, you will watch for any synchronous event that arises that introduces you to someone who may be able to help you achieve your goals. As you do this work in the external world, you must be willing to take the attitude of not being *attached* to how fast your goal happens. If you seem to be running into brick walls, only you can decide internally if those walls indicate bad timing, or if the obstacles are trying to tell you, "Don't do this at all." You must be willing to let the universe send you clues about where and how to design gardens, even though the clues don't look that related to your goal at first. You may not have any idea how to start manifesting your ultimate goal, but your job is to be *clear and focused about your love of gardening.* Surrender is the act of being patient and trusting that God or the universe has heard your intention and is setting about attracting into your life the people, places, and events that will create that intention. Another word for surrender is receptivity.

> "Another notion of freedom was beginning to make its way into my consciousness at this time, far below the surface—the freedom to follow my life's purpose with all the commitment I could muster, while at the same time, allowing life's creative forces to move through me without my control, without 'making it happen.' As I was to learn over time, this is by far a much more powerful way of operating."
> Joseph Jaworski[6]

Surrender also happens involuntarily when you have "snapped," such as when I knew that I was not on my own path, but had adopted someone else's. When surrender happens involuntarily—because you are up against a wall—you have no choice but to acknowledge that what you are doing is not working.

Surrender is realizing that you are not in charge of your life; for people who are very control-oriented, this can be very scary or painful. Later, however, one usually comes to realize that by surrendering to a higher will, he or she was following a deeper signal than the ego's plan. Letting go happens when you focus less on making something happen, and focus more on *participating* in life. Surrender is noticing significant information, and being willing to let that image or intuition lead you somewhere that may not, at first, match your expectations. Our collective belief is that change is difficult, that life is competitive, that resources are scarce, and that everything is a struggle. How many times have you said, "No pain, no gain" to someone?

Our culture teaches that to find our purpose, we must control our future actions and make a plan and stick to it. Paradoxically, the movement we desire comes just at the moment when we stop being so afraid.

To enhance flow, try to limit judging your progress. Instead of fixating on "Am I on purpose?" try to pay more attention to what captures your attention each day, surrendering to and trusting your capacity to self-organize. Surrendering can mean taking in whatever positive flow is coming to you, and letting it become part of your purpose for the moment.

Is There a Limit to Surrender?

You may ask, "How far do I go in my surrender? Does that mean just letting the winds of fate toss me about?" If you feel totally confused, take some action to stop your frenzy—whatever it might be. Pretend you are hitting the "pause button" on your emotional state. If you can, take yourself to a quiet place, or just close your eyes briefly, take a few deep breaths, and let go of the confusion. When you have slowed down a little, remember one time when you loved someone (or even loved your pet). Bring that episode as fully into your mind and heart as you can. Reconnect to that one wonderful feeling that you have already experienced in the past. It's a little bit like putting balm on a burn. Try to stay in this state of love for as long as you can, at least two or three minutes. Notice how you have calmed down. Quietly ask that your inner guidance come forward and give you a simple, clear message about the very best thing you could do right now. Resume your activities, and remember—anything is possible! Research studies have proven that a calm and relaxed attitude increases creativity and even enhances your immune response.

MISS AMERICA

Sharon Ritchie was crowned Miss America in 1956. I first met her in New York in 1991. Her story about winning the crown vividly shows the power of positive consciousness, and how a positive attitude is a lifelong treasure. When I called to interview Sharon, I asked her to talk about her dreams as a little girl growing up in Nebraska. She began by saying, "I was always fascinated by the possibility of being a movie star. I loved going to the movies and dreaming about the glamorous life."

Winning the Crown

"When I was seventeen," Sharon continued, "I won a scholarship to Colorado Women's College. The week before I left for college, my father gave me a copy of the book *The Power of Positive Thinking* by Dr. Norman Vincent Peale. I remember that Dad gave it to me in the evening, and I stayed up all night reading it. I was absolutely captivated by all of the possibilities that can be open to us if we learn how to arrange our thoughts in a positive way to attract positive results. I probably read that book three or four times that week before I went off to school.

"By the time I got to college, I know that I had already changed. I was more outgoing, and had more confidence in myself. During those first few months, I became freshman class president, and chairman of morning meditations in the chapel. I made lots of friends, and good things were happening to me. Because I was settling things in myself, I was more open to others and was more kind. I even greeted others in a different way than I had before.

"That following April of my first year of college, the college offered, for the first time, a beauty pageant, the winner of which would go to the Miss Colorado pageant. Three days before the pageant, a couple of friends talked me into participating. That was such a stroke of good fortune. It was a turning point. Obviously, in looking back, that college was where I was supposed to be in order for this wonderful opportunity to arise. I won. I was amazed, and went home to Nebraska for the summer to work before competing for Miss Colorado.

"That was an important time in my life. I already had the basics about positive thinking, which I took in to the tips of my toes. During those two months, I worked steadily on making affirmations. I exercised both my body and my mind. When I went back to Denver to compete, I was in good shape mentally and physically. Again, I was fortunate, and won that pageant.

"I remained in Denver five or six weeks before going on to Atlantic City for the Miss America contest. By this time, I *knew* I was on the right path. I didn't know if I would win the title, but I knew if it was

God's will I would be okay. I was also very young and didn't know about all the things that could go wrong! I had an absolute faith that the right thing would happen.

"Walking into that convention hall in Atlantic City was extremely overwhelming. It is huge. It seats twenty-five thousand people, and you can play two regulation basketball games at the same time on the great stage. Imagine! This was where I was going to deliver my dramatic reading! This trip was also my first time on an airplane. So much newness! But I was able to take all these mind-boggling things in stride because I had this calmness inside. As you know, there are dozens and dozens of reporters covering these pageants. Interestingly, somehow the word got around that Miss Colorado had an unusually calm attitude, and the reporters got interested in this. I had dozens of reporters coming to interview me to find out what was going on. You have to remember, ideas about positive thinking were a very new philosophy at that time. The reporters were intrigued by what this young girl was demonstrating, especially in this frenetic atmosphere.

"The night of the final competition, I had gone out on a balcony of the hotel at the end of the hallway, overlooking the ocean. I prayed, 'Dear God, if it can be your will, please let me win.' I know this sounds odd, but after I said this, there just seemed to be a feeling like there was an angel in the clouds. In my mind, I heard the statement, 'It will be done.' I was exhilarated! My chaperone was waiting for me, and I turned around to her, and said, 'Iris, I really think I'm going to win. I have this divine feeling.' Of course, she was so afraid that I would be disappointed. I was young compared to the other girls. It was a long walk to the elevator, and I told her, 'I'm going to walk like this tonight on the runway.' There was something wonderful right there in the hallway. I felt a divine presence with me. That was a good week for me," Sharon laughed over the phone. "I won.

"This type of awareness of divine support is much more accepted now. We get help all the time, and it doesn't have to be necessarily something as big as a national competition. Even *People* magazine recently published stories about angels helping people!

"What I have learned over time is how important it is to find a place of peace within yourself and remember to go there when you're upset or struggling. I have gone through many dark cycles where there was pain and heartache, and I needed that place of peace to survive.

"While living in New York, I had the opportunity to hear Dr. Peale speak. I met him afterward and told him how his book had changed my life. I showed him my book with my father's inscription: 'Dear Shari, walk always with your hand in God's and your feet will never stumble.' Dr. Peale was so delighted with those words he even used them in his sermons. Sometime after that, my children and I moved into a new building, and it turned out Dr. Peale was living upstairs. The man who had changed my life was living upstairs from me! I couldn't believe my good fortune. I felt as if God was smiling on me.

"I believe that it is so important to be around people who share your views. In the years when I was working in TV and film, no one I knew was involved in these spiritual ideas. I began to drift away from them myself. But somehow, I'd remember again, and I'd make a U-turn and come back. In the last few years, I have begun to know many people who also share my feelings and beliefs, and I feel I am surrounded by extremely kind people."

I asked Sharon how she stayed balanced.

"It's so important to sit still and mediate every morning," she said. "I imagine putting my hand in God's, and I think about love. When we see greed, corruption, and dishonesty in so many places, we can get lost if we don't center ourselves in what we know is right. We risk losing our way. Those are conscious choices that we can make. Reading books, talking to friends, and communing inside with our higher self, however we imagine that. These are all things that keep us on the path. When we take care of ourselves like this, we're more able to light the way for others. It's an act of service.

"When I look back at my life, I feel my greatest accomplishment is that I have found my way, found myself. I'm very positive about that. I think I'm exactly where I should be."

Always curious about people's actual experience, I asked Sharon how she knew she had found herself. She replied firmly, "I just know it. When you know how to do long division, you know how to do long division. I just know."

THE WOMAN WHO LOVES HORSES

A commitment to approach *everything* from a spiritual point of view can shift a situation that once seemed intolerable. Helena (not her real name) works in a large health care organization, and at the time she took my Pathfinders class in 1994, she was struggling with a boss whom everyone in the office hated. In those days, she had felt very frustrated and unfulfilled. Helena was new to the intuition work we were doing, including working with tarot cards, and guided meditations and tuning in to and interpreting the synchronicities that appeared in everyday life. By working on her inner perceptions, she has been able to completely transform a job she hated into an activity filled with meaning. She has gained a sense of purpose by acknowledging how good she is at her job. She sees that her department really needs her ability to cut through confusion and her ability to organize multiple tasks. She also has come to see that her spiritual outlook is valued by her colleagues, although they might not say it in those terms. After work, she renews herself with her two beloved horses.

When Helena came for her interview, she seemed far more radiant than I had remembered her. She told me she had come straight to my house from riding her horse. I wanted to know how her life was now in comparison with how she was a couple of years ago when she came to the class. Did she feel more on track?

> **INTENTION CHECKLIST**
>
> - A change in beliefs requires change on three levels:
>
>   thought
>   language
>   action
>
> - Be clear about what you want to manifest.
> - Tune in to your thought process during the day.
> - What are you thinking about as people talk to you?
> - Are you listening for an idea that could spark a new line of thinking for yourself?
> - Avoid self-deprecatory remarks.
> - Do you frequently see yourself as a victim of circumstances?
> - Focus on what you want rather than on the obstacles.

Healing and Horse Power

"Without question," she began. "The increase in a spiritual perspective has changed my life—in fact, my life has taken on a completely spiritual focus. If I had to prioritize, my number one priority would be inner growth and learning to listen to my inner wisdom and going deeper with it. In the course of doing that, the external conditions of my life seem less and less relevant. I'm just not putting charges on things, or getting so upset with people. It's so much easier for me to let go of negativity.

"In 1994, I was feeling stuck in the nine-to-five business environment. I was there but I didn't want to be there. I don't feel like that anymore. It's been a realization that I really *do* enjoy the work and the people. At that time, I can see that I *chose* to see work as a trap, but now it seems easier and more pleasurable.

"This shift didn't happen overnight. But, instead of leaving when things didn't go the way I wanted them to, I stayed with it, and doing the *inner* work changed the outer environment. I realized that I really like managing multiple tasks, and solving things even with thirty-two phone calls a day. I had to ask myself why I had been so resistant. I guess I changed my whole perception, and now I recognize how good I am at what I do, and I just let it flow."

"What turned it around for me, I think, was when I started to really *feel* the trapped feeling. I've learned that when something has such a big charge, I definitely need to work with it and get conscious of what is actually going on inside me. I also absolutely understand that when I am telling myself I feel trapped, that will give me the experience of being trapped! On the other hand, if I see work not as a trap, but as an opportunity to express my abilities, everything has a whole different feel.

"I'm getting a stronger sense of my purpose," Helena continued. "While I'm not totally clear about it, I do think that when I am in the moment, and in touch with my inner spirit or the universal mind that is in me, it comes through in my contact with other people. It's hard to put into words, but I guess I am leading by example. *When I am in the moment, I can be in any situation and I almost always make the right choices, and say the right words*" (italics added).

"To get into alignment, sometimes I consciously say to myself, 'There's God here somewhere. Help me to see it. Let the God in me handle this, because I can't.' When I remember to do that, it works unerringly. The situation either diffuses itself, or the person who is uncomfortable relaxes.

"For example, one day a friend at work looked like she was coming apart at the seams. I asked her what was wrong, and she told me about a family problem. While I was listening, I was thinking, 'What do I do with this?' All I said to her was, 'You sound both sad and angry at the same time.' She immediately agreed with that, and really opened up. All I did was validate her feelings, but she came in the next day and said, 'I can't tell you how much that helped me. I still don't know what to do, but I feel so much better.' This was one of those times that I just had the right words at the right time.

"For myself, when I start getting angry or upset, instead of going off on a tirade, I say to myself, 'Let's sit with this. Where is this coming from?' I'm willing to go *into* the anger, and see what I am afraid of. I work with it now instead of stewing about it for hours."

Since Helena had come into our session having mentioned her horses, I sensed this was an area that would tell us more about her purpose and sense of connection to spirit. As soon as I asked her to talk about them, she broke into a huge smile and sat up straighter in her chair.

"When I am with them, it doesn't matter what I'm doing, whether it's cleaning the stalls, doing barn chores, nuzzling them, riding them, or watching them play, the sense I have inside is complete and utter contentment. I have more magic moments when I am with them than anything else.

"One late November night, it was very clear. I had gone up to the barn after work. Not a soul was there. I got my older horse out and saddled him up, and worked him for about forty minutes in the indoor arena. At one end of the arena were huge open double doors. I just stopped at the doors, and looked up. The moon was full and shiny and silvery. I sat there on my horse, taking in deep breaths. My horse was looking up, too, with me, and it just gave me this incredible feeling of well-being and ease and connection. I can just stick my nose in my horse's neck, and I'm at peace. I almost feel my blood pressure go down. It's very definitely a connection with nature. Horses are powerful animals whose instincts are still vibrant and immediate. If they see something that scares them, they run from it. They have this incredible power, and they are so willing to turn it over. They are remarkable in that way.

"Being in communication with them has taught me patience. It is a thrill to be in communication with another species. Sometimes I think, 'If I can handle this twelve-hundred-pound animal, I can handle anything. Working with horses is a very spiritual activity on the emotional, physical, and mental levels."

So it seemed that Helena had learned a lot in the last two years about trusting herself, sitting with her feelings and fears, and acknowledging the importance of her contribution at work. I asked what happened with the old boss who had presented such a problem—and learning experience.

"Like I said, everything in my life is just about the same. The same horses, the same house, but I see my life very differently. It's a different life, and I can't go back. What was really interesting, things had gotten so horrible with my boss that I thought if this doesn't change soon, I will have to leave. About this time, a friend told me a story about a man who was desperate for money since almost all his clients had disappeared and he had no work. He couldn't drum up any business, and he was very intense and tight. Finally, the man said, 'Okay, God, if this is what you want me to learn, I give it to you. I cannot control how this happens.'

"For some reason, this story made a huge impression on me, and I thought, 'Wow, I have no control over my boss, either. I have no control whether she gets fired or leaves. I only have control over myself and how I am in the moment.' I truly let it go, and I slept better than I had slept in weeks. The next morning, she came into my office, and closed the door. She said, 'I'm too stressed out here. I can't handle it anymore. I'm taking a leave of absence.' The very next day after I let it go, and this had been going on for almost two years! It was like having a huge knife in the back taken out."

WHEN INTENTION BRINGS BRICK WALLS

What happens when you intend to start your own business, but find nothing but roadblocks? Have you set the wrong intention or was your intuition faulty? Mary is a thirty-six-year-old wife, mother, and accomplished businesswoman, who had set out to follow a new passion only to find the success she sought in the job she once hated. She had come to my three-month-long class years ago, and I wanted to know what her life was like now. Mary, a lovely, energetic, person one would describe as "spunky," began by saying:

"Now that I've accomplished a successful six years in business, I quit to be home with my nine-year-old daughter and my husband, who is fighting prostate cancer. When I took your class in 1991, I was in a major life transition. I was getting a divorce, my finances had become a total disaster, and I was constantly either terrified or anxious. I was also giving up a lot of unhealthy habits — cigarettes, alcohol, and recreational drugs. On top of that, I was confronting my family's disapproval.

"I had just started a job as a marketing assistant and researcher, and felt very little control with that position. I had to work under someone who lacked vision, and this was very hard for me. I'm the type who either has to lead, or be given a clear idea of where I am going.

"I absolutely hated my job, and when I signed up for your class, I didn't think I could face even going into work every day. I was passionate about starting my own business in the area of financial counseling. Even though I was completely passionate about my consulting business, I was constantly struggling to get it going.

"I guess I really learned that old saying, We plan and God laughs. I kept trying to get away from where I was. I thought one more day of that job, and my brain would explode. Every moment was spent calculating how to find some way to support myself in my own business.

"Finally, I guess I had an epiphany. I was getting nowhere. At some point after our class, I decided to take control of my job. Somebody got fired there and I began to think maybe I could have the satisfaction I was looking for by making this position my own. I thought, 'If this is where I'm going to be, I'll make the best of it.' Since I couldn't seem to get away from it, I decided to completely change my perception of it. Somehow, I had to face that things were not flowing to get my own business off the ground, and I didn't feel I could leave my job because of having to support myself and my daughter.

"But an amazing thing happened. Once I turned my attention *toward* the job, I doubled my income. I got a car and a car phone, and started having fun. I began to design a vision and a mission for the company. As I became more present in the situation, I was much more productive. I remember I kept thinking a lot about the lack of integrity I felt from the company. In retrospect, I think it was *I* who didn't have integrity with the job because I was spending so much time not being present in my work.

"Once I got focused, the company sales tripled. Now I have a lot more confidence as a result of knowing that I can support my family, even though I knew all along that that job was not what I would call my life's purpose. But it was clear that I had to complete something there. Why? I don't know. One night I had a dream that many little dinosaurs came out of my closet, and I knew the dinosaurs were the people I worked with, and that I had been with them for hundreds of years. They are all very good people. My boss had even created my position just for me. There seemed to be a recognition, a link with them. But finally the time came, especially with the demands of my family, that I felt I needed to leave the job.

> "I learned that you don't necessarily have to be doing your life's soulful purpose in order to find soul in your work. I used to think, I don't want to go through life at some dull job just being a work drone. Since then I have realized that we all have to support ourselves, and there is a lot of soul to be found in just working with a community of people."

"In that job, I learned that you don't necessarily have to be doing your life's soulful purpose in order to find soul in your work. I used to think, I don't want to go through life at some dull job just being a work drone. Since then I have realized that we all have to support ourselves, and there is a lot of soul to be found in just working with a community of people. I see some of them as almost family. I was amazed that I could find soul in something that I didn't choose. I now know that you can find soul in your responsibility to others and to your community, whether it's your work, your church, or your child's school. I felt that by accepting my work situation as it was, it gave me a reason to get up in the morning. I realized that my simple acts on a daily basis were able to affect the success of the people in my community. It gave me a sense of purpose. I felt purposeful in that I could bring cohesiveness to the company. I could motivate people by talking about our vision. I got excited about long-term plans and what we were trying to communicate. I enjoyed being able to raise the energy.

"You know, I had been totally passionate about starting my own business. But then I slammed up against brick walls. I was struggling to force my business to take off. At some point, you do have to let go. When I let go, and put my attention on my 'boring' job, my financial life flourished. Money certainly motivated me, even though I would have told you this job was not my life's work."

Mary's story is a good example of feeling as if she *was* on purpose, but hitting a brick wall. I asked her what she thought was the purpose of her passion for her own business in the field of financial analysis?

"I was so excited about learning the information myself," she answered, "that I wanted to share it. I was hungry for that kind of information, and it sure felt like my life's work at that moment. I felt like I could do it for the rest of my life. However, I didn't experience the feeling of synchronicity very often. I really struggled to get everything I got. In retrospect maybe I didn't have the internal structure to carry it off, or maybe that was just not where life was leading me. I now believe that there was something I was supposed to do in the job that was not present in my own business. I hated my job so much that it was hard for me to believe that was where I should be.

"If I have learned anything, it is not to plan, but just take the next step. I was so sure that my own business was right—almost at a cellular level. It's baffling to me why it didn't work out. I see that I needed self-esteem building, and that's what I got in the job. I guess I knew, too, that I wouldn't be in the job forever, either. Karmically that turned out to be where I was being pulled. I stopped fighting it, and it seemed to complete something and then I was released. When I finally left the job, I came away feeling I could be successful at motivating people and creating a community."

FOUNDATION INTENTIONS BECOME BELIEFS

If your life is not going ahead as you would like, you may want to examine any limiting beliefs that were implanted in early childhood. For example, Paul, a musician, said, "In our family, we don't accept charity from anybody." For Paul, this idea might get translated into the belief that he can never accept help of any kind—even when it is serendipitously offered! False independence may create a whole perspective of aloofness, competitiveness, hoarding, suspicion, or even bitterness that limits the ability to follow synchronicities.

In my interview with therapist Colleen McGovern, she had been very adamant about the necessity of recognizing one's most basic beliefs—the ones we take for granted as if they were the only reality. "The main point is to find a way to believe anything is possible. Merely saying it isn't enough sometimes," Colleen emphasized. "Affirmations have become very popular in the last few years. But affirmations are not enough. We have to go deeper to find how we frame our *foundational* beliefs. For example, you can affirm that your life is wonderful, but if you really believe, deep down, that you are not worthy of a wonderful life, that foundation—'I'm not worthy'—will be the one that gets created in your external world."

Let's say you think, "I don't believe I'm talented enough to have a distinct life purpose"; then you have to ask yourself, "What events have led me to believe that?" Perhaps you were constantly told as a child that you were worthless. Try to remember back to the *first time* that you took in a negative judgment. Once you identify where you got your belief, the next step is to realize that your parent (or some other authority figure) was doing only what he or she was capable of at that moment. Beliefs are formed by a process of conditioning that eventually reaches critical mass. You don't start out in life believing that you are not worthy. Sometimes your self-image is negatively affected by only one remark said at a vulnerable time, or you may hear a criticism again and again over time that you wind up taking into yourself as a truth. Once you gain the insight that those comments did not constitute absolute reality, you can choose to rethink your identity.

Colleen suggests the following method for changing a belief such as "I don't have any special talents." "Start by acknowledging that you do have a desire to find your purpose. That is, you do *believe that you have a desire to find your purpose*. Since you can feel the reality of your desire to know your purpose, this alone will start to activate your energy field. The universe will respond whether it sends you a mentor, a new job, or guides you to a workshop or a seminar."

TRANSFORMING TRAUMA THROUGH IDENTIFYING UNDERLYING BELIEFS

Colleen shared with me the story of her niece, who transformed the aftermath of a nightmarish event into a path of self-discovery and transformation.

"My niece E. was violently raped at a U.S. federal academy in February of 1995. She lived with the pain of this event for a year. She believed that she could not shame her family by talking about it, and that there was no way she could buck the system at the academy or talk about it to the authorities there. In addition, she believed that the only way she could get an education was to stay at the academy because she was there on scholarship and there would be no chance to go anywhere else.

"I began to work with E.," Colleen said. "The first thing we did was to look at changing her belief that the only way she could get her schooling was to stay in this painful situation. Over time, she could acknowledge, 'Yes, it would be better if I went to another school'—money aside, because her parents had no money. So the first step was admitting that it *would* be better to go to another school. We weren't trying to figure out how to do that at this point, just to acknowledge that another school would be a good idea.

"Then I asked her to set an intention for being able to attend a new school. I had her practice 'feeling' the experience that she wanted to have at the new school through visualization. I asked her to focus on how she would like to feel in another school. We worked on bringing those feelings into awareness as if she was really there at the new place. She told me that she wanted to experience more freedom and ease. She wanted to be treated fairly (which had not been her experience being a woman at the academy). She wanted, of course, to feel safe. She told me, 'I want to feel like I do when I come to visit you in California!'

> "The mechanism for achieving your desire is already inherent in it. The desire is the visible part. The mechanism—the how—is as yet invisible because you don't know how it is going to reveal itself. If I had ever written down a list of characteristics that I wanted in a man, I would have had only one quarter of these qualities. By focusing only on the feelings that I wanted to experience, I found a man well beyond my dreams.
>
> "You do a disservice by trying to do the work of the creative force that produced oceans and trees. If something can produce the ocean, it can certainly fulfill my intention to contribute to the world better than I could have by trying to control everything."
> *Colleen McGovern*

"She kept allowing herself to feel feelings of safety, ease, and freedom. I told her not to dwell on the money. We did all this work in May. By September, through scholarships, some family money, and work/study that she adores, she was enrolled at the Salve Regina University in Rhode Island. She lives in a mansion that was converted for women students, and has maintained a four-point-oh grade point average.

"She has blossomed. Interestingly, she has received many requests to speak out about the issue of rape. She now realizes that the academy was a far too stultifying environment for the kind of person she is. She is a visionary and there was no scope for that there.

"E. is a good example of how our early upbringing can cause us to see life in only one way. Her father is an alcoholic and her mother is very old-fashioned. Few people in her family went to college, and there were few role models for self-development.

"E. now believes that her rape has turned out to be a gift. Before this happened, she was fiercely independent and would never ask for help. This may sound strange to some people, but going through such a traumatic event taught her that she had to learn to ask for help. She is a different woman now, because of expanding her beliefs about what is possible, and by learning that she is not weak to ask for help. There was no rape crisis line in Newport, Rhode Island, and E. has already completed the process of setting one up."

TALKING TO YOURSELF

What would you like to have happen in your life?

What would have to change for you to have this thing happen?

What is your worst fear at this moment? Describe that fear on paper very specifically. *For example:* "I'm afraid that I will never find my life purpose. I'm afraid that I will be stuck doing something below my abilities forever. I'm afraid that I don't have what it takes to succeed."

Where do you think the fear comes from?

Rewrite your fear as a positive statement. For example: "I'm afraid that I will be stuck doing something below my abilities forever." *Rewrite it in your own words to say something like:* "Life is presenting me with wonderful opportunities to get paid for what I love to do— and what I do well."

CHAPTER 8

Using Intuition to Follow the Movement of Your Life Purpose

⁘

Every time you ask for guidance you receive it.

GARY ZUKAV[1]

LISTENING

If you think God is going to hand you a game plan for your life, you're right. There will be messages and clues that point you in the direction that you were born to take, but it won't feel like God is giving them to you—unless it does, in which case you have just had a transcendent experience. You may or may not have something inscribed in stone. However, God *will* speak to you. You may remember the old story about a man who was trapped on top of his house in a flood. He prayed for God to rescue him. A boat comes by, but he declines to get in because he is waiting for God to rescue him. A helicopter drops a rope to him, but he refuses to take the rope, because he is waiting for the appearance of God. If you fail to notice the messages or opportunities that come into your life, then you, too, will feel abandoned. Feeling isolated and trapped by seemingly intractable obstacles causes you to feel powerless and victimized by external circumstances.

One of the greatest virtues you can cultivate in finding your life purpose is the simple act of listening and becoming aware of what's coming into your sphere of activity. For example, I was at a New Year's party talking to a couple about metaphysical ideas and writing in general. Standing next to us was a man named Richard who was trying to make tapioca in the hostess's microwave. "I'm a stove top kind of guy," he said ruefully, opening the microwave door for the third time to see if the tapioca had thickened yet. "I know what you mean," I agreed amiably. He took the opening to say, "I overheard you talking about writing. Wow, writing. That's just the last thing in the world for me. Writing is so hard." He paused for a breath, and said in a sort of sideways manner, "Several people have told me that I should write a newsletter, but I just don't write."

> "Intuition must be 'set in motion' by a question. The question focuses your intuition and tells you what you need to notice in the world around you."
> Laura Day[2]

"So what do you do, Richard?" I asked in a New Year's party kind of way. "Oh, I do environmental counseling. You know, people who have allergies to stuff in their house. I talk to them about the alternatives, and sometimes I have to tell them that they're going to have to move to solve the problem." Interested in this newly emerged occupation and thinking maybe here was a story for this book, I asked him if he was satisfied with the work. Did he feel that this was a good use of his talents at this time? Did he feel he was on his path? Obviously surprised to be asked such questions about his destiny in life at a New Year's party, he replied, "Oh, who knows. I don't know. Yeah, I guess it's okay. Actually, I like the counseling. I always seem to be teaching people something, and I like that part of the job. It's just the money. I'm not making enough money at it." Richard asked me what I did, and we discussed books for a while. I don't know why but I felt there was something I was supposed to learn from this conversation with Richard from the way he had said, "I'm not making enough money at it." For some reason, I found myself telling him the story of how the opportunity to write the first guidebook for *The Celestine Prophecy* had come into my life. I had had two people tell me to read the novel, which I did. Following that, I had begun to work with the principles with my clients, which led finally to my agent saying, "Why don't you write a proposal for a guidebook to the novel?" "I generally listen, now, when people tell me things!" I laughingly told Richard.

> "Sensitive expression, entailing carefully chosen words spoken from the heart, has the power to move people to tears or laughter—to inspire action that can change the world in ways large or small."
> *Dan Millman*[3]

"So, Richard," I continued. "You just mentioned that you need to make more money in your environmental counseling business. And you started this conversation by telling me, a complete stranger, that people have been telling you to write a newsletter. I'd say that you need to write that newsletter, and that maybe you aren't even going to have to write it yourself. You are probably going to have someone come into your life very shortly who writes newsletters!" He was already nodding his head, as I was speaking, and gave me a shy smile. "I think you're right." He appeared to be almost done with his tapioca and we parted for the moment.

"People Have Been Telling Me"

If people have been telling you all your life that you are a natural teacher, have you been listening? If people come to you on the weekends to fix their bicycles or tinker with their dryers, is there a handyman business waiting to happen for you? If you are a workout fiend, interested in health supplements and good nutrition for yourself, is this a natural interest that could be developed into a profession? For the next two weeks, write down every idea or suggestion that comes to you that seems significant. Notice what you overhear in others' conversations. Notice whom you attract into your life that may be out of the ordinary. Notice what articles fall open in magazines. Did a new subject present itself two or more times in the two-week period? Do not judge any of these ideas in terms of how hard or easy they would be to achieve! Just write down anything that sounds like a message directed to you, and see if any themes unfold over time. After two weeks, if you don't have many messages, extend your record keeping for another two weeks.

If you think you have identified a trend, ask your intuition, "What could I do to take a step toward doing more of [what it is that attracts you]?" Now is the time to turn up the volume on your listening skills! Set a priority to make one phone call or take a new step within the next week. Two excellent books for getting started on your path are Barbara Sher's *Wishcraft: How to Get What You Really Want* and *Live the Life You Love.*

DISCOVERING ONE'S PLANE OF CONSCIOUSNESS

At the age of twenty-one, Joseph Campbell, a man of immense heart and intellectual power who would become one of the world's greatest tellers of timeless myths, wrote in his journal, "A day of musing. Whether to go to work or to go to college for another year is the dilemma that has me guessing." With a deadline for fall registration looming, Joseph decided to give his father's hosiery business a try. After a month or so of working, he reflected in another journal entry:

> After lunch time dragged worse than ever. I talked with Miss Torpie [one of his father's employees] for a while—she told me about the time when Uncle Jack Lynch worked at Brown and Durrell's [the hosiery business], and I had a queer thought. I thought that if he had planned to dedicate his whole life to hosiery, he was lucky to have died when he was still young and free. Business, as I have seen it so far reduces living men to dull machines, that go on from day to day working at stupid tasks with not the slightest idea of what they are working for. Tom O'Keefe remarked this morning that he worked today so that he might live to work tomorrow—and he didn't seem to be very excited about it.[4]

Since young Joseph started asking his fellow workers troublesome questions about how they felt about their work, he began to stir up some existential unrest. By the time he left his position, his father was actually rather relieved for him to continue his search for a meaningful life elsewhere!

Joseph Campbell was continually working a self-improvement plan that included developing his physical strength as well as learning new ways of thinking. At the same time that he put his father's business behind him, he began to read and study the ideas of such seminal thinkers as Krishnamurti, Aldous Huxley, and Ernest Holmes, author of *The Science of Mind* and founder of the Church of Religious Science. At one of Holmes's lectures, he received an answer to one of his questions. "[He said] . . . that to discover scientifically the plane of one's consciousness one should jot down notes for a period of four or five weeks on the things that interest one. It will be found that all the interests tend in a certain direction." This turned out to be "the precise technique that would allow Campbell, at a later stage of his development, to know that it was 'mythology' that would be his subject."[5]

As Campbell began to learn to discipline his thoughts and mind, some of his concern about his destiny began to ease. He wrote in his journal:

> "I vividly remember a schoolteacher who came up to me during a workshop and announced: 'I am so glad I teach kindergarten.' Well, I was too, since she seemed so very vibrant and alive, but when I asked why she was so happy with this prospect I was less than thrilled with her explanation that only in kindergarten were the children allowed to 'mess with things,' to cook and taste and touch and smell and really get into the thickness of the mystery of their environment. In the first grade, then, comes 'society's teaching time,' when we learn 'about' rather than 'with.' "
> *Jean Houston*[6]

The awful weight which seemed to settle on my head when I realized that my college days were things of the past & that I was lost to know what I should do for the rest of my life, seemed to rise up from me, and I am now convinced that thru relaxation rather than thru struggle I shall discover the plane of endeavor to which I am designed. I am going to rest comfortably in the assurance that my subconscious will find its own level.[7]

ARE YOU INTUITIVE?

Yes. There is no way that you could have survived this long without being intuitive! Our early ancestors were very much in tune with their intuitive faculty as they hunted game, kept a weather eye on the skies, and uncovered the healing properties of plants. Intuition is a natural ability that arises from a deeper level of intelligence than our conscious mind, and without which we could not live. However, about five hundred years ago, our Western minds, in a natural evolution of mental development, began to believe that everything could be understood by rational, deductive thinking. We looked for a logical cause for every effect, and since we could not see the cause of intuitive information, we dismissed or marginalized our inherent intuitive faculty.

> "One of the most common questions students of intuition have asked me over the years is 'How can I be sure I'm intuiting and not projecting my fears or hopes?' In other words, 'How can I tell when a hunch is intuitive (that is, valid) and not something simply made up or a random lucky guess?'
>
> "My standard response is 'You *don't* know.' I'm not being facetious; that's the whole challenge of using intuition."
> *Laura Day*[8]

Intuition is our energetic diagnosis of an energy field of information. Intuition is sensing movement toward a future event. It is direct knowledge that does not arise from training. It sees the whole and presents a solution *en tout,* or all at once. Mathematicians are famous for getting the answer to a scientific enigma before they have the step-by-step rationale.

Intuition may be the self-organizing factor that steers our attention to the path that bears fruit. Somatically accessed, intuition is often described as a gut feeling, or a tingling of excitement, or a click or light bulb experience. Mentally accessed, it is the capacity to pick up information you weren't consciously aware of, but which, when the time is right, you find you now know—you suddenly know something that you never knew you had learned in the first place. "How did I know that?" The ability to anticipate trends and make decisions based on relatively undifferentiated data often turns out to be more valid than trying to make decisions on conventional data and fact sheets built from historical records.

A highly evolved use of intuition is being able to find meaning in symbols and synchronicities. The more we focus on finding meaning for ourselves in "chance occurrences," the more we increase our intuitive power. Deepening our connection to our current surrounding increases our ability to follow the guidance of our inner purpose. All things are connected!

PAYING ATTENTION

We all possess this ability, *and* there are ways of enhancing it and using it more effectively. To increase your ability to use the guidance of your intention, keep in mind these points:

- Your psyche is always organizing around incoming data.
- Each event or piece of information has a meaning or purpose for happening.
- Your reactions to information or events tell you something you need to know. (Get into the habit of noticing your inner reactions and feelings. Throughout the day, ask yourself, "What am I feeling now?" or "How am I feeling about this situation?")
- Dreams often present information that is useful to your present situation.

INCREASING CLARITY

To strengthen your intuitive ability, therefore, you need to become more sensitive to body signals such as stiff necks (which usually indicates you are locked into a power struggle and/or feel overwhelmed by too much to do), headaches, stomachaches, or sleeplessness. Instead of taking these annoying or painful symptoms for granted, take the attitude that they are trying to get your attention about something. Trust that they hold a meaning for you.

Next, take time for quiet reflection to listen to their message. Instead of trying to "figure out" what they mean from an intellectual point of view, however, get into a dialogue with them. Try writing out your reactions in a stream-of-consciousness method to let the feelings tell you what they mean. Ask yourself, "If I knew that *anything* I chose to do right now would be successful, what would I decide to do right now?"

Intuition seems to come unbidden from external events, and seems to reside in a deeper layer of awareness. One person, when thinking about a certain plan, might experience intuition as a prickling of the skin. Another person might wake up one morning and "hear" with the inner ear a message: "Call home." Or another person might realize that her thoughts keep returning to a certain idea: "Maybe I should take a computer class." All these are forms of intuition.

TUNING IN

> We may think that intuition should give us complete certainty, and an exact plan. Usually, when we are crying out for CLARITY, we are really asking that we get a message from the universe that *guarantees* that we have made the right choice, that it will lead to a lot of money, that we will not have to make major changes, and that we will stay safe for the rest of our lives. We aren't asking for clarity, so much as a guarantee that everything will work out right in the manner in which our ego imagines it.

Slowing down and doing less is great for increasing your intuition. Try setting aside one night a week (or even one or two hours) without turning on the television or radio (music is fine, but commercial breaks will be disruptive). If you can, don't even read. Pet your cat, or allow yourself to daydream and relax. Do nothing.

Mark off on your calendar one or two hours of some day in which to just do nothing—preferably outside. Keep that date with yourself just like any other appointment.

Another intuitive exercise is to spend a half hour staring out the window and looking at clouds. What shapes do you see? The ability to see meaning in shapes means that you are tuning in to an inner voice that is organizing your reality. That voice responds to any inner question that is highly charged—such as "What is my life purpose?" Or, for example, if you have been wondering whether to leave your job, notice what images are popping out of the clouds! As simple as this visualizing exercise seems, it allows you to "exercise" your intuitive muscles every time you ask yourself, "What does this mean? What do I see here?"

Knowing that you have a reliable intuitive faculty can give you great power. Hunches are free and they happen instantaneously. Intuition is notoriously clever and happens most when we shift our rational mind into an unfocused state. It is the wellspring of our creativity, our guidance, and our ability to take the road less traveled—more often than not leading us to our heart's desire.

Penney Peirce, expert intuitive and author of *The Intuitive Way*, recommends the following exercise for testing multiple choices for intuitive problem-solving and decision-making. If you are considering two or three career choices, for instance, you may have already visualized yourself doing them to some extent. This exercise allows you to make your natural process a little more intentional.

ONE-MINUTE INTUITION REVIEW

Before you go to sleep, review your day. Try to remember anything that stood out. Think back, "Where did I feel uncomfortable?" What was happening? What did I do that felt "against my grain"?

Upon awakening, where does your mind go? Before you get up, tell yourself that you are going to feel as if you were just about to head out on your vacation. Maintain that loose, expectant mood for as long as you can.

Remember, God is your source of supply.

TESTING YOUR ACTION PATHS

Step 1—Select three options. Write down three of your top options for whatever you want to test.

Step 2—Choose one of the options. Imagine that option as if it were in front of your eyes. Now imagine that you actually enter into the scene, as if you were walking into a movie. Imagine it happening *now.*

Step 3—Feel your feelings. As you imagine your first option, notice your *immediate* physical reaction. Do you feel anxious as you imagine your scene? Do you feel excited and anticipatory? Do you feel heavy, fearful, or overwhelmed at the idea you are imagining? As you keep that awareness of what is happening to your body, strengthen your imaginative scene by fleshing it out with all the senses—*hear* yourself in your option, *smell* the scene, *see* the people. Would you say this option makes you feel more expanded or contracted? Hot? Sweaty? Comforted? Happy? Relieved?

Step 4—Imagine the future. Next, move your imaginative scene into the future—*to the next four to six months.* Now what reactions do you feel? Is there a change from relief to anxiety? From a sense of foreboding to feeling fine? Note whatever change happens in your body at this future date.

Step 5—Move your imaginative scene ahead one year. Continue to feel your physical reactions. Does this option seem okay in the beginning (Step 3) and then feel strained or heavy in one year's time (Step 4)? Did your option start off badly, but change for the better a year later? Did it start out fine, but become unendurable after a while?

Step 6—Be neutral. After fully assessing your first option, clear your mind of all those images and sensations, and become neutral again. Repeat the process for each of the other options.

Step 7—What if you did nothing? When finished assessing the most obvious options, repeat the imagination process one more time with the choice of "doing nothing." Do you feel relief at doing nothing now? Or does doing nothing actually produce tension and anxiety? As you project into the future, when does it feel appropriate to take action?

Peirce suggests, "When using this technique to make decisions, concentrate on the choice that gives you a feeling of *deep comfort*, not superficial ease."

FORCE THE QUESTION WITH A COIN TOSS

Another technique that gets you in touch with your intuition is to ask a question, flip a coin, and see how you feel about the result.

Take a coin and decide if heads is yes or no. Think of your question, then flip the coin three times, to see if it comes up with a yes or no answer. Immediately pay attention to how you feel about the answer. Relieved? Disappointed? Energized? Deflated? Fearful? Not good enough? Excited? *This is your intuition talking to you.* It is as simple as that. This is the beginning of the *clarity* that you were seeking. Receiving this information about your energy state lets you see where you are in alignment or out of alignment with your path.

HOW TO STAY IN TOUCH
WHEN YOU FEEL IN A MUDDLE

"When you're feeling a sense of ease and flow," says Penney Peirce, "you're receiving messages from your 'superconscious mind.' As soon as you start noticing tension, confusion, snags or struggle," she claims, "you've probably shifted to your subconscious mind and are trying to solve your dilemma by using your own willpower alone. When you're using self-will, or being willful, you're missing a vital piece of intuitive information that would return you to a grace-filled way of living."

Struggle and effort usually indicate a conflict between different motivations within your psyche, and with which you are out of touch. For example, you might want to buy a house that is inexpensive and sound, but that lacks beauty. If you feel torn about buying it, your need for beauty is struggling to make itself known before you commit to something long-term.

Once an idea about taking a new step comes into your mind, it's a good policy to do something about it immediately. The quicker you act on internal energy shifts, the more quickly you can return to the flow. Otherwise, if you procrastinate on taking a new step, that unexpressed energy may turn stagnant and you will wind up feeling tired, frustrated, or depressed.

Peirce suggests that if you don't feel in touch with that ease and flow of your superconscious mind (Soul Self) try mentally "letting go" for a few minutes. Let your mind go blank or hang limply like a loose muscle. Stare out the window, or breathe consciously. In order to realign with the flow, fill your body with a feeling of love and kindness. Bring to mind a specific memory of a love-filled time (e.g., climbing a mountain, getting applause for a presentation, kissing your lover, or cuddling your cat). Sit in that feeling memory for a minute. Notice the next thoughts that come, because they will be originating from a source much closer to your soul. Listen to your inner advice, then relax, and trust that more guidance will show up shortly. Don't struggle to get a complete "life direction" message from your soul all at once. The right intuition will show up gradually.

GIFTS FROM INTUITION AND DREAMS

Dr. Marcia Emery, author of *Dr. Marcia Emery's Intuition Workbook* and a consultant who does intuitive training work with business executives, met me for lunch to discuss how intuition can be used to find our next step. Her own story shows how clues appear to help us through the obstacles that arise on our path. She had told me that she had at least fifty rejections of her first book, *The Intuitive Work-book*. I asked her how she resisted getting discouraged. She smiled and said:

"Two things. I had a clear knowing inside myself that this book had something to say to people, and that it *would* get published. I can't tell you how I knew that, but I did. It's almost like I heard the book saying, deep down, 'I live. I live.' Second, I don't listen to the naysayers." She laughed, and went on. "I also believe in the wisdom of my dreams. For example, I had recurring dreams of letting my female cat out of a cage, and she was so happy. Now I don't really keep my cat in a cage, obviously, but I felt the female cat was a symbol of intuition, which was the subject of my book, and she was happily coming out. In another dream, I was in a hospital and a doctor was telling me, 'The baby didn't live.' Then he called me back and said, 'Your baby's been revived.' Shortly thereafter, the book was accepted, but there were modifications that I needed to make.

"I look for signs of encouragement or for a new direction. I will follow up in some way on any leads that come to my attention. I am very patient!"

What happens, I asked, when we become aware of an intuition, take a "logical" action to follow it up further, but nothing seems to come of it—as we saw in Mary's story in the last chapter? Was the initial intuition wrong or irrelevant?

"I used to travel a lot," she answered. "And I would frequently read the airline magazine, *Hemispheres*. I liked it and decided I'd like to write an article about intuition for *Hemispheres*. Over the next few months, every time I saw the magazine I'd think ever so briefly, 'I want my article in this magazine.' Finally, I finished the article and sent it in. The editor told me the subject of intuition was a little iffy, but she finally accepted the story. She liked the emphasis on how business executives can integrate both their intuitive and logical de-cision-making processes to improve their success rate. They entitled the article "Power Hunches." I liked that title so much I now use it for my seminars. *When I am clear, really clear, the way is shown and whatever I need is provided*" (emphasis added).

"This kind of providence happened again when I was trying to decide if my husband and I should move to California from Michi-gan, where he had lived for fifty-eight years. I was attending a con-ference in San Diego, and happened to be having dinner on Friday

SIMPLE WAYS TO INCREASE INTUITION

- Spend time alone every week for one or two hours. Puttering, tinkering, or listening to music helps relax and free the rational mind.

- Notice people in cafés. Make up a story about their lives.

- Look at clouds and imagine different shapes in them.

- Every time the phone rings, ask yourself, "Who's calling? A man? A woman?"

- Before picking up your voice-mail messages, guess how many people have called. Guess quickly without trying to "figure it out."

- Buy a pack of metaphysical cards such as tarot or animal medicine cards. Pull one card each morning and see what it predicts about events of the day or week. Look for references to the card in daily life.

- Before going to sleep, ask your dreams to answer a *specific* question. Write down whatever you remember from your dreams. Remember:

    The beginning of the dream tells you what the issue is.
    The middle of the dream tells you what you must do to resolve it.
    The end of the dream shows the outcome if you pursue this path.

- When interacting with *anyone,* silently look at them and see the beauty in their eyes or face. See them as a soul. Consciously send them blessings or loving energy, and notice how your interaction improves or what information comes that is useful to you or your life questions.

- In the morning, ask that you meet helpful people or be given useful information to move you toward a specific purpose.

- Start your day with hopeful expectancy for good things to come your way.

night with Jeffrey Mishlove, the director of Intuition Network, and Inge Lillie, an intuitive financial forecaster. I had mentioned that I didn't know what to do since my husband was going through a deep clinical depression and didn't particularly want to move. Jeffrey turned to Inge and asked her what she thought was the problem. Inge, after a moment's reflection, started writing down the intuitive information she was receiving and said to me, 'You are not clear about what you want. Get clear.' That night I decided that I definitely wanted to move to the West Coast.

> *"When I am clear, really clear, the way is shown and whatever I need is provided."*

"On Sunday at lunch, I 'happened' to sit next to a woman, and I casually remarked that I was looking for some kind of house-sitting or animal-sitting opportunity so that I could preview the Bay area and also San Diego and Phoenix as a potential home. She said, 'In a few weeks, I am going to China for a month, and I need someone to watch my cats.' I was astounded at how easy and fast things were happening! My husband and I came out to house-sit, and having a chance to experience this area, too, he got excited. We bought a house where we were cat-sitting out in Berkeley.

"Oddly enough, the new house has a skylight in the bedroom and when I saw it, it triggered a memory of a dream I had had of just such a skylight in a house that was situated near the water. I remember having awakened from that dream extremely happy, but had forgotten it until I saw the exact same thing in 'real' life. This really confirmed to me that the house was right. Being in California has absolutely been the best place for me to develop my intuition training program."

I was curious how she made the transition from a successful career as a university professor and clinical psychologist to an independent intuition consultant to businesspeople.

"Well, it was interesting. I had no real interest in anything of this nature until I had two dreams that were precognitive, showing two automobile accidents that happened exactly as I dreamed them. I was very shocked by this. I also started getting incredible numbers of déjà vu experiences with people. Sometimes I argued with them that we had already had a certain conversation! Also at that time, I started having what I secretly considered 'brilliant' insights in my counseling work; I got all puffed up about these new insights until I realized that it wasn't coming *from* me, but *through* me. I didn't talk about any of this, but the synchronicities kept growing.

"One day a student told me in the most oddly emphatic way, 'Go get your cards read' and I thought she was talking about playing cards. I didn't have any idea that she was referring to tarot cards. When I did get my tarot cards read, I was told some information that later proved true.

"What was happening, I think, was that I was being shown, without doubt, that there is a lot more to consciousness than I had learned as a 'straight' psychologist. I'm delighted to have the sci-

> "Everything I learned along the way has served to give me a fuller picture of how people work and create."

entific background of my psychology degree, because I now feel that my work is focusing on how to bring these insights back into the mainstream community — whether to other psychologists or to businesspeople. Reflecting back, I even see how my early training as a dancer fueled my creativity and helped me balance my intuitive side with my logical side. Everything I learned along the way has served to give me a fuller picture of how people work and create."

MAGIK — LISTENING ALL THE TIME

In our next story, we meet Laura Adkin, executive director of MAGIK — which stands for Movement and Acquisition of Gifts in Kind. MAGIK is a nonprofit agency, which takes recycling to a new level. Through her organization, an incredible cornucopia of unwanted, donated goods moves from corporations into the hands of social service agencies whose clients need them. In the process, many lives are changed. In her work, we see clearly how one person can make a huge difference to a vast number of people.

Laura's own search for life purpose reveals two major insights. First, we see that early hardships and later good fortune prepared her psychologically to create a unique career. Second, she attributes finding her life's work largely to listening to her inner voice.

Laura Adkin and her computer work out of a seven-thousand-square-foot office in the Hunters Point area of San Francisco, California. Most of the time, she may not even see the items that are donated since agencies pick them up directly from donors, once the computer matches donors with needs. I interviewed Laura to find out how she came to develop this simple, original, and beneficial concept into a fulfilling career for herself. I wanted to know how she had gotten to where she is, and what life experiences had shaped her path so that this new concept could be brought to fruition. Many of us think from time to time, "There has to be a better way." Or, "Somebody should do this (whatever product or service we see a need for)." But too often we don't follow through on our intuitions and bright ideas. How did Laura Adkin do it?

"I would call this business benevolent waste management. It's simply a different kind of Robin Hood experience. I used to have a 'real' job, doing media work where I met a lot of celebrities. I worked on world hunger issues, and I worked with a lot of architects and designers. Everything I did led me back to doing the same thing, which was working between haves and have-nots. I have two degrees—one in fine arts and another in psychology. I became an art psychotherapist, but when I worked for social welfare agencies with families, there was always one thing that was missing. People would get therapy or maybe receive medication in order to function better, and then they would go back to the community. But often they would go to live somewhere, and they would have almost no resources such as furniture or even a bed to sleep on.

"Following my social work and media experience, I was hired by the American Institute of Architects. They wanted me to work as a social commentator on the services that would be needed to design effective housing for different homeless populations. I found that none of the social agencies had anything to give people, and the designers often had way too much of everything. I began to realize that they needed to meet each other, and that there was a niche here to be filled.

"My early upbringing helped me resonate with people who have very little. My parents divorced when I was very young. I was brought up by my maternal grandmother until I was four. She was very religious and wonderful and made me feel that I was a gift of the gods. She was also very poor. By contrast, neither my mother nor my father seemed to feel I was at all important. My father, in particular, let me know that I didn't have the power to make any changes. Oddly enough, my mother, who literally abandoned me a couple of times, gave me the message that I could do whatever I set my mind to do. With such a painful family experience, I became clinically depressed in high school, and didn't talk for over a year.

"In 1974, my whole life changed to the opposite when I met a very wealthy family, who adopted me. By this time, I was a single mother with a four-year-old daughter, and they gave me a home in Washington, D.C. I try to imitate this family's way of giving—with no strings attached—today in my own work.

"It was so miraculous how I met these people. I was introduced to them through a man I was dating. They are old enough to be my parents, and they had a family of their own. They were more interested in me than anyone in my own family had been and more supportive. Education was extremely important to them. She was a Yale Law School graduate and heiress. We shared the same values, whereas no one in my birth family shared the same values about education or service. I am very much more related to my adoptive family. I had asked the universe for a family and I got one!"

"I soon made a decision to go to junior college, and as soon as I did that, everything began to fall into place. I became interested in everything that was not like my previous life."

After working for a while as a therapist in Virginia, Laura decided to take a year off and volunteer as a media person for a nonprofit organization in Los Angeles that taught people how to farm and raise pigs in Chile. The AIA later hired Laura because of her social work and media experience.

"I became even more familiar with the needs of nonprofits. I started to introduce the businesses who had things they didn't need to the nonprofits who had nothing. What I liked about this work was that it provided small, concrete things that people needed to do the work *they* needed to do. If you give someone a typewriter or a computer, or a desk, or a chair, they can deal with ten people that day that I could never talk with.

"A lot of great stuff comes through here. But I don't have a problem giving things away. In my life, I've had nothing, and I've had everything." Reflecting on Laura's path, I mentioned facetiously that she must have had some past lives where she possessed great wealth but hadn't learned to share it. She laughed and agreed.

"I think I must have been either Marie Antoinette or the queen of Sheba," she joked. "Apparently, I was never meant to own anything ever again, but I'm supposed to be in charge of more tons of stuff than any woman on the planet!"

From a brief review of her past, we can see that life shaped Laura first by giving her an experience of deprivation, and the subsequent desire for self-sufficiency. Once she broke out of thinking that others were in charge of her life, she could begin to envision a future that was not dependent on what had gone before. She could revision her identity. Next, life gave her experience in two worlds. One was the world of great wealth, which she experienced personally through her adopted family, and later, professionally, with big corporations. The second was the world of nonprofit organizations, which give a helping hand so that others may do what *their* life purposes require. Throughout all her experiences, intuition kept showing her where the need was for her unique perceptions. Developing self-sufficiency and seeing the value of responsibility at an early age, she was able to create a career for herself that was something completely new. Interestingly, life gave her the exact experience of having nothing and receiving everything from her adopted family—the same experience she would later give to others. I asked her what she feels about her life purpose at this point.

"I don't have a real clear answer. I wake up in the middle of the night, and I'm still having a dialogue about my purpose. What I've had to learn to do is to listen all the time—even to things you wouldn't ordinarily listen to. Whenever I look at anyone, I simply see them as another representation of whatever this thing called God might be. It doesn't matter if it's an alcoholic person. That's God as an alcoholic person living on the street. It doesn't matter if it's Jeff Bridges, one of the smartest and most educated men I've ever met in my life. It's another face of God. My purpose is mostly about experiencing everything and about listening.

"When I was little, I wanted to be President. I remember when Dwight Eisenhower ran in 1956. I wanted to be President, and I actually thought I could be President until the seventh grade, when I found out I couldn't be because I was a girl. In seventh grade, there were five or six girls who were interviewed by a representative from

Vassar. I was one of those girls. I think if I had had any support at all, I could have been a contender."

MAKING SENSE OF WHAT WE RECEIVE

Our last story in this chapter is from Donna Stoneham, an organizational development consultant. In addition to her full-time career, she is also working on her Ph.D. in transformative learning. Donna is one of the most focused, funny, and original people I know. While most of her clients come from large mainstream businesses, her focus is on raising awareness around spiritual values in business. Her story shows us how intuitions and dreams help guide us and reinforce where we need to be.

"About a week after my graduate program started in 1994, I had a dream. I orient my life a lot around the information I receive from dreams. Liz, the woman on the faculty who was instrumental in getting me into the program, was in the dream. All twenty-two of us students were sitting in a circle. We were all in spirit form, and, as souls, we were dancing around Liz. She was telling us, 'You have come back together this time to do a very important work in the world.'

"I've held this dream in my mind for about two and a half years. Recently, we've been getting ready to do our demonstration of competency, similar to orals. Our group is doing a workshop called Exploring Our Cultural Trances. In the process of our demonstration of competency, we split into three groups. One group is working on the soul of our cohort group. Another is working on a video, which shows our eighteen stories, and what we've learned about how we've come to be constructed, what we've come to do, and how we have become awakened to issues such as racism. As I watched the video, I began to weep. I realized that the video was the manifestation of my dream, and this is the work we are doing together. It's a powerful piece. This weekend I've been thinking a lot about soul groups, and why people come back to work together."

As Donna was talking, I had an eerie sense that each of us has agreements to work with people, and that at certain times we have our appointments to keep to move each other along.

"Six years ago, I would have had to pretend that I knew what I was doing, even if I didn't."

"I would say," Donna continued, "that the biggest difference in who I am today, versus who I was six years ago when I left the corporate world as an employee, is that I finally realized that it's not about what you do, but about who you are. I came to understand that it was my willingness to face the truth about myself, and to show up as authentically as possible that would make the difference in having a meaningful life. I try to live from my core and my spirit, versus doing something because someone else might like it.

"For example, I did a seminar on women's leadership in Napa last week for a group of businesswomen. We went around the circle, and talked about why we were there. I said that I was there because I had spent the last six years trying to reclaim my feminine side. I had always operated in a very male-identified kind of way, as the only way to be successful. In the last six years, I have tried to develop my creativity and intuition and softer side. To be able to talk about how important my spirituality is, was a big benchmark for me. I found that I could be vulnerable and still be in charge. That seems to be where power comes from.

"Six years ago, I would have had to pretend that I knew what I was doing, even if I didn't. We are all in this together, and we're all struggling to find our path, and we all have things to teach each other.

"There have been a lot of changes. For example, driving myself into the ground and being out of balance is no longer an option. I'm not willing to live a life so out of balance. Six or seven years ago, I was not conscious enough to know what was going on. I had colitis. I got sick a lot. I was cranky and miserable. I'm not willing to do that anymore. My big realization was that I can make a choice about where I want to go or where I don't want to go and what my boundaries are. I may still jump in the fire before I realize it, but I get out much faster now. I am much more aware of how I allow myself to be a victim. Now, when things happen, I look for the lessons. It's not about what people are doing to me anymore. It's about what am I supposed to learn that will help me as a teacher and a learner."

I asked how she had made the transition from being an employee to being a freelance consultant.

"I had been laid off from three different companies for downsizing and different reasons over a period of three years. It was finally like being hit with a sledgehammer. Something seemed to be going on that was bigger than me. I made a decision that, no matter what it took, I was going to find out what it was that I was here to do. I was going to face myself and liberate myself from the many things that I had felt had enslaved me.

"I went on a deep spiritual journey for about a year and a half. It was the most excruciating time of my life because I didn't have any of the old diversions. I did some very deep healing on issues that I felt had gotten in my way. These things had caused me to feel like a victim. I didn't try to spiritualize it or transcend it. I really went into it, and stayed as long as I needed to be there. Then I moved on. But it was the first time I hadn't tried to escape the pain. My priority and my foundation is my commitment to finding and fulfilling my destiny.

> "I have come to realize that if I follow my dreams and intuition, and follow what has heart and meaning, it always works out. It may not work out how I think it's going to, but it always works out for everyone. When I try to control or make things happen, it rarely works out."

"The pieces still are coming together. I do some very traditional things in business, but it's a doorway in to doing some other things. I do some individual work that is more leading edge. I used to drag people down a path I thought was more appropriate. Now it's like 'Do you want someone to walk with you?' I just help them see that a path is there.

"Much of my work in the outer world is generated by my work in the inner world. My work with the women's leadership—Wisdom Weavers—came right out of a dream. My dissertation came out of a dream. I have come to realize that if I follow my dreams and intuition, and follow what has heart and meaning, it always works out. It may not work out how I think it's going to, but it always works out for everyone. When I try to control or make things happen, it rarely works out."

What happens, I asked, when she gets called by a company she doesn't like? Does she feel it's her mission to work only with compatible people? Does a difficult place mean that she's not supposed to work there?

"I don't think I'm only supposed to sing to the choir. I worked with one company last year whose CEO was so shut down and so disinterested, that after a couple of months I could see that he didn't really care about his people at all. He saw his people as mechanical beings, who could be replaced at a whim, and he only saw what they could do for him. My focus was to try to help the people see that they had options and they didn't have to stay there. I'm happy to report that after working with them for three months, three people left. That was a victory—not for him—but for them. I try to look for what the need is, where the healing needs to take place. Sometimes it works, sometimes it doesn't, but I'm not going to stay where there is not some sense of being welcomed. Nobody gets served in that process.

"To free ourselves, we have to look honestly and see where we have been in prison. I ask people, 'What does it take for you to take responsibility and step up and liberate yourself?' I believe that we have to see how all of our life's experiences have gotten us to where we are today. I look back at my life now and it's so clear. Now when I'm in a place and I can't see the sense of it, I trust that it does somehow make sense. That is liberation to me."

TALKING TO YOURSELF

What aspects of the preceding stories touched you? Jot down a couple of thoughts, and reread them in six months.

Which of the intuition practices in this chapter appeal to you? Would you like to commit to doing one of them this week?

Take the time to write down at least one dream and ask, "What is this dream telling me that I need to know right now?"

CHAPTER 9

Increasing Creativity
and Developing Your Abilities

⌒⧖⌒

Meaning is at the core of the creative process and of storytelling. . . .
When it is our own life story we are telling or a story from our lives,
we become aware that we are not the victims of random and chaotic
circumstances, that we, too, despite our grief or feelings of insignifi-
cance, are living meaningfully in a meaningful universe.

DEENA METZGER[1]

Creativity is our natural talent for shaping potential energy into form.
We are born to create our lives within the medium that "life" provides. Some of us sculpt our life out of mud and seawater. Some of
us fashion together a glorious life that is as complex, quirky, and
unexpected as a Rube Goldberg contraption. Some of us paint ourselves into a corner, while others seem only to press a button and be
transported to fame and wealth.

Creativity is the key to the life you want. When we talk about living
with a sense of purpose and fulfillment, we are talking about creating
life. Within the boundaries of your beliefs, you can create your
dreams and desires. You have already created everything in your life
through your previous choices. Even though you may not love the
results, they stem from the choices you made, which seemed necessary or desirable at the time! To see how creative you are, look around
at where you are sitting at this moment. If you are in your home,
what have you given the most attention to? Whatever that is —
whether it is a coffee table you built, your collection of music that
you organized, or the home office you put together — that is what you

have been drawn to create. Are you satisfied with what you see? What would you like to change?

CREATIVITY STARTS AT HOME

In order to increase your creativity, you have to make room for it. Even though our mind is striving to know "What am I here to do?" I believe it's important to start looking for answers in one's immediate surroundings and energy field. What have you created so far? What area of life is beckoning to be resolved, enhanced, or transformed? Is there any area of your living space that cries out for order, completion, or balance? Are you living with a brick under one corner of the couch? Have your plants all dried up? Is your porch light working? Is the bathroom floor littered with clothes? Is your closet a nightmare of discarded stuff that hasn't been moved in five years?

You could start to move your own creativity by clearing out unused or broken objects in your home. Accomplishing these seemingly simple tasks has the power to clear the mind and let you feel a sense of control. Many times we want to work on the *big* issues of our life, like our life purpose, but the "little" issues are blocking our energy and so we do nothing.

CREATING A CHANNEL FOR
YOUR STREAM OF ABUNDANCE

We exist within an energy field. While it is invisible to our physical senses (unless you are able to see auras), you may be very surprised when you begin to work more consciously on this field. Start to imagine how energy flows through your house or apartment. Imagine that a stream of abundance is at your front door, waiting to flow into your house. You open the front door to let in the flow of energy. What happens to it? Intuitively, where would you say the energy slows down or stops? Is there a wall in front of your door? Does your furniture create any physical obstacles to easy movement through your rooms? Does energy rush right through from the front door and out the back door?

To change the flow, you may want to move your furniture around. Experiment. Sometimes common sense tells you that your living space is not harmonious. If you want to know more about how spatial layouts affect different areas of your life, there are now many good books on the ancient Chinese art of fêng shui. Many Westerners are now using fêng shui to situate their new homes in harmonious relationship to the natural surroundings, as well as to create a better energy flow inside their homes and offices. Believe it or not, this system proves to be extremely useful in clearing up blocks to your career, fame, health, creativity, and abundance!

As you work on your house, closet, or yard, think to yourself, "I am creating a channel for energy to flow into my life and take me where I need to go."

THE POWER OF MANDALA WORK
TO INCREASE PURPOSEFUL CREATIVITY

Another nonlinear, intuitive, and un-common approach to drawing out creative energy as you ask for answers about your life purpose is to draw a mandala. Usually, the first thing we do when we

> "Experience is not what happens to you; it is what you do with what happens to you."
> Aldous Huxley

are looking for a new job or change of career is to sit down and rewrite our resume. A resume requires that we think about what we have done and which elements of our experience to highlight in order to attract a new position. In the resume process, we work primarily from our ordering, logical left-brain creativity. In contrast, drawing a mandala activates our right-brain creativity and gives us another dimension of influence on our energy field.

Even if you have never been "good at art," you can stimulate creative energy by creating your own power mandala. The circular shape of a mandala is a symbolic representation of cosmic order. Think of your mandala as an activating force working through your attracting field of purpose. Within the embrace of the mandala, you will draw symbols for the people, places, qualities, and opportunities you wish to attract. The activating ingredient for your mandala is your intention and desire. Be as clear as you can in specifying what you wish to attract, and be willing to surrender to a greater divine plan as well. This is your spiritual "future resume." Once it is made, give thanks to God or the universe for already having provided that for which you ask. Know without doubt your needs are already being met.

Many years ago, I was introduced to this process of making mandalas, and I would create them with specific amounts for the money I wished to make each month, and so forth. I would then put them away so they would not be disturbed (I usually put them in my underwear drawer!). Several months later, whenever I got around to straightening out my drawer, I would find these old mandalas. Usually, by that time, I would find that everything on the mandala had manifested, and I might be making even more money than I had asked for! A friend told me she introduced this technique to social workers in the department of a hospital. They were trying to write a grant proposal, and their mandala work was followed by success in all areas of their requests.

Try it yourself.

To make your mandala, you'll need a large piece of paper (larger than 8½ by 11 inches) and an array of colored pencils. One day when you can take an hour or two, sit down and put on some quiet music. Begin to focus on what you'd like to bring into your life. A new career opportunity? More money? Better health? A new business partner? A lover? A good, affordable car? Recogition for excellence in your field? Try to visualize one or two achievements that you would *love* to have in your life.

After meditating a bit on your goals, draw a circle. Spend a few minutes just looking at the blank circle. Draw a smaller circle in the center of your big circle to define a central core to your mandala. In this core, draw a symbol for your spiritual source.

> **"Your life proceeds out of your intentions for it."**
> *Neale Donald Walsch*[2]

Next, meditate on what you want to manifest or on your desire for helpful people to come into your life. Soon you will be inspired to make some doodles, symbols, and pictures on your mandala. Let your intuition choose the colors that feel right. As you work on your drawing, periodically look at the whole circle to see where it needs balance. As you work, invest it with your spiritual yearning to be shown your true self, your true path.

Stop as soon as you feel your energy wane. If your mandala still feels unfinished, put it away in some place where no one else will see it. Once you have finished, put it in a special place of honor. Let its energy radiate and attract what it is that your heart needs. You can make as many mandalas as you feel inspired to make, but don't force yourself to work on them when you are too tired.

If you are attracted to exploring mandalas more deeply, I highly recommend the books *Mandala and Mandala: Luminous Symbols for Healing* and *Drawing the Light from Within: Keys to Awaken Your Creative Power* by Judith Cornell.

CREATING WITH MUSIC

Anytime you wish to tap into the landscape of your intuition, turn off the phone, get comfortable in your favorite chair, and turn on some uplifting instrumental music. Before you start listening, write down in your notebook a question you wish to ask. Then close your eyes, start the music, and let your imagination create a scene. You might even visualize your higher self appearing to you while the music takes you into the scene. If that seems hard to do, "pretend" you see your higher self. Pretending is a good way to practice receiving intuitive images.

> "This faith in the process is the only goal or purpose I need. What happens as a result creates and generates its own purpose. So I don't question the purpose beforehand; I've already accepted the process as the purpose . . . let it be, let it keep growing, and something will happen. And what happens generates its own purpose."
> *Anna Halprin, dancer* [3]

What answers, messages, or symbols appear to you while immersed in the music and the landscape? Let a story come forth. Record in your notebook whatever story, details, or messages you create. If nothing seems to make sense in a linear way, write down in the center of the page any detail or idea that impressed you the most. Let that central idea stimulate any associations or further questions. Draw a line to the association, and surround your central idea with these associated thoughts. You now have a constellation of thoughts around a central idea. What is the organizing theme? What is the relationship to your current questions?

Over time, the images you received may make more sense or suggest new directions to explore about your purpose or question.

LOOKING AT LIFE UP CLOSE

We can also increase creativity by becoming more conscious of details. The following simple exercise can provide you with surprising insights!

Next time you are out for a walk in nature, look for a special rock, leaf, or other natural object. When you return home, sit with your object and look at it closely for five minutes. Next, describe all the qualities you see in the object in your notebook. Ask yourself such questions as: "What is the message of this rock?" "What does this rock remind me of?" "If this rock were my future, what does it look like?" "Why did God make this rock?"

> "This sudden shifting of all one's forces, these about-faces of the soul, never occur without many a crisis; the majority of artists avoid them by means of distraction, but that is why they never manage to return to the center of their productivity, whence they started out at the moment of their purest impulse."
> *Rainer Maria Rilke* [4]

Let your description sit for a week. After a week, reread what you have written. Then, rewrite each of your entries as if it were the story of your own life. When appropriate, substitute "I" or "me" or "my" for what you wrote about the rock, and read the story of your life! For example, you may have written "This rock reminds me of a small mountain that is bathed in the setting sun" and "This rock is sharp, small, dark, but has many colorful marks that look like single-celled animals." And "If this rock were my future, it looks hard, many-faceted, and rounded on top." You now have the elements of an intuitive, imaginative story of yourself.

You might rewrite these elements as: "I am like a small mountain that is bathed in the setting sun. I am sharp and small. Part of my awareness is in the dark, and I can't see much because the light is setting. The setting light suggests a time of closure, or time to finish something and go to sleep. I admire the colorful marks or parts of myself that I have already developed in the past—like single cells of activity. My future looks hard, but there are many facets or avenues that I could look into. The rounded top of my future makes me think that I am climbing to something that is rounded (smooth and comforting) and attainable."

Reading the preceding theoretical story may sound interesting to you, or it may sound stupid and far-fetched. But when you actually write your *own* story, it will be much more powerful and meaningful. You may be fascinated, amused, or inspired by the information you receive from your own creative depths!

ESOTERIC CONVERSATIONS

Try another uncommon approach to dialoguing with your intuition with the following exercise, which has been adapted from *Tarot Constellations* by Mary Greer.

Using only the twenty-two major cards of your favorite tarot deck of cards, ask to be shown information that will help you more clearly see your life purpose. Select one card. Study it closely. Ask the following questions, and record the answer to each question in your notebook:

1. What is going on in the card? Describe everything you see.
2. How do the figures in the card feel? Describe this in detail.
3. Next, rewrite the basic elements of the actions and feelings of what you have written as if you were describing yourself in a story. What do you see that is meaningful? Date your story, and *make a note in your appointment calendar to reread your story in six months.*

You might also try this same technique with postcards of favorite paintings or any art book you have. Look for paintings that have strong appeal to you.

CREATE A CHANGE OF SCENE

Changing the scenery is one of the first things we normally think of doing when we are restless and searching for new opportunities. What country has always intrigued you? France? The South Seas? Africa? The Seychelles? If you are free to fly away, great. But what if you are constrained by responsibilities and lack of finances? Actually, a limitation itself can provide you with a great deal of opportunity to increase your creativity. Limitations often force us into doing things we would never have conceived of doing. Remember, *anything is possi-*

ble. You can have a great time stirring the pot of your travel desires right in your own town. When you begin to flesh out a daydream or follow an intuition, you are creating a new path of opportunity for the unfoldment of your life purpose.

> **"We write in the moment. ... Watch yourself. Every minute we change. It is a great opportunity."**
> *Natalie Goldberg[5]*

If you think your life purpose has something to do with collecting French antiques or studying French cuisine or learning how to build French intensive gardens, you are on a French trip! Even if you think you'd just like to go to the south of France and gaze across the fields of wildflowers to get your juices flowing—that's an intuitive, creative urge. What to do?

For visual reinforcement, track down some pictures with which to make a travel collage. Put a picture of yourself right on top of the Eiffel Tower. Find out who teaches French in your town, and see if you can go for an informational interview for ten or fifteen minutes to find out about where they come from. Maybe they have relatives who would like to trade apartments with you for two weeks. Let your nose for things French lead you around. Get something French into your life every week. Making even tiny connections with people around your French theme will start to build a sense of accomplishment and, at the very least, give you some pure fun. In that state of mind, you will be open to a vast array of paths and influences that might create a channel for unexpected meaningful encounters. Not only will you expand your field of opportunity, you will be having fun—a good way to keep the energy flowing.

WEAVING MANY THREADS

Even when we have a strong and visible path in life and receive recognition for our work, we ourselves may not always be able to discern just *what* it is that we are doing. My friend Eleanor Coppola came to my mind as I wrote this chapter. She is a good example of someone who has explored a myriad of creative paths. She masters whatever she does; nevertheless, she still wonders about her ultimate life's expression. Her story is about creative *breadth* and variety.

I have known Eleanor and her family since the late 1970s, when we formed a women's support group. She has been married to film director Francis Coppola for thirty-three years. They have two grown children, a grandchild, and a huge extended family throughout the world. When she was fifty, Eleanor and Francis lost their eldest son, Gio, in a boating accident. Ellie has always been one of the most genuine people I know. Never glib or thoughtless, she is a quiet force in her family for stability, support, beauty, philosophical understanding, and common sense. The strongest connection between the two of us is our mutual love of art, pattern, fabric, color, and psychological analysis. I wanted to know how Eleanor might describe the purpose(s) of the complex path she walks with her family involvement and creative interests. In her characteristically straightforward style, Eleanor told me:

"It has always seemed to me that *other* people have a single life purpose that they develop and become an expert at—for example, a carpenter or cinematographer or painter. All my life I've tended to compare myself with people who are experts in their field," she said. "When I was a child, I wanted to be an elementary school teacher, and at the same time I wanted to be like my dad, who painted in watercolors. I remember being utterly frustrated because I couldn't paint as well as he could. This is almost a theme for my life. I think I've always struggled with feeling small and insignificant compared to some larger-than-life figure.

"In college, I got a degree in applied design, which included textiles, ceramics, jewelry, graphic design, and so on. I began to create cloth murals for architects and interior designers. Then I had an opportunity to assist the art director on a low-budget film being shot in Ireland. Francis was the writer-director.

"Six months later, we were married. I hadn't realized that Francis had very traditional Italian views on marriage—the wife stays home. We had two children right away, but I always managed to have a room in the house for my own studio. For several years, I continued doing commissions for architects, but as Francis's career took off, we were away on locations so often I had to discontinue my projects.

"When we lived in San Francisco in the late 1960s and early 1970s, I became very involved in photography, and had an exhibition of my work. Shortly after that, the urge to do big, minimalist drawings came over me like a fever. I had a show of drawings, sold one to a museum and others to art collectors. Then the fever passed and I began working on conceptual art installations with my friend Lynn

Herschman. That's been my pattern. I would become adept at each thing, but then my interest would shift."

I well remembered these artistic outpourings of Ellie's. Her work always had a certain mark of being a distillation of *something*—a deserted storefront with black-and-white tiles around the doorway, a woman changing clothes in front of a mirror, an empty living room with a blurred television set keeping itself company, an abstract grid of ever-paler parallel lines.

> **November 14, 1976**
> **Pagsanjan**
>
> "Today it is still raining. I was talking to Francis about it this morning. He was saying that there has been some really difficult obstacle during each phase of making this film [*Apocalypse Now*]. In Baler it was the helicopters, at Iba it was the typhoon, at the French plantation it was the actors, at Kurtz Compound, in the beginning it was Marlon, then it was Dennis Hopper and not having a scripted ending. Now it is physical difficulties. There has never been a day when you just went to work, worked real hard, got what was intended and that was that. Tonight there are going to be one thousand extras for the big shot in front of the temple. It is raining hard. There will be more mud than ever."
> *Eleanor Coppola[6]*

During the years her children were in high school, Eleanor went into business with a friend to design and manufacture designer lounge-wear inspired by Japanese kimonos, which included fabrics she hand-painted. More recently, she has designed costumes for ODC, a well-known modern dance company. In addition to her drawings, conceptual art, photography, and fashion and costume design, Eleanor became more widely known for two other accomplishments. *Notes*, her nonfiction account of the making of the film *Apocalypse Now*, was well received and opened the door to writing and public speaking. Some years later, her documentary film on the same subject, *Hearts of Darkness*, won numerous awards, including an Emmy.

"One of my goals has been to balance my projects with rearing three children, supporting Francis in his work, and taking care of the family homes and related businesses. We've developed property in Belize, and recently expanded our vineyard and winery business. No matter what's happening, I'm always involved in these enterprises as the interested partner.

"I'm again doing something that I did not set out to do—shooting a documentary on how Francis works with his actors. We recently went to Memphis on location. I have always accompanied Francis in order to keep the family together. This time, I decided to look at it as an artistic retreat, a chance to concentrate on my own work. I got a small office in the production building, with a beautiful window overlooking the Mississippi, where I could watch cloud formations and barges on the river. I began to work on editing and writing the script for a video project. Every morning at seven-thirty, I would go with Francis to the location for about an hour. By nine, I was in my own office for the rest of the day, and I loved it.

"One morning when I went to the set, a very interesting improvisation with the actors was in progress. The assistant director said, 'Ellie, you should be shooting this,' and before I knew it, a whole scheme developed for me to make a documentary about Francis's directing method. Once again, I found myself turning towards something new. Shooting this video has been exhilarating and frustrating. I've made one mistake after another, but I've gained new insights into acting and directing and there are moments only I could have captured."

"What do you think has been the thread in your art life?" I asked. "What has been meaningful to you in the art?"

"Art has always been an essential part of me. I see things in my mind's eye, and I want to make them. Then my practical mind says, why? My goal for the next ten years is to let myself make the things I see.

"Recently, I made some doll clothes for Gia [the daughter of her son, Gio, who died before she was born]. She was visiting me, and when her friends and the rest of the family left, she was bored. So I took her to the fabric store to let her pick out some material to make a skirt. Instead, she made a beeline for these little padded dolls. We spent the next two days making clothes for the dolls. After Gia went back home, I bought her another doll and made some more clothes. I was enjoying doing this, yet I was feeling uneasy. I long to do the small things and I'm surrounded by the large things that need my attention. Our culture says bigger is better, and I'm often on the wrong end of the spectrum, observing the minutiae of life.

> "My own art has been almost like research for something else. The art I did not set out to do is more manifest than the art I intended. The thread in all my work is that my form keeps *evolving*."

"One of my purposes has been to be a stable element for my family and at the same time to express my talents within the limitations and opportunities of family life. My own art has been almost like research for something else—the art I did not set out to do is more manifest than the art I intended. The thread in all my work is that its form keeps *evolving*. Maybe my life is about weaving—weaving together the public and the personal, the large and the small, the extraordinary and the ordinary. Observing the ordinary in the context of the extraordinary has always fascinated me."

FACETS OF THE INNER GEM

In our next story, we meet an artistic and spiritual seeker who has always followed his passion. Glenn Lehrer is an accomplished goldsmith and gemstone artist who creates one-of-a-kind carvings and sculptures. A leader in this unique field, his work has been shown in museums, and he has won national and international cutting awards. Published dozens of times, his designs have been on the cover of several trade magazines. There are only a handful of artists here and in Germany who do this kind of work. In contrast to Eleanor Coppola's story, his path seems to be a continuing search for *depth of experience* and creative expression.

"All these years, I just pursued what I wanted to do because I loved it," Glenn told me. "Now my industry is recognizing my work and seeing in it a major trend for the entire industry. I guess that's when you really know you are doing your life purpose. I've always thought, 'When you can't see the light [or the purpose], you go out and do what makes you happy. You won't be good for anybody anyway if you don't make yourself happy.'

"When I left high school, I did some wandering around the country before I went to college to study liberal arts. In 1971, I began to have a spiritual awakening. I would be able to psychically hear and respond before the teachers asked a question. I had an out-of-body experience, where I walked through a wall into the yard and looked back and saw my body. I also had samadhi experiences where I would transcend this realm and go to other levels or dimensions. I was greeted by a being of light and was actually given the physics of the atomic world. This was before *The Tao of Physics* [by Fritjof Capra], and I was not a physicist, but an artist. It was too uncanny. There was too much synchronicity for it to be just fantasy. I began to study Eastern philosophy and worked with some teachers here.

"After about a year of college and after having these experiences, I decided I was going to travel the world. I traveled mostly in France, Italy, and Greece, where I studied the classical art of the country. By the time I got to Greece, I still didn't feel quite fulfilled. I had tasted this other dimension and had awakened to pure knowledge, and I was curious to know how this all fit in.

"I remember riding in a bus going over a mountain pass in Afghanistan, sitting next to an old man with a Winchester rifle on his knees and bullets across his chest. He was a tower of manhood. He was calm, proud, and secure. At that moment, I knew I had reached some understanding about how to be in the world.

"So here I am, twenty years old, halfway across the world, living in a very different culture. It opened my heart. People there spoke more from their heart than their mind. It was quite an awakening. These people eked out just enough to live each day, but there was such joy in them; I had never seen that joy growing up in California. It almost stunned me. They were looking at the world in a completely different way.

"I lived in a tiny little ashram in southern India and just meditated for months. I still had no direction as far as a career goal. I wasn't even looking for that. I let each day bring the synchronicity, and just pursued it. What I now do as an artist has been an extension of this period, in the sense of following my intuition and natural flow.

"I left India and came home to California, which was a greater culture

> "People who were more often in flow were especially likely to feel 'strong,' 'active,' 'creative,' 'concentrated,' and 'motivated.' What was unexpected, however, is how frequently people reported flow situations at work, and how rarely in leisure."
> *Mihaly Csikszentmihalyi[7]*

shock than living in Asia. I was confronted by all these concepts I thought I had left behind. Just getting off the plane and seeing the commercialism was almost overwhelming. In terms of sustaining a livelihood, it took me a year and a half to get back into the culture.

"One day, my older brother handed me a polished quartz crystal. Something went off inside me and I knew this was something I could get really involved in. I had no background in gem cutting or jewelry, although I had done a little goldsmithing, oil painting, graphics, and photography. All of a sudden something happened inside me. Here was an artistic medium that also challenged my mind the way no other medium did. Because I had had those samadhi experiences years earlier, I could feel the aliveness in that stone.

"I went back to school and studied geology, chemistry, mineralogy, and math. I thought I wanted to be a mineralogist. As I was studying, I found that I already intuitively knew some of the principles. Here was a form where I could combine two elements of myself—the artist and the scientist. It gave me a great feeling of power. As I played around and explored, I found that it was the first medium where the end result was exponentially greater than my initial creative vision. That's when I knew I had hit on something that would grab and hold me—where I could never know it all, and it would hold my interest. It's been twenty years since then, and I continue to have new ideas around it. I have hit my mark. With gem cutting, all the elements of my life came together, and it took me to a different level.

> "They were to come to the meeting prepared to listen rather than to present, prepared to create and synergize rather than to defend and protect. . . . The release of creative energy was incredible. Excitement replaced boredom. People became very open to each other's influence, and generated new insights and options. By the end of the meeting an entirely new understanding of the nature of the central company challenge evolved. . . . A new common vision began to form."
> Stephen R. Covey[8]

"The pursuit of my purpose has not always been easy. There were times when things were so bad I went out and sold encyclopedias and waited tables. Sometimes you can't see where you are going. When you don't feel the world is supporting your efforts, you have to reach back to your life purpose, and remind yourself how you've learned to survive so far.

"I tell people, if you don't know what your destiny is, just do whatever interests you. Have fun. Don't worry about what you can do with it, or if it will make money. Follow the passion. See where it takes you. For example, I get up and surf every morning. I've done this from childhood. I've had a pod of dolphins jumping over me, and seals swim by me. I continue to look for things that give me passion.

"Another thing is important to keep in mind. You will never know everything. That is not a defeat. Curiosity and searching for new ideas keeps you alive. When you stop learning, you stop growing. Your life has its own energy for seeking a state of perfection. You can never reach it, but something in your DNA seeks its highest state of existence. That is a law of nature. That is why crystals are like the fruit of the earth.

"Crystals are like concentrated knowledge pressed into crystalline form. They are the culmination of life force coming together in time and space. The crystal shows nature's urge for symmetry and perfection. Our life purpose is like that—purposeful curiosity and imagination yearning for balance and beauty. In the process of seeking that symmetry, you and your soul reach a state of excellence. What happens is that life becomes elegant, you don't struggle to accomplish. You creatively imagine it, and life is there. After twenty years, I can say I know that as a truth.

> "Our life purpose is like that—purposeful curiosity and imagination yearning for balance and beauty. In the process of seeking that symmetry, you and your soul reach a state of excellence."

"I am not just an artist for my own sake. If I do my work or someone else does theirs, then more creativity will be accessible to everybody. In my own small way, I am bringing more beauty into the world. Beauty is one of the spiritual principles of life.

"I had no traditional training in my work. I learned it all on my own, and I've taken it to extremes. Because of that, I've failed a lot. You have to be willing to fail a lot in order to discover what doesn't work. You just recover and keep coming back. There is a power greater than you; but it isn't outside, it's inside."

"The planet is already changing, and I can feel myself being a part of that macrocosm. Feeling joy in what you create sustains you and helps you do your part in the world."

YO!

Our final story of this chapter comes from David Inocencio, thirty-three. David is living his dream job as the education director of Pacific News Service, a nonprofit media service dedicated to bringing a diversity of voices and ideas to the public. PNS publishes YO!, Youth Outlook, a newspaper written by young people. David had been recruited in 1995 to become the director of education — an opportunity that seemed to come at exactly the right moment for him.

After being hired, David and *YO!* editor Nell Bernstein launched writing workshops held inside the Youth Guidance Center—a detention center for youth who have been convicted of everything from carjacking and drug sales to murder and rape. Through these writing workshops, David and his team are transforming some of the most troubled children into budding writers. For most of these young people, this is the first time that anyone has ever asked them for their opinions on the complicated forces that have shaped their lives. Even though most have little education or experience in writing, a chance to be published and heard gives them a new sense of what's possible, a new sense of identity, and a passion for communication. His story demonstrates the great power of intention to be of service and how it led him directly to his life's work. His story also clearly shows the power of creativity to unlock the heart and soul of young people.

David sat on the desk of his office in San Francisco, and began to tell his story:

"I had been working in photography until I was twenty-six, and although I loved it, I knew it wasn't my calling. I had a deep-seated interest in working with young people at risk, and I got tired of just talking about all of the ills of society. I wanted to do something about them. I went back to school in my twenties and got a degree in social work. I was so focused, I knew exactly where I wanted to go.

"After I got out of school, it seemed that things just started falling into place. As it turned out, I never even had to go on and get a master's degree. I'm continuing to grow and I'm touching the lives of the people I wanted to touch.

> "The simple fact remains, however, that the stronger and more radiant we are, the more we can serve as a positive influence in the world. *The more happiness we bring into the world, the better it is for everyone.*"
>
> Dan Millman[9]

"My first big break came in meeting Marynella Woods, who became my mentor and friend. One day, she gave me the keys to a jail cell so I could interview one of the inmates to get a feel for this work. I loved it. I quit my job in photography, and focused all my time in going over to Juvenile Hall and just listening to the young people. I became a caseworker advocate and learned to work with both lawyers and judges. Even though it was unpopular with the old guard, who didn't like people from the community coming into the Center for

Juvenile Criminal Justice, we started a groundbreaking program where kids had a choice to participate in new behavior, such as drug treatment, going to the Omega Boys Center, keeping a curfew, getting a job, or going back to school. We worked closely with them, and because we had small caseloads, it was very successful.

"However, I was always on call, and by the age of thirty I had developed two ulcers. So when [editor] Sandy Close called to offer me the job at PNS, I was thrilled. I was particularly impressed because this agency manages to bring together, in an unusually harmonious way, a very diverse group of young people.

"I wanted to maintain my contacts at Juvenile Hall because I felt those voices needed to be heard—there is so much raw talent there. Our first experiment was a girls' writing workshop, and it has since grown to include all the units.

"We started a column in YO! called Letters from Lockdown, but the need was so great and the writing was so incredible, that one day we decided to publish *The Beat Within*—a newsletter written by incarcerated youth. The name just came. It is only circulated to the kids in Juvenile. It's a raw voice and we want to keep the circulation small. Kids who would never speak to each other otherwise are learning about each others' lifestyles.

"It's hard for a lot of them to express themselves. A lot of their writing is dark—themes like loneliness, suicide, revenge, fear, and violence. We want to keep the voice of the writers, but as we work with the kids, we also try to promote peace and unity instead of bolstering racism, violence, and hatred. We are careful not to let them incriminate themselves."

For example, in one issue of *The Beat Within*, the editors asked the young writers to talk about "the game." The editors asked, What is the game? How do they view the game, and do they see themselves as winners or losers? Does the game play you?

J. B. wrote:

The game of your life is to be in a gang! Winning and losing is really simple. When you lose, you lose your life. But, you win by surviving. When you first play the game you are under the best players. To become the winner you must respect and show loyalty to the game. Don't be too eager to play, 'cause think of how many lives you take to become the "A" player in the game. It could come back to you!

Angelo, aka Lil Play-Boy, says:

When I think of the game I think about trying to survive. There's always some player haters trying to take me out. But it's not going down because I am a crazy ass.

Philly Phil writes:

The game starts when you're born. To me the game is about life, but you know others might say "the game" is the dope game. With the dope game that's nothing but a one-way street, you either find yourself locked up or dead. The other game is the street game, which is practically the same thang as the dope game.

In any of these games there are winners and losers. The winner is the one who succeeds in life, and reaches his or her goals. The losers are the ones who fall behind, and lack the skills to use their minds. In any of the games we play, it's all about money. We need it and gotta have it. This is my philosophy on the game.

While much of the writing is sad, angry, or depressing, some, like Michael's, is reflective:

I feel like a bird locked in a cage, wishing, hoping I had some "nade" [marijuana]. But for now, I'm trapped in this cage. But on the other hand, I like being in this cage, because it's a good time for me to think. I go deep down inside myself and find the reals about my true self, a young man.

One former resident of the Youth Guidance Center, eighteen-year-old Carter, aka Mr. Blackbird (and now a member of the YO! staff), says:

I've been shot twice, stabbed a few times, almost stomped to death, and run over twice in a car accident. I want them [in Juvenile Hall] to know there's a different world out there. There's more to life than juvenile hall or gangbanging.

David Inocencio says that he tries to teach the young people something that he learned from his girlfriend, who taught him that through challenges we become strong. "I tell them, 'Your faults are your power.' They can use what they know, what they've lived through, to educate other people. When I tell them that, I can almost see them take a step back as they register the idea that their faults are their strengths."

Our interview came to a close, and David smiled. "I can't believe that I'm actually doing something I dreamed of doing, and I've met my goals. Somebody asked me what I wanted to be doing in five years, and I can't answer that. As far as I can see, there is plenty of work ahead of us, and I don't feel stagnant. I know I don't want to become a bureaucrat. I want to touch the lives of these young people. I'm so grateful that it's all fallen into place."

TALKING TO YOURSELF

Write down any insights that occurred to you as you read the stories in this chapter.

Notice what details jumped out at you in the various stories.

Take a moment to reread the story you liked the best, and give it another title based on what the story meant to you.

Make a mandala.

What could you do to clear up any energy drains in your life? Write for five minutes, describing what you would do. Start by saying, "I would like to get my creativity moving . . ." and let your stream of consciousness creativity pour forth. Follow through with action on what you write.

PART THREE

DEEP WATER

CHAPTER 10

In the Void

It had never occurred to me that feeling empty might actually be a route to something deeper and richer within."

TONY SCHWARTZ[1]

WHAT IS THE VOID?

Each of us has had, at one time or another, an experience that strips away our normal feelings of knowing who we are, or our general at-one-ment with the world. Like any continuum of feelings, the void may enter our lives in different degrees. For example, you may feel generally down about life, and tell your friends, "I'm depressed" or "Nothing's happening; I feel so blah." Or "God, I wish this waiting was over." Or even, "Nothing is working. I don't know where to turn. I feel like I'm going out of my mind."

While clinical depression may be one expression of the void, its roots may lie in physical conditions such as hormonal imbalances or other disease processes and is beyond the scope of this book. Likewise, if your depression or dissatisfaction lies in unresolved traumas or past feelings, you may need to seek professional help for specific issues.

In terms of the search for a meaningful life, the void, however, has its place as a necessary, natural, albeit disturbing, spiritual passage.

Paradoxically, the signature sign of the presence of the void is the feeling of the *absence* of something. We feel out of sorts, cut off, and alienated. We can find nothing to look forward to. We may feel that life is not worth living if it's going to look like this!

> "For this reason, internal chaos needs to be cherished as the indicator that an underlying assumption, world view or self view needs to be brought into question. Once the limiting structure is seen and released, more space becomes available. In this way, chaos can be seen as the fuel or energy which can guide us back to Quantum Consciousness."
> Stephen Wolinsky[2]

The void may be stimulated by an unexpected and unwelcome life change such as a divorce or job loss. It may also come upon you *before* these precipitating events. Its message seems to have something to do with not feeling connected to life, not feeling recognized or useful, and not feeling that there is much purpose to anything. Even if you have a fabulous career, plenty of money, and friends and family, you may still feel the void. Mystics have referred to this deep alienation as "the dark night of the soul." Dark, because we cannot see our way out of it and cannot understand what is being asked of us. The metaphor of night, however, suggests that there *will* be a dawning, counting on the physical reality that day does follow night. Linking this cloud of unknowing to the soul signifies that our deepest essence is occluded from us at this point. Nothing short of the soul is at stake in the true void. Our question rings out, "Has God forsaken me?" Or we may think, "I'm lost. I can't connect to anything."

Sometimes our void looks like lying around the house, staring out the window more than usual, puttering around the yard and collecting unemployment checks. Sometimes we formalize it a bit more and leave the country, install ourselves in an ashram, or go backpacking alone for a week.

As we seek our life purpose, we may be even more prone to the void. Why? We have repeatedly mentioned that discovering our uniqueness and using our talents often requires that we walk a different path. Even if we explore the world synchronistically, using our intuition and uncommon sense, we may lose sight of our goal whenever we seem to be out of the flow. It's important not to take the void personally. This, of course, is the very thing we rush to do.

IS THERE A PURPOSE FOR THE VOID?

The void does not mean that you are a bad person, that you have a character defect, or that you have even made a mistake. The void is bigger than you are. Rather than coming down hard on yourself as a failure, it might be more productive in the long run to think of the void as a rite of passage, an initiation to the next level of your life. It is a time of germinating the seeds of your new self, and a time-out while your inner processes sort, clear, and present you with new insights. In indigenous cultures, this time of life is traditionally given over to working with one's inner spirit guides or going on a spiritual quest in order to emerge transformed with a new and deeper perspective on one's life and purpose.

> "Often you almost literally fear you'll die if you stay in that emptiness, and in a sense that's true. A given sector of the personality will die if you don't keep trying to fill it up. But there is something deeper . . . [this emptiness] is very spacious, and it's anything but deficient. It is the beginning of opening up to our true selves—to the empty space in which everything arises, to the ground of our fundamental nature."
> *Sandra Maitri[3]*

The void gives us an opportunity to end some part of our development, and to prepare the ground for new growth. Whether or not we know it consciously, we are undergoing a psychic reorganization of our attracting field of purpose. We are integrating the lessons of the past, and pruning our old views of ourselves and the world. Imagine, then, that the void is a period of death and regeneration.

Leslie Lupinsky, a career and life coach who practices in Albany, California, likens one aspect of the void to a sapling tree. "You have to water a sapling, and make sure it has good sun and earth. After a while, you see these precious, tiny little shoots start to appear. The void is like that little tree."

HOW CAN WE LIVE THROUGH THE VOID?

The void is a natural part of life. It is normal and appropriate to slow down from time to time in order to let new things come to the surface. But we get so used to a certain level of productivity that when we withdraw from our normal pursuits and haven't yet established a new rhythm, we feel "off track" or "out of it" for a while. Often during these times, we are forced to rethink what we have been doing. There is a natural process of review, as we hunt for "what went wrong" or "why is this happening?"

Many times when we are at our wits' end, we tend to think in black and white. For example, we think of ourselves in terms of being either good or bad. We decide that others are either saints or devils. We think our life is in the toilet and everybody else is happy.

The most evolved way to handle this period of life — not to say that we can all easily achieve this — is to accept it and really allow ourselves to feel all the feelings that arise — anger, loneliness, sadness, hopelessness, frustration, and so forth — without being *attached* to the state as if it were the whole of us. It's important to remember that our heavy feelings will not last forever.

Although the void serves its own purpose when it enters our lives, we still may look for ways to lighten its effect. Bruce Biltekoff, a teacher from Buffalo, New York, says about his encounters with the void, "I find that there are three things that help get me out of the void. The first is meditation because it brings back the *presence* of something. The second is true communication. When we can share messages with each other, it's a gift. When you can speak with someone about things that matter, you go beyond your despair. This goes all the way back to the Bible with the idea that 'when two or more are gathered together, I am there.' Sharing insights and sharing a story with someone I resonate with restores me to myself.

"The third thing that helps me deal with the void is performing some kind of action, which I would call right action or service. I think doing any of these three things moves you forward. When I am in that void place, I have to tell myself to have faith. I also know now that this change from absence to presence is only a moment away. All you have to do is stop for one moment. If you are in a dark room and light a match, the dark is instantly transformed. No matter whether you meditate, truly communicate with someone, or take an action, you will transform your darkness. It's like a switch of the channel. No matter what your void is, external things won't change it for long."

Glenn Lehrer, the gemstone artist we interviewed in Chapter 9 has had plenty of experience with these deep inner spaces.

"What I have learned is that the quiet times are the most powerful

times. Now I welcome them, because
I'm not being disturbed. But it took me
years to see that. I suggest that if you are
doing something you love, even though
the world is not knocking at your door
for it right then, use that quiet time to
dream even broader. Take your dreams

> "To do things beautifully,
> to handle ugly problems
> beautifully, with a deep
> regard for the sacredness of
> the human status—that is
> the Divinity in each of us."
> *Pir Vilayat Khan*[4]

even farther. I know that sounds crazy, but I never stopped imagining
what I wanted to accomplish, and I kept my dream alive. Those quiet
times are the best time to do this because the world is quiet and I
can go deeper and farther out with my thoughts.

"One of my favorite teachers, Lazarus (a discarnate spirit guide
channeled by medium Jack Purcell), calls the quiet times the Narrows. The Narrows are like winter, when our collective consciousness goes in and goes deeper. It is in the quietest times, when it
doesn't look like anything is happening, that growth is unfolding.
As you go deeper into your trust, your center of creativity, or your
passion, it will come back tenfold. It's hard to see at those moments, but if you allow your mind to soar with whatever your creativity is, it will come back.

"It's important to learn to be comfortable when you are in a time
of the void. If you are pursuing your life purpose, you have to be
comfortable and admit the shadow—the part of yourself that you have
buried away or refuse to admit about yourself. There is a lot of creativity there when you are struggling against something bigger than
you are. If you look to ancient cultures like the Tibetans, the reason
they deify the monsters is not that they are enthralled, but that when
they get in touch with them, they are liberated by them. We don't
have those kinds of rituals to get in touch with the dark side. We
don't look at it; we deny it."

YOUR RELATIONSHIP TO POWER

Usually when you are experiencing the dark night of the soul or the
void, you feel powerless or disconnected from a source of hope or
light or certainty. If that is how you feel at present, reread the "Power-
Loss Analysis" section in Chapter 5. If there are relationships in your
life that you can do something about, begin to ask for support in

making those changes. You may need to see a therapist, or perhaps engage the listening skills of a good friend.

One man who had been fired in the previous month said:

> "It is useful at times to admit to yourself that you don't know your way and to be open to help from unexpected places. Doing this makes available to you inner and outer energies and allies that arise out of your own soulfulness and selflessness."
> Jon Kabat-Zinn [5]

"When I lost my job, I felt afraid and angry at the same time. Afraid that I would never have a meaningful life, and that I would be drained by the forces I was letting control my life. I was angry out of frustration that I was letting other people control my life. My fear prevented me from taking any action. I felt like I had dropped into a black hole. I panicked and thought that these changes were dangerous and that everything I might do would be unfruitful.

"The funny thing was that it looked to me like my employers were controlling my life, but I was really just handing it to them. I had tried to meet their expectations and even exceed them, but I wound up just living to please them.

"I couldn't believe that they didn't want me anymore. But I finally realized that the firing had freed me. I had to really live through that time of fear and anger and humiliation. I'm starting now to see that my question needs to be 'How do I apply my true abilities and interests? How do I express my own life? How do I start doing those things that people have always said I was great at, like writing, and being funny?'

"I figured out that I have four months before I have to get a job. I have stopped worrying about finding a job and continuing in that career [software programmer]. I'm going to take it one month at a time. The first month has been about relaxing with the idea, and just getting past the panic. Now I'm reading, meditating, walking, and riding my bike. I'm writing again."

HOLDING YOUR CENTER DURING CONFUSION, CHAOS, AND FEAR

We can see that sometimes our life has to disintegrate before it gets restructured. This is the period when we must retreat, simplify, and let go—like letting a horse "have its head" as it wildly runs back to the barn, or letting the airplane right itself when you let go of the controls. Your tendency will be to "hold on" to something. Here are some practical suggestions for working with the forces of the void, instead of letting yourself get sucked into the downward spiral of self-loathing, apathy, or panic.

> "Authentic needs are the needs that are always met by the Universe."
> Gary Zukav[6]

1. *Look at your foundational belief about the void.* Notice that you have two major choices in *your beliefs* about the void. The first is to plunge into the belief that you did something wrong, that your friends have more luck than you do, or that you are doomed to mediocrity and a meaningless existence. The second belief is that this time is a natural part of life, and that some kind of change is being required of you. *Choosing* to see the void as natural and *necessary* has the effect of opening your energy field to the emerging information. Like water, go with the flow.

2. *Assume there is a purpose to this time, even if you don't see it yet.* Take a metaview. Imagine one of those maps you see in the mall—with an "X" indicating where you are as you stand looking at it. You are at one stage of your life between the past and the future. As the ancient Chinese book of wisdom, the *I Ching*, would say: No blame.

Whenever we take the position of being a student of life, we are automatically open and receptive to new direction. If we, on the other hand, tell ourselves that life is unfair and struggle against our fate, we are operating with a victim mentality, which automatically puts us in a one-down position and creates a power loss. *Remember, there is a purpose for everything.* If you let fear rule your actions, you tend to block the advantages or lessons of the void. One of the advantages of the void is that everything *is unknown to you, and thus you have no limiting preconceptions about what might or might not happen.* Another advantage is that much of your normal activity is disrupted, opening a new space requiring new choices. You are forced out of your comfort zone.

3. *Ask yourself, "What have I been tolerating?"* Review what was happening just before you entered the void. Something in your life required changing. What was it? The time has come to make that

change. Life coach Leslie Lupinsky has her clients ask themselves this question while they are gestating in the void. "When you are willing to see what you have been tolerating, and decide not to keep doing that," she says, "you tend to experience an amazing boost in energy." Asking yourself this question identifies, at the very least, a place where you have stagnant energy. Like lighting a match in the dark, facing the things in yourself and in others that you have been putting up with can shift your entire world very quickly. Ask yourself, "Where am I treading water?"

If you *know* you should move on from your job or from any other situation in your life, but have been stalling on making changes, your buried emotional energies *will* emerge to get your attention. *However, your repressed or denied feelings will look as if they are coming from other people in the external world.*

> "Care of the soul's *fathering*, therefore, requires that we sustain the experiences of absence, wandering, longing, melancholy, separation, chaos, and deep adventure. . . . In soul time it takes ten symbolic years to establish a solid sense of *father*—that is to say, odyssey takes place eternally."
> *Thomas Moore*[7]

4. Feel the feelings. When you panic, acknowledge the fear. Give yourself time to really feel your emotions. Writing out the events that have happened is a good way to stick with your process and allow it to tell you what you need to know.

5. Give yourself quiet time to be alone. One of the primary purposes of the void is to give you plenty of time for self-reflection. Don't plunge into relationships or spend all your time on the phone getting the opinions of your friends. You may have to be creative in finding time alone if you live with others. If you have just lost your job, don't force yourself to go on interviews when you're panicked or tired. Give yourself some time to heal and listen for the gentle wisdom of your inner voice. Being alone with yourself moves you to your place of power—the place where your internal shift is going to happen. The temptation is to move things around in the outside world and try to be in control.

6. See the void as a perfect time for self-renewal. This idea might take some practice if you have a habit of being self-critical or pessimistic. It takes a good sense of self to go with the emotional roller coaster that the void often presents. However, on your "good" days in the void, begin to think of small things you can do to enjoy the present moment. Try to stay as current as you can—avoiding regrets about the past and fears about the future. Being in the void is the time when trust is most important. Look for the benefits that this time offers. One of the best things you can do for yourself is spend as much time in nature as possible.

7. *Do less.* When life crumbles completely, and you find yourself in a divorce, out of a job, or facing life without the normal buffers and securities, you must listen even more acutely to the small signals within you telling what needs doing, and how to be. This requires doing *less*, spending more quiet time in meditation, and doing only what is necessary. Don't expect yourself to be superperson at this stage.

8. *Deepen your spiritual connection.* By focusing on the universal truths more consciously, you will connect your energy field with that of the universal field of wisdom. In this open state, you will draw strength directly from the universal source, not your usual illusory places like job status, romantic love, denial, and victimhood. "Holding on" in the void requires focusing on what you want, and staying in the present. Let the long term take care of itself for the moment. Notice when you start to spend energy on regrets. Holding on in the void is, metaphorically, more akin to surfing or gardening than to building.

9. *Look at your "lie."* Another powerful self-evaluation process for counteracting the feeling of being cut off from life purpose is that of becoming

> **"I remembered what the palm reader outside of Albuquerque had said a long time before: 'You're going to go some place you've never been before. Where you know no one. Into the deep north. You'll do this for the love of a man.'**
>
> **"Minnesota was certainly as far north as I had ever been."**
> *Natalie Goldberg*[8]

WHAT TO DO IN THE VOID

Doing any one of these will start a flow of energy.

Look at your foundational belief about the void.

Assume there is a purpose to this time, even if you don't see it yet.

Ask yourself, "What have I been tolerating?"

Feel the feelings.

Give yourself quiet time to be alone.

See the void as a perfect time for self-renewal.

Do less.

Deepen your spiritual connection.

Look at your "lie."

aware of the ways in which we reinforce our limitations. In her coaching practice, Leslie Lupinsky asks people to look closely at the stories they tell themselves about themselves. "For example," she says, "we all seem to have a basic 'lie' that we have been telling ourselves since the age of two or three, reinforcing it any time we feel helpless. It could be something like, 'I'm too little to do such and such,' or 'I'm too old now,' or 'I'm not good with money and never have been,' or 'I'm not smart.' The lie is always a version of ourselves that reinforces what we perceive to be an inherent limitation. It's our excuse, or the statement we go to when things get hard."

ORDINARY OVERLOAD OR THE VOID?

Sometimes life feels overwhelming and many of us have a tendency to "globalize" everything or "eternalize" everything. We think our life is completely out of control (globalizing the problem), and that it will *always* be that way (eternalizing the situation). In reality, we simply have more than we can handle at the moment. When demands on our time accumulate, we begin to feel bad about ourselves. For example, one day Richard, one of the men in my class, called me in high frustration. He had been feeling very much in the void, not being able to sort out whether to sell his business and pursue his painting or get a corporate job. All of a sudden, life seemed too much. The tax board was demanding an accounting and payment of past-due sales tax. His customer orders were piling up. His art exhibit date was impending, and his paintings needed organizing, and on and on. In the space of a few minutes on the telephone, we discussed some options. On page 209 is a list of things you might try yourself when you need to regain your footing for the moment.

TWO VOIDS

In the following stories, you will hear from Stephen, whose void has stretched for several years as an existential question, and from Sandra, whose void followed a peak.

Stephen, in his mid-forties, drives a van shuttling elderly people back and forth from their nursing home, and also freelances for a

SHORT-TERM TIPS ON HANDLING AN OVERLOAD OF TASKS WITH CONCOMITANT FEELINGS OF WORTHLESSNESS

Be

Breathe deeply and consciously.
Feel your feelings as clearly as you can. Cry, stomp, or rant.
Bring your attention back to Now.
Stop thinking about the future and the past.
Trust that there is an inherent purpose in what is happening.
Be grateful for the simple things in your life.

Do

Decide how to simplify the next twenty-four hours.
Cancel nonnecessary events.
Go to a park bench or café for thirty minutes.
Take along index cards or blank paper.
Get out of your head. Write down *each thing* that you feel you
    have to do in the next week on one card or one *small piece* of
    paper.
Put your cards into piles according to priority.
Decide what can be delegated to someone you trust.
Hire someone short-term who can handle some of the menial
    tasks.

Ask and You Shall Receive

Ask, "What do I most need right now to support me?" Pray for
    that.
Give your fears and confusion to divine intelligence to handle.
Trust your process.
Notice when you start to regain energy.

cable television show on spiritual subjects. Bright, articulate, and obviously on a spiritual path, Stephen shared his deep feelings of turmoil and inner dissatisfaction with his current lifestyle—an accurate description of what it's like to be in the void.

Revelation or Resignation

Steve began by saying, "I feel lost, which for me feels like huge self-doubt. There have been times—years ago, that I experienced a tremendous power coming through me. I had amazing synchronicities happen that seemed to be taking me somewhere. I had major break-throughs where I felt the Christ energy, and felt the connection be-tween all people. At that time, I was even able to heal with my hands. I seemed to be totally opening up.

"In the last ten or fifteen years, however, I feel like I have become contracted and am just living in the ordinary world. I lost my access to this higher energy and these events. Because of all those transcen-dental experiences that took me *out* of the world, I find I don't have that much ambition anymore. But I'm also not happy with where I am financially or in relationship. I wish I had more comfort and more money, and I'd like to be able to travel. I'm limited by money.

"I feel like the spiritual path can tune you in or it can drive you crazy. Before that, I had led the regular life. Went to college, joined the service, worked in business, got married, and followed the rules. One day in my twenties, I had an out-of-body experience, and in that brief time outside the body, it was like the flash went on. I thought, 'If I can be outside my body, then I am not my body,' and it changed my whole view of the world. I started doing a lot of reading in the psychic realm of past lives. I was starting to make the connection of asking the universe for support, and getting messages. I also got into reincarnation. I had a transcendental experience in my room, and I felt this loving, expansive energy. At that moment, all my animals came up to me and my friends and sat on our laps. That made it very real for me because I wasn't in my own subjectivity, because the animals were also feeling it.

"Then my focus changed out of the psychic phenomena. I felt I was moving in a whole new direction, and I could see myself on a path that was expanding, and the oneness of everything. I saw that God was in all things. That's why the synchronicity worked. It seemed to be responding to the needs in each of us. I felt there was a magnificent intelli-gence that is aware of any particle at any given moment. Along with my own flowing with events, I thought the whole world was doing this. A few years later, I started realizing that not everyone was doing this. It was kind of a letdown.

> "Either I am lost, crazy, and screwed up, or I am found and on a difficult part of the path."

"I have two feelings about my life. Either I am lost, crazy, and screwed up, or I am found and on a difficult part of the path. When I had that higher experience, I shifted my level of understanding about life, but somehow I didn't feel I had earned it. I had no teacher or guru to follow. By then, I knew that I was responsible for my life, so I knew it had to be my fault. A period of self-doubt and blame came in. My energy kept going down and I kept seeing all my faults. Why was I given these high experiences? I still really have no understanding. Why me? Why in this manner? I didn't have a guru to explain things along the way.

"Right now it's hard for me to accept where I am. I'm bored with my job. It's not creative. People say we are exactly where we're supposed to be. I can't accept that."

Stephen is very frank and forthright about his feelings of discouragement. Even though he has gained a good deal of awareness, it seems that two attitudes are keeping him in a state of struggle. First, he spends a lot of energy focusing on the past. He continually turns over the situation that opened him to higher dimensions as if he has to figure it all out and understand completely *why* this happened to him. During his conversation, he said several times, "I didn't ask for this [transcendent experience]. I had no one to help me through this. I can't find other people to confirm why this happened to me."

Second, he makes *the questions themselves* bigger and more important than himself. These questions keep him in confusion. Confusion justifies inaction and underachievement. By waiting to know the answer to an unanswerable question, he keeps himself in limbo. The question sucks away his power in the moment. Interestingly, instead of incorporating the realization of the oneness with all

> "Guild members, we are told, would begin their day with the master in prayer to the guild's patron saint before turning to the work, and prayers of one kind or another punctuated the whole day. Throughout the day there was the closeness of man to man, the sense of one another's existence, and the exchange between the experienced workers and the novices: the meeting of eyes, the showing and the watching, the speaking and the listening. How different from the usual factories and workplaces of today, where little is 'handed' from man to man, where eyes rarely meet, and the human voice cannot always rise above the noise of machinery; where men in their isolation from one another begin to feel a kinship only with their particular machine."
> **Jean Martine**[9]

things, he lets the experience separate him from others. In the void, he creates the same self-doubt that he felt when living with his mother, who continually eroded his self-confidence. Psychologically, he has internalized the criticism of both parents. Menial work allows him to avoid living up to his father's expectations. On the other hand, fixating on the transcendent experience encourages him to feel "special," without feeling that he "deserves" it.

On the psychological and personality level, Stephen's void experience oscillates between grandiosity and painful self-criticism. In the grander scheme of things—on a spiritual level—spirit had offered him an opening into another dimension that is part of the purpose of this lifetime. For whatever reason—and the reason may be complex—Stephen seems to have gotten stuck in the *phenomenon*, letting confusion, self-doubt, and dissatisfaction rule. Instead of listening and trusting that he will be shown the way, he lets his inner critic run his life and create his response to the world.

FROM THE FLOW TO
THE FALL

Another description of the void comes from a woman I'll call Sandra, who went from being the popular owner of a café and bookstore to the target of community rumor. At first, she loved owning the store and being there every day to greet her customers and help them select books on various subjects—many of them self-help and spiritual subjects. Many people came on the weekends and evenings to hang out at the coffee shop, browse, and chat. Sandra was in her element, and made many friends—or so she thought.

> "There were a lot of good things that happened, but the egocentric part was not acknowledging the possibility of the shadow side of being adored."

"In the beginning," Sandra told me, "I loved being part of helping other people grow and learn—it was like being a messenger or a guide. The first couple of years, the energy was so strong it was almost palpable. It had the siren call of being adored. I guess I knew that my customers were not seeing my real self, but I enjoyed being the focus. Being in this energy allowed me to connect with people, and I had a lot of intuitive flashes about them. There was no separateness. There were a lot of good things that happened, but the egocentric part was not acknowledging the possibility of the shadow side of being adored. I began to play with the dark side by dressing outlandishly or saying controversial things. It was Dionysian energy—intoxicating and passionate. It was life-affirming and contagious, and it was bigger than the local community energy. A lot of the subject matter of our conversations bordered on the unconventional, almost inappropriate, the dark magic. At the time, it felt positive. The store was an orgy of the love of learning and of information that was not available anywhere else. It was also a pragmatic business and it seemed to work very well. I loved the people and they loved me.

"The energy level started to fall in early 1995. Something changed. It became a struggle. I was tired. The adrenaline rush was over. For example, one customer who came in all the time, suddenly felt I wasn't paying enough attention to her. Another customer said, 'You seem too busy to talk to me.' I was tired, empty. The party was over. I started resenting some of the people who came in and wanted to talk for two hours, but didn't want to buy anything. Then they started not feeling as loved.

"Just at this low ebb, someone offered to buy the store. At first, the sale seemed to be well-timed and synchronistic. I said good-bye to my customers, and visited the store periodically to advise the new owner as requested. A few weeks into this new stage, things started to deteriorate, and I could feel people were starting to become negative around me. The new owner seemed to be taking on my persona, while at the same time, circulating negative rumors about me. She became like my shadow. She started dressing like I did. She went to my hairdresser, and frequented the same place I go to eat.

"The store was not doing well. I felt her hatred. I assume this is my own internalized rage. Now there is such resentment coming toward me, it upsets my sense of balance. I feel like Humpty-Dumpty. I feel shattered. I feel betrayed by those people who were so close to me who are now siding with her. I can feel their coldness as much as I used to feel their warmth.

"Now my energy is drained. My power is gone. I pray for strength and courage. It's ludicrous and melodramatic. Am I into the drama? I feel deflated, defeated, and embarrassed and humiliated.

"I have to go inside, but there's nothing to hold on to. There's no anchor. The store was my constant, and I have no place to stand, no place to be. It triggers all my betrayal issues from childhood, not trusting that people will be there if you aren't perfect. If you're not all light and perfect, you get crucified.

"I feel I am on my knees and I am crawling. It feels like rotting and it feels hopeless. It just feels horrible. If it weren't so public, I think I would go into denial. It is so hard to go to the grocery store and walk with my shoulders back and head held high. It's hard not to run to a friend who will just say, 'Everything will be okay.' Two of my friends don't give any credence to the dark side. They just tell me to ignore it.

"When you're in this void, everything that you hold most dear goes. You feel alone. It shatters the sense of who you are. There is no identity for me now. What's new for me is the pain in my heart. I have always been able to handle this stuff by reading and being intellectual about it. I can hide in my rationalizing, 'Oh, that makes sense.' But now even my eyes get sore when I read too much. Now I have to handle this pain. Something has moved me to have to feel it rather than shrug it off. I'm a mess.

"What is the purpose of this time? I guess my soul wanted to go down some other road, but I wouldn't listen to the little signs. Something is forcing me to stop going wherever I thought I was going, and turn in another direction. Unfortunately, I see no other direction. I know there is a call to move in another direction, but it isn't obvious. I have stopped doing almost everything.

"This is testing my whole faith in the spiritual world that I was teaching everybody else. Now I wonder, maybe there is no spiritual dimension. Maybe this is all there is. It is so hard to have my faith shaken. Add to that, I feel like my youth and looks are going.

"I always thought that as long as you believed that help is coming, and that there is meaning in your misery, you can hold your breath a little longer. But, *is* there meaning or truth? Or is that just a survival technique that we created? These are the types of questions I am asking."

THE VOID FORCES US
TO DETACH AND MOVE ON

Sandra's story helps us to see that even when we are "on purpose," we have to keep moving and responding to what we have attracted into our life. In her case, she began to feel tired and drained, and withdrew her psychic energy from the store. Following that, an opportunity presented itself to sell the store and take a different path, and she was right to move on. However, by keeping herself in the capacity of adviser to the new owner, she maintained an *attachment* to that old life, which kept her in the situation. Her statement "It felt rotten" is an apt metaphor for something that has been spoiled, is old, and has been left too long to be viable. Feeling the dark energy was her sign to pull back, get quiet, and listen to her inner guidance. By staying even a little attached to the old glamor, her shadow (her unrecognized aspects) started to run her life. The dark side of her former status—she had been almost a guru or celebrity—was so outwardly directed that she lost sight of her own self.

> "Raising your vibration changes your relationship to everything. Since your personal objects are attracted to your vibration, when you change your vibration you may go through periods of selling things, losing things, or buying new things."
> Sanaya Roman[10]

The void now gives her a chance to remove her energy from her former "glory," and trust that something else will be there. Her statement "I see no other direction" is a call to get quiet, but it's difficult to get quiet when we are invested in the past. Self-doubt usually comes when we cling to something we thought was the true self. Life always changes, but we try to solidify our gains. Sandra was invested in seeing herself as the guide, the one to whom everybody flocked. Consequently, she lost the ability to learn from the situation and was not living her true purpose in that role anymore.

TALKING TO YOURSELF

What touched you in these stories?
How often do you visualize a negative outcome for something you hope

might happen (for example, when you are waiting to hear about a job, or wondering if someone will call you)?

If you currently feel empty or "in the void" describe any specific thoughts and feelings.

After writing down your thoughts and feelings, notice any insights, or physical shifts that occur.

If there was a purpose to this time, what do you think it might be?

What do you wish would happen right now? Write out your wish on a three-by-five-inch card, as if you already had it (e.g., "I feel energized and on track with the purpose for this stage of my life"). Date the card, put it in a drawer, and forget about it.

CHAPTER 11

The Shadow and Life Purpose

∞

*If we imagine ourselves as being every bit as huge, deep, mysterious,
and awe-inspiring as the night sky, we might begin to appreciate how
complicated we are as individuals, and how much of who we are is
unknown not only to others but to ourselves.*

THOMAS MOORE[1]

WHAT IS OUR SHADOW?

The shadow, a term coined by Swiss psychologist Carl Jung, is a
psychological concept describing all the things we either cannot accept about ourselves, do not like about ourselves, or do not wish to
look at.

While we tend to characterize our "dark side" as some unpredictable and probably evil force that has the power to make us do awful
things, the shadow is more accurately the storehouse of *all* our unrecognized personal material—including undeveloped talents. We
may have dismissed some of our talents because early in life we believed and accepted other people's negative judgments about us. We
may also have denied the value of these talents because they seem
impractical in the face of the workaday world. These dismissed but
good qualities are called the "bright shadow."

The shadow is created because our ego, constantly trying to control
our world, sorts out things that don't fit the picture we have constructed for how to survive and be accepted. The shadow begins to
build in early childhood, when we hide away parts of ourselves that

218   THE PURPOSE OF YOUR LIFE

were criticized or ridiculed by our parents. As we go through puberty, we stash away more of our unacceptable parts as we seek acceptance into our peer group. Not only do we struggle with our own shadow, but we may also be caught up in the unrealized dreams and shadow characteristics of our family or in the community consciousness of some other tight-knit group, such as religious sect. Jung believed that children were destined to act out the shadows of their own parents! The final story of this chapter, for example, describes the journey of comedian Jim Burns to differentiate himself from the shadow of his family system.

By the time we are in our twenties, we have already created a persona, or outer aspect, that we show the world in hopes of being loved and accepted, in hopes of succeeding. If we have not given much thought to our purpose in life—or to examining our social and family conditioning—then we are still living mostly to meet the expectations of other people (spouse, family, boss, or community).

It may even be that we are most at risk of meeting our shadow when we have gained success. For example, if one is on the high road to material success, feeling important, thinking she has accomplished something special, she may push down any feelings of self-doubt. Those nagging feelings of doubt are held at bay in the back of her mind—or in the shadow of her full conscious understanding. We have all watched people, who when they are flying high, begin to think they are beyond ordinary conventions or rules. In their drive to achieve, they dismiss any feelings of emptiness (the nascent tendrils of the void) and disregard their need to stay in touch with the spiritual dimension. The ego loves to claim success as its own achievement, and *control* as its handmaiden.

These rejected parts, like unruly children, are very much alive in the dark and will make their presence known when one least expects it.

The shadow is seen in the habits we can't seem to break. It's the lie we tell ourselves about ourselves, which was discussed in Chapter 10. The shadow may come through our life like a firestorm in uncontrollable urges, breakdowns, and contradictory desires. Or it may lie on us like a wet rag, dampening our enthusiasm for life and oppressing our creative energy.

HOW DOES OUR DARK SIDE AFFECT
OUR MISSION IN LIFE?

If you are working without joy, only to pay the rent, you may have shoved into the closet of your shadow all the dreams you once had—relegating them to the realm of childish fantasies inappropriate in the "real" world. Instead of nurturing your life purpose, you may have put it aside in the dark, closing the door on the idea that you can ever achieve fulfillment.

> "Jung thought that, while the unconscious certainly contained elements of personality which the individual might repudiate, it also contained the germs of new possibilities, the seeds of future, and possibly better, adaptation."
> *Anthony Storr*[2]

When we have allowed ourselves to get smaller and smaller, we wind up living without the fullness of our being. Without the full spectrum of the spirit we were born with, the unfolding of our life purpose tends to be thwarted or stunted. Although, to be fair, many geniuses make their mark in spite of, or because of, severe challenges or character disorders! But if our goal is to take an uncommon approach to finding our place in the world, then the shadow is a domain that is not usually visited by our egoic drive for success.

YOU AIN'T ALL BAD—WANNA BET?

Our first step will be merely to become aware that our dark side is not necessarily bad, although that's usually what we think it must be. Perhaps, when your mother was mad at you, she told you over and over that you were lazy. If she said it enough times, a critical mass of your psychic energy turned this idea into a belief within you. "Laziness" became part of your self-identity. Now fast-forward to this moment. When you think about your search for life purpose, you may, without even being consciously aware of it, think, "I'll never find my life purpose. I'm not motivated enough. It sounds like so much work. I've never been much of a student. What's wrong with just vegging out? I'm no genius. What's the point?" Or a thousand other excuses will pass through your mind around the shadow constellation: "*I am lazier than other people.*"

AIN'T I GREAT?

Even success can bring out shadow qualities. If our crowning moment is achieved at the expense of others, or riches and fame are attained without the balance of self-reflection, one may be at the mercy of what the Greeks described so well in their tragic dramas: hubris. Hubris is the dark side of living one's purpose or achieving success with little sense of humility or connection to the sacred. Hubris is that overweening pride, excessive self-confidence, or arrogance that may creep in just at the moment we feel that we have made it.

John R. O'Neill, president of the California School of Professional Psychology, in San Francisco and author of *The Dark Side of Success*, outlines the telltale signs of the emergence of hubris:[3]

"Endowing ourselves with special gifts." When we begin to take on certain airs of self-inflation, such as believing that our judgment is infallible, that our position is invulnerable, we are seeing the shadow's face.

"Killing the messenger." This refers to those times when we refuse to hear information that is contrary to what we want to hear. Instead, we surround ourselves with "yes" people. We don't see the handwriting on the wall.

"Needing to command the performance." When we must structure all business meetings rigidly in order to maintain our position, or when we manipulate social gatherings and engage in territorial power struggles, we are being driven by our hidden insecurities.

"Living on higher moral ground." Whenever we are feeling self-righteous and thinking we have the only truth, we are ripe for the fall. There are many examples of politicians, religious leaders, or social activists who, in the name of right action, seem to be working with their own personal shadow.

OUR UNRESOLVED SHADOW MATERIAL MAY NEGATE OR BLIND US TO INTUITION

As I was writing this chapter, Joan, a freelance insurance agent making a transition to hypnotherapy, called me to get the number of someone who could produce a set of hypnosis tapes that she had been wanting to do, but had been putting off. Joan had not been talking long before I realized that she was describing some of the very concepts that I wanted to include in this chapter.

She told me that she happened to be in the process of doing some written homework for a personal growth group she attends. The homework was to make a list of repeated patterns and negative behavior in order to recognize them. Next, she told me, she was to try to discover what the lesson was in each of the patterns.

Joan is in her late forties and quite beautiful. Petite and vivacious, she has been very successful in the life insurance business. About seven years ago, when I met her, she had just earned a hypnotherapy license. As far as I knew, however, she had never really developed this second career. Her insurance business seemed to provide enough money that she had no real financial need to make her counseling business profitable.

> "Jung [believed] that . . . men became neurotic when they were in some sense false to themselves; when they strayed from the path which Nature (or God) intended them to follow. By listening to the inner voice, which manifested itself in dreams, fantasies, and other spontaneous derivatives of the unconscious, the lost soul could rediscover its proper path."
> *Anthony Storr*[4]

THE DRIVING FORCE OF THE NEED "TO BE CHOSEN" CREATES AN INAUTHENTIC CHOICE

Joan began to tell me about the difficulty of changing what she called her people-pleasing behavior.

"It seems to be a lot easier to make a list of negativities and flaws and stay focused on those flaws, than it is to change my behavior with people. Instead of going into the question of why I fixate on getting other people's approval, I just keep seeking approval. I see very clearly that I am continually motivated by the fear that I will always be alone because I will be rejected and 'not be chosen.' So I get caught up in 'Pick me, see me, don't leave me out, choose me.' My behavior around others is mo-

> "And if we have put away so many of our angers, spontaneities, hungers, enthusiasms, our rowdy and unattractive parts, then how can we live? What holds us together?"
> *—Robert Bly*[5]

tivated by the thought, 'Who do you want me to be so you'll choose me?' But the irony is, even if someone *does* choose me, I don't believe they chose the real me because I was never being really authentic in the first place! I was only being a certain way to get their attention. Therefore, I can't trust them because I 'sold' them a certain persona. To get accepted, I'll run through so many different, and falsely accommodating, behaviors that any authentic part of me gets entirely lost. So when they do respond to me, I don't know what part they were responding to—the real me or the false me! Therefore, I can never trust the relationship or really settle into it. I just keep trying to figure out which behavior they responded to. What did they like? so I can do more of that."

Joan's self-disclosure was quite remarkable and courageous. Just listening to her spinning through these ever-increasing webs of delusion made me dizzy, and I could sense her utter frustration and disgust along with a strong commitment to change this unfulfilling habit. She was clearly describing the effect of her shadow.

"I'm beginning to think my life purpose might be just to learn to trust myself," Joan continued. "For example, in every one of my failed relationships, I knew, intuitively, what was going on from the very first moment. But in my need to be chosen, I would ignore or negate my own intuition or thoughts by telling myself, 'I don't care. I don't need that' or 'It will change.' The dominant drive was always one thing—to be chosen."

PATTERN RECOGNITION

In order to have all of our creative energy available to be fully in our power and "on purpose," we must be in present time. If our energy is being sidelined and drained by trying to control our unacceptable patterns, we feel scared, insecure, doubtful, and sure that we cannot be worthy of fulfilling a larger purpose in life.

Take a moment to read the list of patterns that follows. It's sometimes easier to see problematic patterns in our *personal* relationships. Ask yourself, "Am I motivated by any of these patterns in my personal relationships?" If you see yourself engaging in some of these behaviors—and we all do at one time or another—with your family or friends, you may also be unconsciously resorting to them in your career life. As you read through the list, try to avoid being hard on yourself. Each of us learns to cope with life in the best way we can when we are young. Some of our strategies work for our best interests, and others work against our best interests. Keep a sense of humor about these tendencies.

> "The bigger the bag [shadow], the less the energy. Some people have by nature more energy than others, but we all have more than we can possibly use. Where did it go? . . . When a woman puts her masculinity into the bag, or rolls it up and puts it into the can, she loses energy with it. So we can think of our personal bag as containing energy now unavailable to us. If we identify ourselves as uncreative, it means we took our creativity and put it into the bag."
> Robert Bly[6]

Negative Patterns of Behavior

- *Lack of discernment or good judgment.* Do I jump into friendship or intimacy too fast, and then get scared and pull back? When I commit too soon, does it make me feel trapped, causing me to "back out" of things? Do I overlook obvious signs of future trouble with a company because I am so desperate to take any job? Do I listen to my instincts about a prospective boss or company? Do I fail to state clearly to myself what it is that I value and want to have in my life?
- *Overaccommodating and people-pleasing.* Do I always try to please everybody by using many different personas—flattering, overly rational and businesslike, flirtatious, cynical, too nice, too accommodating, or any other behavior that is motivated by the desire to "be chosen"? Do I say one thing to my coworkers, and then talk about them behind their back to others? Do I feel appeasement is the best form of feeling in control? Do I feel I cannot live a full life because my life is not my own?
- *Craving recognition.* Do I have a pattern of wanting recognition for everything I do? Am I doing something because I get lots of money or recognition, rather than doing something I enjoy? Do I try to ingratiate myself with the boss because she is in the power position?
- *Talking too much.* Do I have to control the conversation, or take center stage by incessantly talking, or talking about myself? When I notice people distancing themselves from me, do I try to keep talking faster to keep the connection going? Is it difficult for me to listen? Do I frequently interrupt business meetings with jokes or silliness?

- *Suspicion and secretiveness.* Do I feel I must keep certain ideas to myself so others won't steal them or beat me to the punch? How does my suspicion keep me from gaining support (e.g., on a project) when I need it? How do I *specifically* distance myself from others? What *specifically* about someone makes me become distrustful?
- *Withholding love.* Do I use silence or smoldering, unexpressed anger to let people know that I am upset, without giving them a chance to talk it through with me? What subtle forms of withholding energy do I use in the workplace?
- *Resisting authority and cynicism.* Do I tend to become elated only when I have made someone else feel inadequate or wrong? Do I see myself as a lone ranger, or the only one who sees "the truth" in a group situation, although I do nothing constructive to change anything? What do I *specifically* feel when I have one-upped someone? How has this sabotaged my progress in the past when I really wanted to succeed?
- *Self-righteousness.* Do I feel most powerful right after I have been "proven right" in a situation? Do I watch for ways that I can use my knowledge and surpass my friends or colleagues? Is it inordinately important for me to be right all the time? Is it very hard, or impossible, for me to admit any oversight or misjudgment?
- *Unwilling to commit.* What does commitment really mean to me? What do I think I have to give up in order to be committed to something? Does remaining uncommitted make me feel more secure, *because then I always have open-ended options*? What *specifically* do I feel when I have many options? Am I addicted to the *potential* of a career, job, or project? Am I always waiting for that big break or that big client? If I hate my work, do I secretly set myself apart from my colleagues, because I believe this is not my "real" work?
- *Committed to something that will never work.* Do I believe that I have to struggle to make something work even when I am getting every sign to let it go? Do I work marathon hours or take less money than I am worth?
- *Always thinking there is something better than what you have.* Are you always fixated on some golden future that never comes? Do you take small steps toward your goals, or give up because your goal seems too big and impossible? Are you chronically dissatisfied, and

constantly let everyone know it? Can you truthfully acknowledge your strengths and achievements?

- *Automatically assuming your needs will be met by the other.* Do you bring your needs and childhood inadequacies to the relationship instead of your strength, kindness, and openness to learning about the other person? Do you expect that people can read your mind and provide everything you desire when you desire it?
- *When things get tough, I get going.* If a circumstance doesn't satisfy you, do you check out? Do you decide *everything* is wrong with your workplace the minute things get difficult or if you get a new boss you don't like?
- *Fear of change.* When you reach a new level of responsibility or recognition, do you then fear that you won't be able to maintain it?

UNRAVELING THE PATTERN

If you resonate to one or two of these patterns, write down your insights on an index card. Keep it where you can see it, and let it remind you of the work you are doing to release your attachment to this unproductive behavior. In working with these shadow patterns, our goal is to bring them into the light of awareness. Without judgments against yourself, make a clear intention to work on making better choices in the future. Ask to be given opportunities to heal these patterns. Remember, change doesn't always happen overnight. You have been coping with life by using these patterns. They have been a big part of your complex nature, and they have also contributed to your uniqueness. Try to avoid taking the stance that these patterns are awful or that they make you a bad person. Judgments against yourself merely feed your shadow. Use these patterns to observe yourself, and learn how they might lead to new choices. Interestingly, from a spiritual point of view, working with these patterns may be an important part of your life purpose! In any case, becoming aware of them *engages* your soul's purpose for spiritual awakening.

For example, let's say your pattern is self-righteousness. Ask yourself, "What am I afraid will happen if I were shown to be wrong

"Awakening to the original seed of one's soul and hearing it speak may not be easy. How do we recognize its voice; what signals does it give? Before we can address these questions, we need to notice our own deafness, the obstructions that make us hard of hearing: the reductionism, the literalism, the scientism of our so-called common sense. For it is hard to get it through our hard heads that there can be messages from elsewhere more important to the conduct of our lives than what comes through Centel and Internet, meanings that don't slide in fast, free, and easy, but are encoded particularly in the painful pathologized events that perhaps are the only ways the gods can wake us up."
James Hillman[7]

about something?" Think back to a childhood memory when you made a mistake. What were the attitudes of your parents, teachers, and peers toward making a mistake? Do you blame others for your problems? If so, you will keep creating power struggles all your life. Because you learned in childhood that making mistakes resulted in losing love or security, you pushed your fear of being wrong into the shadow. Thus, the need to blame others becomes vital to the ego in order to maintain the illusion of control. To grow beyond this fear, you eventually have to realize that you can make a mistake and "not die" — as you feared as a child.

If your pattern is overtalking, ask yourself, "How would I feel if no one in the room spoke for ten minutes? What about silence makes me afraid?" The next time you are in a meeting, practice being quiet and feeling any tension in your body. Later, when you have time, remember these bodily sensations and write them out as if they were "voices" speaking to you.

In the next week, just begin to notice how you get angry at yourself for certain things. Notice how you talk to yourself negatively. Try to see how you are spending your precious life energy in ways that literally suck the life out of your cell tissue. Just becoming aware of this self-bombardment will start you on the path to reclaiming your power; however, you may want to work on these patterns with a therapist to deepen the process.

MAKING PEACE WITH YOUR FLAWS

Life is a constant flow between ebbs and tides. We wake and we sleep. The day dawns and the night enfolds us. We have our bright side and our shadow side. Problems arise in the external world when we *project our unacceptable qualities onto other people.* Then we struggle to control others or change them, always feeling like a victim of circumstance. With little awareness of our responsibility in situations, we suffer inner conflict and self-doubt.

Ideally, as we express our authentic spirit in meaningful activities, we begin to live in a state of balance, where we accept and work with what we've got— who we are. Often, we are so busy trying to meet the expectations of our nine-to-five jobs, or attempting to fulfill the unlived dreams of our parents, that we scarcely know *who* we are. In order to fulfill that unique complex of what we call our life purpose, it is very helpful to let go of judgments—of self or others.

> "When we become impatient, we literally devalue ourselves and our connection to the divine Holy Spirit. Impatience is a failure to trust in the universal intelligence, and it implies that we are separate from the all-providing spirit."
>
> *Wayne Dyer[8]*

Instead of judging ourselves, it is more useful to think of our "flaws" as a vital inner characteristic that wants to be heard. For example, can you see your need to tinker and doodle as part of your creative process and not just lazy inaction? Try to understand what *purpose* your flaw might be serving—whether it's positive or negative. The things you hate about yourself may provide you with a wealth of uncommon sense, once you release them from the judgments that keep them in the dark.

AN ENTRYWAY

Interestingly, Joan, the insurance agent, began to consider that her patterns could be an entryway to a much deeper level of self-knowledge.

"When I started the insurance business, someone asked me what my goals were, and I said, 'Fame, fortune, and recognition.' For me, money means, 'I did it right.' It means acceptance and it means love. I think that's why salespeople get so angry when clients leave them. The loss of income means, 'I didn't do it right,' or it means that their client is going to someone whom they like better, or who does the job better.

"In college, I first studied psychology. When I quit psychology, I said it was because it was too hard, but my real fear was that I didn't think that I could do it right. My secret thought deep down was, 'Who would come to *me* anyway?'

"When I was little, we lived on a farm, so I gravitated to wanting all the princess things. Right from the beginning, I had the desire to be special—to be chosen. I always tried out for song leader, cheerleader, and baton twirler. I was on the student council, but that was not nearly as important as being picked on looks and charm.

"My biggest fear is that I will be alone because I didn't do something right. Because of that fear of being alone—and this is so hard for me to look at—I am always mentally screaming out, 'Pick me! See me.' If someone *does* choose me, then I still have the same fear. I'm afraid they will judge and criticize me, and then leave me, reinforcing my fear. I'm always focused on myself. I constantly compare my body to women at the gym, or on the street, seeing how I match up.

> "My biggest fear is that I will be alone because I didn't do something right."

"It's becoming clear to me that the deepest lesson in my life—one that enters into absolutely everything I do, at least so far—is to learn to accept myself and have compassion for myself. When I can value the me that is not constantly performing, I will be able to trust that people are responding to the real me, and not a cardboard stand-in."

Joan's life purpose at this time, more than finding the right career, may be the healing of a deeply held self-perception, which may even be a karmic pattern carried over from a previous lifetime.

"I've been very focused on my health in the last year. In the past, I totally focused on the *beauty* of my body and my weight. Last year, I got really sick, and now my focus has shifted to the *health* of my body. But even as I'm getting healthier, I'm starting to think about getting plastic surgery again. It's still the old fixation on the perception that I'm not okay the way I am.

"I am consciously working to shift the focus from my drive to be chosen. I also began to watch my thinking process and beliefs, such as, 'My money has slowed down because I haven't done my business right.' I start thinking that I should have done it the way they [her life insurance mentors] told me to, versus trusting myself to know how to do it my own way, which has been very successful in the past," Joan said. "The hard part of trusting myself is, I guess, knowing *which* voice to trust. Should I listen to the critical voice that sounds like my old trainer and mentor? Should I listen to the voice that says I work best when I'm doing more of a soft sell than a hard sell? My insurance business voice says, you should be out there prospecting. That's the part I hate, and I want to give up doing things I hate."

FINDING THE TRUE VOICE

As Joan talked, she seemed to answer her own question about which voice to listen to.

"I am most successful when I do my work my way. For example, I do a lot of business by mail and phone, which is unusual for insurance. I have consciously done my selling without guilt, pressure, or shame, ever since I had my own experience of being sold insurance by the intimidation method. I guess I am going against an accepted strategy of the industry, but I found the experience so demeaning.

"I can see that selling insurance has been good for me, in that it helps me feel recognized. When people call me sight unseen and want to work with me because their sister referred me, it makes me feel very good."

In Joan's story, we see that a specific career may have been consciously chosen to make a living, or it may have been unconsciously chosen to heal an unrecognized part of the psyche. Or both. Once we face our fears, life begins to change. Joan told me that recently she took a big step in her ability to receive both positive and negative feedback.

"I was in a training situation," she said, "where I hypnotized a client, and then was evaluated afterwards. The client told me she felt like she had really benefited from the work. On the other hand, a colleague who observed me criticized my pacing and technique, which were the very things the client liked. Two things happened for me. For the first time, I was really able to hear and accept the client's positive comments without doubting their validity. Secondly, I was also able to receive the critical information without feeling absolutely rejected. I was able to take in both comments as constructive information and to use them to balance my techniques. I can see that both my professions offer opportunities where I can work through this central personal issue of being okay."

WHERE WE LOSE POWER TO THE SHADOW

In the box on page 231 are brief descriptions of negative behaviors that do not allow us to contribute the best of ourselves to the world; nor do they bring us true happiness. We must consider, too, that overcoming these challenging tendencies may be a big part of our soul's purpose for being born.

> "Therapy seeks not only to dissolve armor but to introduce flexibility and conscious choice to what had been a rigid, unconscious, defense structure. . . . The shadow . . . contains not only the dross of our conscious life but our primitive, undifferentiated life force, a promise of the future, whose presence enhances our awareness and strengthens us through the tension of opposites."
>
> John P. Conger [9]

Because our habits are so ingrained in us as part of our coping strategies, in truth, we often may not even see ourselves having them. We may, at first, see them in the actions of other people, not even realizing that they are a part of ours, too.

It would be unrealistic to think that we can clear these tendencies wholesale in one grand scheme designed to "fix" ourselves, thus enabling us to achieve a brilliant new future. It is much more helpful to see these behaviors as ongoing patterns that represent *reality* in our thinking. Once we become aware of even one behavior, and intend to stop putting our energy there, our self-organization automatically starts producing different outcomes. Recognizing these patterns allows us to shift our process of responding to events. In the beginning, we may struggle not to fall back into old habits, but once we experience some success, we automatically feel more "on purpose." New behaviors become new habits. One day, we realize, "Hey, life's pretty good now. How did that happen?"

As you begin to recognize your patterns, remember:

HOW WE LOSE POWER

The Victim/ Overaccommodator	Reactionary	Fear of Failure
Daily Situations	Daily Situations	Daily Situations
Frequent retelling of painful events (e.g., "When my husband divorced me . . ." or "My childhood was so bad that I never . . ." Downplaying your strengths in conversation (e.g., "I'm not very good at . . ." or "I've never been able to . . ." or "I don't seem able to . . ." Feeling that others think you are weak, unintelligent, or unsuccessful Second-guessing someone's "real" motivation toward you Working too much and feeling resentful about it Constant complaining Obsessing about past conversations or encounters	Thinks those in authority are fools Uses sarcasm and cynicism often in conversations Quick to argue; looks for small transgressions to prove a point about someone Distrusts others' motives Feels others are unrealistic or stupid	*Frequently* dwells on not having enough money, education, contacts, charisma, ability, etc. Keeps doing more of what is not working Procrastinates Fears being a bag lady; fears letting someone down Always alert for doomsday scenarios; thinks pessimism is the best defense
	Controller	**Fear of Change**
	Daily Situations	Daily Situations
	Frequent power struggles Constant sense of urgency Works hard for recognition Feels pressured to achieve Is always giving advice Is secretive and suspicious Talks compulsively	Frequently tells others, "I don't know what to do" or "I'm so confused" Compromises and defers, then feels resentful Feels hopeless or helpless but justifies current situation as necessary (e.g., "I need the paycheck" or "I have to keep the family together," or "No one else will hire me")

- Give yourself permission to be on and off purpose, knowing that any process has cycles.
- When you catch yourself in the middle of an old habit simply come back to center, and tune in to your intuitive guidance in the moment.
- Appreciate your path, your propensities, and your process with a sense of humor and compassion for yourself.

LIGHTENING THE SHADOW

As you learn to notice the *specific* ways you judge yourself or discount your abilities, you can support this growth by aligning yourself with age-old spiritual principles. In the box on page 233 are several universal practices that will help you attract what you need to find your life purpose. Notice that if you consciously navigated your life by any *one* of these ideas, you would be living in alignment with your spiritual path.

Donna Stoneham, the organizational developer whose interview with me was presented in Chapter 8, discussed these ideas with me one day. She commented:

"I have a story on the principle that when we are on purpose, we are *living mostly in present time*. About three months ago, I was driving home from a training and I had an epiphany in the car, and I began to cry. For the first time in six years, I thought to myself, 'Donna, you are in exactly the right place at exactly the right time.' It was a huge realization. I was always the overachieving, type-A personality. I'm always living six months in the future, instead of noticing where I am at the moment and enjoying whatever that is. I suddenly saw that everything I am doing at this stage of my life *is* important, *is* meaningful, even though it doesn't look like my expectations of where I wanted to be. It was liberating to realize this.

"On the principle that *I value ordinary life*, I can't tell you how many times lately I have felt grateful for the beauty around me. I'll get tears in my eyes. Being able to carry that sense of the mundane into the next effort or activity completely shifts how I do what I do.

"I always knew that changing my life is an inside job. In my old life in the corporations, I felt it was what you did in the external world that made the difference. I was constantly living like a lab rat,

HOW WE LIGHTEN THE SHADOW

Daily Practice

Notice that if you do any one of these principles, you do them all.

I trust myself to make the right choice.	I accept what is: the good, the bad, and the neutral.
I trust there is a purpose for everything.	I keep coming back to the intention to love.
I live mostly in present time.	I surrender to a higher order.
I value the ordinary life, but may live an unordinary life.	I strive to fully engage and participate with all of life.
I am willing to take pain without blaming.	I am kind to myself and others.
I realize that reality is created by thought, language, and action.	I keep a sense of humor and openness.

scurrying around trying to do the best work, work the longest hours, do the right things for the right people. After I started meditating, being clear about my vision, and accepting myself the way I am, my life turned around. There were some lean years in the beginning, but I always trusted that if I was doing my work and God's work, it would all come together."

TRACKING YOUR PATTERN DURING ONE WEEK

Photocopy the table on page 231, titled "How We Lose Power." Keep the copy in your pocket, wallet, or purse as a reminder of what you would like to change. Make a check mark next to any behavior that you become aware you are engaging in. By the end of the week, you should have a good idea of the amount of energy you lose in these directions. Simply increasing your awareness of your behavior will send new messages to your field of energy, attracting new situations. Another benefit of this practice is that you will automatically increase your ability to stay in the present. Also be aware that life might get more challenging while you learn new ways of participating in your relationships!

FREEING OURSELVES FROM HABITUAL CRITICISMS

The following story provides us with a good example of how to reclaim our creative energy by refraining from negative mental preoccupations. My friend Gilberto Munguia, a highly respected cellist and founder of the Chamber Music Festival in San Miguel de Allende, Mexico, happened to call me as I was writing this chapter. As he related how some of his professional struggles had resolved themselves, and how much happier he was feeling, I realized that his story was about the shadow. I asked him to what did he attribute the positive changes in his life.

"I got rid of the obstacles within myself," he was quick to reply. "Somehow in the past few months, I began to realize that I have always gone around with this feeling that some bad thing was going to happen. You know, like waiting for the other shoe to drop. I somehow always had this inner unsettled feeling, like something was going to come and slap me down. After I pinpointed that in myself, I saw it as what it was—a thought pattern that I continued to re-create every day. There is no external reason for this dread. Somewhere in life, I had latched on to this fear and was hardly aware that it was there every day. I can't tell you how different I feel now. I just feel happy. I'm not harassed by every little thing that happens anymore. I'm happy in my work. I know why I'm playing [the cello]. I feel like I'm surrounded by love and God and life.

"I can see the last two years have been pushing me in this direction. We try so hard to find out who we are, and we try to discover what our life means. We read books and try to find answers, and all of a sudden the door opens and there's a beautiful field in front of you. Once I saw the beauty of life, it felt like I always knew it was there, but I had forgotten. All we have to do is remember where we come from and that life is a continuing creation.

"I had been reading Neale Donald Walsch's book, *Conversations with God*, and I was loving it and wondering, 'Is this the truth? Is life about creating?' I went outside and was standing in a field under the stars and was asking this question, 'Could this be true?' At that moment a falling star went by like a huge rocket. It was so amazing, and I realized that God knows everything that we're thinking. It really hit me: Life is not a discovery but a creation. We create, and we have to take responsibility for where we are, and then we go on. The fascinating thing is to notice, 'I don't like this part of my life,' and then, by watching your thoughts, you realize how your life corresponds to your thinking. It's like being on *Star Trek*. You think, I want a chicken dinner,' and it suddenly appears!

"I believe that all of us have a little inner voice that we *turn off and on*. We can be very self-indulgent and go off in a rage, and pretend people are doing things to us so that we can justify drinking or smoking or shopping or any reaction. That's much easier to do than saying, 'Wait a minute. My life might not be going as I want it to right now, but whose responsibility is that?'

"A while ago, I had major financial problems, and heavy responsibilities with the Festival that really weighed me down. I could not see any purpose to any of this. But it forced me to go back to my musical roots in order to rediscover who I was and who I had started out to be. I realized that the feeling of being held down was really because I had not been expressing myself enough musically. The fountain of creativity had been bottled up. I had polarized my choices into an either/or situation. Either being a cellist or being the festival director. But I had to face myself. 'Okay, Munguia, what is it you uniquely give to the world, and what also feeds you and your soul?' I started to practice more and more. I started getting a few concerts here and there, and now I'm playing better than I ever did. I'm in touch with a higher place in myself that has always known how to play the cello. I get done in an hour what I used to get done in four hours.

"What made the difference was that I made a commitment to myself. I have had a passion for the cello since the age of five. I think we need to get in touch with those primal desires, and realize we are still that same person.

"Like Walsch says [in *Conversations with God*], don't ask for anything when you pray, just give thanks for what you have. How lucky I've been! It's extraordinary. Despite all our negativity, we can renew ourselves in an instant as soon as we make that shift in consciousness. If one percent of the population is thinking like this, it affects everyone else. Like when I had the thought and the star flew by. If we are meditating on these things, we are affecting the energy field and even the people who are sleeping, literally and metaphorically, are getting the effects.

> "A turning point happened for me one day when I was driving downtown in San Miguel. All of a sudden I realized that I had been criticizing everyone I passed."

"A turning point happened for me one day when I was driving downtown in San Miguel. All of a sudden I realized that I had been criticizing everyone I passed. 'Oh, look at that hat! Look at those pants!' I was sending out nothing but negative energy. I decided to stop doing that. I decided to just look and not criticize. By the time I got back home, I was so full of joy and energy. I realize we wake up with one hundred percent joy, and in the first two hours we spend a lot of that available energy by criticizing or complaining. Or we invest our energy in staying tied down by our past history.

"I start out the day now thinking, 'I can make a miracle with God's help. It's my day. It's my creation!' Just examine yourself and you discover everything."

FAMILY SHADOWS—GROWING OUT OF THE FAMILY MYTH

Our next story shows how we can be under the influence of the shadow of *our family and even our entire community*, misinterpreting this dark cloud as something that is a fault *within us*. Jim Burns is a good example of someone who had to deal with the unresolved shadow of his parents, and the unspoken rules of what it means to be—in his family. Jim left an early, loveless marriage and a "good" career as a schoolteacher to search for something deeper that seemed to be calling him. He now lives in California, is married to the love of his life, and is pursuing his dream of writing and performing uplifting humor.

"When I was twenty," Jim told me, "I had a conversation with my dad not long before he died. He opened up his heart, and let me in on all his secrets. He was an electrician, and he told me that he loved doing the electrical work, but he had never cared for the business side of it. Then he started telling me that he had never felt that Mom was satisfied with him. He felt she wanted more than he could give. He felt he had disappointed her in more ways than one—even in the way he had dressed, for example. Since he had diabetes, and had lost some of his toes, he wore tennis shoes and white socks, in order to be comfortable. He thought she wanted someone who dressed better, and would take her to nice places.

"The funny thing is, just like my dad, *I* got married in my early twenties. I started teaching elementary school, although I really didn't enjoy it that much. From the honeymoon, I knew I had made a mistake. I kept trying to please my wife, and started sacrificing myself and downplaying my own needs. We got the right house, and then we worked on getting the right furniture. About the age of thirty, I was at a point I call my midterm. I looked at my whole life and none of it was working.

"For example, my wife would look at the teacher pay scales for the next thirty years and feel good and secure. I looked at it and thought, 'I'm done? This is as good as it gets? I just plug in and go?' I felt like life was over. All of a sudden, I realized I was having the same feelings that my dad was telling me that he had had. Just like Dad and Mom, I didn't feel I was the kind of man my wife wanted. Believe it or not, I wear tennis shoes and baggy clothes just like my dad! From the outside, my wife and I seemed to have the perfect relationship. We got along well in public. We had a nice house. But it was all hollow. I realized, 'Wow, another thirty years could click by, and who knows, I could be saying the same things to my son.'

"We were Catholic, and no one in our family had ever gotten a divorce. It was a huge, dramatic experience. I knew that I was going to look like the bad guy with my mom and my brothers.

"In those days, I actually thought that it would have been easier for me to commit suicide than to get a divorce. Rumor had it that my grandfather did commit suicide. I thought, 'Man, I want to, but if this has happened before me in this family, I want to stop the cycle.' Apparently, our family does not deal with emotional stuff. No one was being open with their feelings. If you felt anything that was not acceptable, it wasn't allowed to be aired. This was not healthy. I guess that's why I moved to California.

"I told everyone I was moving to pursue a career in comedy, but I think I was really pursuing my own life and freedom. Ironically, at the time, I was collecting clowns. It was my brother who made me aware of the symbolism. He said, 'You know, it's interesting you like clowns because they are sad. They're smiling on the outside and hurting on the inside.'

"I spent the next five or six years in therapy. I found it amazing that we attract people who fit into our blind spots, so we can work on our healing. I guess the gift that came out of all my challenges was learning who I am, and accepting that, and loving those qualities.

"During my healing process, I stopped drinking alcohol and became a vegetarian. I started meditating, and I could feel this as a source of wisdom. I liked it. This is where I want to stay. I know I was drinking to kill my feelings. This was when I felt I wanted to hurt myself or someone else. Suddenly, it just clicked. I realized, 'Drinking is not a good choice for you.'

"I was working in clubs on the road, but even that began to seem not so desirable anymore. I realized that I didn't want to just get a cheap laugh while people were drinking. It was like being on two different planes. From my own experience, I knew that if they were drinking they were closed down, and not comfortable with feelings. I think laughter can help the spirit, but a lot of comedians are just perpetuating ignorance. The jokes are hurtful and ugly. I want to do comedy that lifts the spirit.

"When I look back at my life, my path looks like it was meant to go the way it has for a reason. I can see that I was learning valuable lessons by being a teacher, and being in those classrooms with the kids. I've written my own one-man play, called *Both Sides of the Desk*. It talks about my experiences both as a kid in the schoolroom and as a teacher. I want to speak about tolerance, and about diversity as a positive thing. I want to talk about acceptance. Maybe even though people are laughing, they will start to think.

"In the past, I felt I had to *make* things happen, *make* people laugh. Now I feel I just have to be the best person I can be, and work on my spirit. The most important thing is to be open in the moment, and trust that I will receive messages that will be funny on a higher plane. Most humor is based on racism and stereotypes that make fun of people in a hurtful way. I want to stress the commonality of people and the shared vulnerability that we have. There are no top dogs. That's where I feel comfortable now.

"I'm also married now to the most wonderful, talented, and beautiful lady. As I was getting dressed for our first date, I thought, 'Do I wear the tennis shoes or put on loafers?' My tennis shoes are those black-and-white high-top Converse shoes. I decided to put on the tennis shoes because they are my favorites. Karen's first comment was, 'I love those shoes!' I got married in those same shoes, although I did buy a brand-new pair.

"I've managed to shift away from going on the road, and now work in town. Right now I'm the emcee at the Icehouse in Pasadena. This has given me a breather to make the transition over to performing full-time. One thing that helps me sort out confusion on my life path is to write. I've kept a journal for fourteen years. When I'm confused or have a problem, I specifically visualize my confusion or the problem, and then give it to God. Karen and I have done this together at the beach. We visualized putting our problem into our hands and blew it to the ocean. It worked.

"Even though I'm still in debt, today's bills are paid. There is a wonderful peace, and yet there is an excitement that things are unfolding. I do believe that we limit ourselves by making plans, because wonderful things have come that I wouldn't have planned. On the outside, other people may not see my life as wonderful, but this feels like where I'm supposed to be, yet I won't be here for long because everything is moving. The thing is, you have to accept change and let it show you where to go."

TALKING TO YOURSELF

Talking to Your Shadow

What if the denied or repressed parts of ourselves harbored an overlooked, uncommon wisdom? What if those inner parts held precisely the information we can't seem to find by any other means? Nancy Rosanoff, intuitive consultant and trainer and author of *Intuition Workout*, suggests the following exercise to explore the wisdom that may be locked away in the deep recesses of your shadow closet.

Step 1. Pick one career or job that you would *never* choose to do. Write it down.

Step 2. Now imagine a person who would *love* this job or career, and who would have the perfect skills for it. Imagine that he or she has done this job all his or her life.

Step 3. Next, imagine that you are sitting with that person. Ask him to tell you what makes him (or her) good at this job. Ask him to describe several qualities, characteristics, or skills that he has that uniquely fit him for this job—the job that you, yourself, would never choose to do.

Write down what he tells you. How could the message your imaginary person gives you be applied in any current dilemma in your life?

One man said, "I would never want to be an assassin. But I imagined someone who was one, and he told me that, in his work, he had to be very precise and detached. Being precise and detached was actually very relevant, and helped me solve some of my current problems at work."

A woman decided she could never be a sumo wrestler. When she began her imaginary conversation, the wrestler told her that in order to be good at wrestling, one has to be willing to go to the mat. "You have to be willing to commit to your actions with your body, not just your head," the wrestler told her. "You have to be willing to get down and dirty." This information turned out to be extremely relevant to her present life issues.

Another woman did the exercise a little differently. She wrote down five careers that she had thought about entering in college, but had talked herself out of because of fears of failure. She said the exercise brought back all the dreams she had had, as well as giving her a chance to look at her fears—a very emotional experience. She realized how she had cut herself off in the past.

This type of imagination exercise brings us information directly from the shadow side of ourselves, and is often something that is surprisingly pertinent to whatever obstacle we are currently working on. Keep playing with a variety of "unacceptable" occupations and tap into this uncommon wisdom.

CHAPTER 12

Transforming Obstacles

❦

What matters is not so much whether an interference has or does not have purpose; rather, it is important to look with a purposive eye, seeking value in the unexpected.

JAMES HILLMAN[1]

HOW WE CREATE OBSTACLES

Life sometimes seems more like an obstacle course than a course in miracles. What if there was a purpose to our obstacles? In this chapter, we are going to look at how we create obstacles out of potential energy by the way we choose to see "reality." We will also explore how to move into relationship with our so-called obstacle, and tap into its wisdom.

Obstacles are a part of life. Our magnetic force field is continually opening channels here, closing channels there. Every now and then, we decide we want to move in a certain direction, but are blocked by something we call an obstacle. Usually, we approach an obstacle in one of four ways.

These four beliefs, in the left-hand column, represent the traditional, commonsense Western response to problem solving. While it's true that much in life can be resolved by taking a straightforward, assertive tack, it's also true that such assertive straightforward approaches don't always work. Without throwing out logic and reason, we may find that we achieve richer or deeper solutions to our blocks

With the Commonsense Approach	With the Uncommon Approach
You:	You:
1. See the obstacle as negative, or	Are willing to see the obstacle as *meaningful information,* rather than as a negative thing, or
2. Believe that success is on hold until you get rid of the obstacle.	Look for the *purpose* of the obstacle, which will aid ultimate success, e.g.,
	What do I need to pay attention to?
	What attitude do I need to change?

	Is my timing right?
	    What have I been overlooking?
	    Is there a better way than I thought?
	    Am I ready to have what I want?

3. Believe the obstacle to be an *external* block, which prevents you from achieving your desire or life purpose.	Realize the external obstacle represents an *internal belief.*

4. Believe it can be "fixed" by using external methods of control, such as logic, objectivity, rational problem-solving, money, or urgent, aggressive action.	Resolve the obstacle by being:
	    clear about what you want
	    intuitively receptive
	    willing and able to identify the root belief that created the idea of the obstacle
	    willing to take action
	    willing to make changes
	    willing to let go of something

if we also look for the symbolic meaning, or uncommon sense, within the obstacle itself. Instead of *attacking* the problem, we also have a choice to *listen* to the problem, and receive information about ourselves from the problem itself.

FEEDING THE PROBLEM

Bring into mind one of your current concerns or problems. Can you feel its "denseness" in your energy field? Your problem may just be a vagueness about how to find your life's work, such as: "I have no idea what I love to do. I love to do lots of things."

Worry feeds our problems. Talking about our problems over and over again gives them even more power over us. The more we talk, the more they seem like a solid barrier that prevents us from finding or creating something that really satisfies us.

Most of us are *very* good at focusing on the things that we are afraid might happen, rather than on the sweet picture of what we hope would happen. Take a moment to reflect on the kinds of doomsday scenarios you run past your mind every day ("I'll never be able to retire." "I'll never find my soul mate." "I know I'm gonna get laid off." "What if my contract doesn't get renewed? I don't think there are that many good clients out there." "The competition is brutal." "I can't keep up.") Whenever you catch yourself in this habit of focusing on negative scenarios, remember the principle, *What you focus on, expands!* Train yourself to stop this doomsday thinking the minute you notice yourself doing it. Put your palm on the center of your abdomen, breathe, and ask yourself, "What am I afraid of right now?" "What do I need to do right now to get connected back to my center?" Practice *suspending* the negative scenario, the negative talk, the negative *assumptions.* Imagine that you want to *neutralize* the energy in your mind, and bring in a memory of something that uplifts you. Learning to suspend negative thinking without attaching to doubt, guilt, fear, and self-criticism is an ongoing practice not unlike strengthening your muscles through regular exercise.

If we are to engage our path in life successfully, we must become skillful at handling problems, setbacks, and roadblocks. As we grow spiritually, we understand that our thoughts and intentions direct the flow of our energy. We recognize that synchronicities and intuitions

> "Most times we try to ignore disturbances—until the heart calls our attention to them as possibly important, possibly necessary.
>
> James Hillman[2]

come to guide us when we need direction. Since we also know that our effectiveness in the external world lies in working *within*—with our attitudes and perceptions—then problems become less immutable and daunting when we focus on our internal processes. This perspective puts us back into a position of choice and self-empowerment. We can use those processes as opportunities for growth and development. Retraining our thinking, however, may not be accomplished overnight, but persistent practice eventually adds up to new behavior.

"Real" Problems

What about "real" problems such as losing a job or not having enough money to feed one's family? People sometimes ask, "Did I create the downsizing of my company?" "Did I create the transmission going out in my car?" When accidents or traumas happen to us, we are forced to come to grips with this occurrence. *How* we come to grips with it, *how* we make choices around these events, determines our subjective, or inner, reality. We may not have created an illness consciously, but *how* our illness is seen, experienced, and worked with *is* our creation.

It is counterproductive to assume we have created every misfortune in our life, as if we had made a *conscious* intention to do so. That kind of thinking tends to lead to guilt or despair. Nevertheless, a sincere willingness to acknowledge that we have certain beliefs that have created our situation will enrich our approach to working through obstacles.

Either/Or Thinking

Obstacles arise where we can see only limited options ahead. Remember the last time you went around in circles trying to make a decision involving two choices? How did the problem get resolved? Sometimes, *either* choice will take us into fruitful experiences, or, it could be that we are stuck because we intuitively know that *neither* answer is the right one. Often when we create a dual choice for ourselves, this seesaw serves us in an odd way. It keeps us stuck so that, in the standoff, we are forced to look for a third option we hadn't even considered. Chances are, if you can't make up your mind completely about a choice, neither option is truly the best one. I have often found that, with time, a third option appears.

Working *with* circumstances may take you someplace you would never have gone on your own. Just for a moment, imagine your obstacle is an ally. Remember that this obstacle is somehow an outgrowth of a belief (albeit unconscious) or part of your life process. Are you willing to trust that it has a purpose?

> "The future need not be a repetition of the past. Frequently one is caught by a paucity of imagination which conceives of the future only in terms of rearranging past events or experiences that are already known. Persistent attempts to explain the unknown in terms of what is already known, can lead to blind repetition of unsatisfactory patterns that limit growth and restrict possibilities."
> *Frances E. Vaughan*[3]

Keeping Alive Past Traumas Diminishes Internal Power

In Chapter 11, we explored how we lose energy to various thought processes (refer to "How We Lose Power" on page 231). In learning how to transform obstacles, we need to make sure that we are not filtering our creative ideas through old traumas. For example, Sara's obstacle was that she could never bring herself to ask for

> A problem, and the opportunity for working *with* it, and working *through* it is, paradoxically, the path of spiritual growth.

a raise from her rather domineering boss. "I was molested at six," she rationalized, "so it's hard for me to confront older men." John, whose finances were verging on bankruptcy, justified his lack of control by saying, "My dad was so tight we never had any fun. I promised myself I would live a little now when I can enjoy it."

When we base our identity on past negativities, we automatically face the present with contracted energy and frozen beliefs that limit healthy new choices.

If the Obstacle Feels Familiar

If you had a heavily conflicted childhood, you may still be programmed to *see problems everywhere. Unconsciously, you re-create the tense atmosphere of your early home environment because it feels familiar.* Problems can sometimes be a way to perpetuate the familiar feelings of how life was experienced in childhood *even though, ra-*

> "The shadow comes to us in the form of a thorn in the side, a person or event that appears to block our expansion, interrupt our joy, and negate our plans. The shadow comes to us in the area of our greatest blindness, an area of inferior development where we are least able to defend ourselves, an area where we are least subtle and least differentiated."
>
> John P. Conger[4]

tionally, that would seem counterproductive. For example, if mother and father were always anxious and concerned about problems, we, as children, would have had little choice but to assume that was the normal way of being. If we got attention for *solving problems or for taking care of others in childhood*, it's likely that this might *still* be the way we unconsciously look for self-esteem now. By the same token, if we got love and attention by *having* problems in childhood, we may unconsciously continue to create and use problems as a way of getting attention today. Continually creating problems, lacks, and hassles is a convenient way to avoid taking *any* steps toward our real purpose in life.

Build, Build, Build Those Obstacles

One day, I was working with a client on her career plans. She started by saying that she had been on disability and was anxious to get back into her former job as an occupational therapist. But she said, "I know I have some obstacles to work through before I can do that." As soon as she said that, I had the intuition to question the statement. I suggested that she examine her underlying assumptions that she *had* obstacles. She said nothing for about thirty seconds. Then she laughed. She immediately recognized how attached she was to a belief in work, in obstacles, and having to earn anything good coming to her. After all, her whole life purpose was tied into being an *occupational therapist* — helping people work, work, work to regain their place in the world. She later wrote me that that work on beliefs had deeply affected her view of herself and her situation in a favorable way. In her case, the timing for such a rapid, transformative perception was perfect. She had been ready to make the breakthrough.

Hiding Behind Obstacles

Sometimes we choose to see an obstacle in order to justify not taking a new step. We voluntarily give up our power. The obstacle gives us a good excuse not to face our truth. Many people hold on to their confusion, never allowing themselves to make *any* tentative steps toward change because it's never "quite the right time." If you think you might be hiding behind your "limitations" (e.g., I don't have enough money to go to computer school), you are not alone! Most of us resist change.

CREATING A RELATIONSHIP WITH YOUR OBSTACLES

If It's Not Working for You, It's Not Working for Others, Either

If you have a problem between yourself and another person, realize that some internal change is required. Be willing to accept that the impasse has happened

> **When something is not working, we tend to do more of it.**

for a reason, and know that if you feel out of alignment with someone, they feel it also. If something is not working for one person, it's also not working for the other one. How many times have you heard someone say, "Gee, I'm glad you brought that up. I have been feeling the same way." My own experience of this, recounted in Chapter 1, happened when I kept working harder at the financial counseling business, and getting worse and worse results. It was not working for me, or for my clients, or for my colleague.

Taking the Uncommon Approach

Instead of immediately labeling our so-called obstacle as "bad," or a "block," and pushing it away, let's think of it, first of all, as a mass of energy. It is a pattern of energy that has arisen in our field. At present, we cannot see "around it" or "through it." However, we have attracted it into our life. If we go back to our premise that everything has a purpose, then we must assume that our obstacle, too, has a purpose.

Perhaps if we choose to approach our obstacle intuitively, as if looking for a message, we will be able to see the seeds of a solution. By playing around the edges of the obstacle, we may see where we need to change our thinking to get an even better result than we had first hoped for. Working *with* an obstacle requires that we turn *toward* it. Our intention, in this case, is to form a relationship *with* it.

Who Knows If It's Good or Bad?

The ego's job is to help us survive, maintain control, and feel secure. Our ego is our sense of self, as distinct from our sense of connection to All-That-Is. In order to understand, cope, and maintain its integrity, the ego is constantly evaluating whether something is good or bad. We do not like to be thwarted in our plans; nor do we like to be taken by surprise by events out of our control. While the ego is a necessary energy pattern, we need to be able to see beyond its confines when we engage with the universal energy field. Becoming aware that we are part of a much larger cosmic plan, or soul's purpose, quickly teaches us how limiting it can be to make snap judgments about whether a delay or a setback is in our favor or not. Author and depth psychologist Frances E. Vaughan recounts an often-told Zen tale that teaches us the value of an open attitude to problems and setbacks:

> A farmer who had just acquired a stallion came to the Zen Master in distress, saying, "Master, the horse is gone, the horse is gone!" for the stallion had run away. The Zen Master replied, "Who knows if it's good or bad?" The farmer returned to his work feeling sad and miserable. Two days later the stallion returned and brought with him two mares. The farmer was overjoyed and he went to the Zen Master, saying, "The horse is back and has brought two others with him." The Master replied, "Who knows if it's good or bad?" Three days later the farmer was back again, crying because his only son, his only helper on the farm, had been thrown from one of the horses and his back had been broken. He was now in a body cast and could do no work. The Zen Master again replied, "Who knows if it's good or bad?" A few days later a group of soldiers came to the farm as they were conscripting all the young men in the area to fight in a war. Since the farmer's son was in a body cast they did not take him.[5]

Try using this phrase "Who knows if it's good or bad?" for a week or so as you encounter life events.

Maintaining Responsibility but Not Identification with the Obstacle

In handling obstacles resourcefully, we once again come face-to-face with paradox: The problem *is* ours to deal with, and yet the problem *is not the whole of who we are.* Our best stance is to understand that an obstacle has purposefully appeared in our field, and yet, we must take care not to become so identified with the obstacle that we keep ourselves forever inside its limitations. Just for a moment, bring into mind any current problem you have. Notice how your mind defines this thing in order to solidify and give shape to what is, essentially, a mass of feeling energy. The mind works by defining and shaping energy in hopes of being able to gain more control. Often, when we think about our concern or worry, we are completely identified with this problem *as a part of ourselves.* We would say, "Yes. This is how I am. This is me. I have this certain problem right now." Or "I have *always* been like that. I have *always* had this problem."

The content, or specific issue, of problems, of course, can run the full range of the human condition. One person's problem might be "I want to make more money and have more fun, but I don't know how to make a change in my life. Where do I start?" You may have one major conflict or several circumstances that feel extremely limiting to you.

In the case of a personal flaw or shortcoming, you may feel trapped by this fault, a prisoner within; for example, you may feel, "I'm a procrastinator, and I know I'm not fulfilling my potential." You believe that you *are* the problem. How many of us believe: "I am old." "I am undesirable." "I am overweight." "I am not good at social gatherings." "I feel like I'm invisible and no one sees the real me." This is the lie we tell ourselves so that we don't have to leave our comfort zone.

> "Has exile helped you? Have you found strength in it?"
>
> "Oh yes! Without a doubt. I can try to tell you why. When, at some point in our lives, we meet a real tragedy—which could happen to any one of us—we can react in two ways. Obviously we can lose hope, let ourselves slip into discouragement, into alcohol, drugs, unending sadness. Or else we can wake ourselves up, discover in ourselves an energy that was hidden there, and act with more clarity, more force."
>
> *His Holiness the Dalai Lama*[6]

Your thoughts about your problem concretize it. Since it seems utterly real to you, you *accept* the problem as a fact—which causes you to continue to *react. Instead, try to become aware of how you shape potential energy into "problems" or "conflicts" in the first place.* Ask yourself, "Why have I defined this situation as a problem?" Our reality looks a certain way to us because inside ourselves we are completely identified with it.

Become Your Observer Self

Notice that you are reading this page and taking in these ideas and deciding if you think they are true or not. A part of you, the Observer, is continually witnessing yourself. The Observer is your eternal, unchanging self. The Observer has no problems. The Observer *is*. It is the core You that exists within the universal flow of energy.

Imagine that the Observer exists in the space at the end of this sentence.

Notice that the Observer exists in the morning when you wake up, and before you remember your problems. Notice that the Observer is free and unaffected by passing events or emotions or even concerns about whether you are fulfilling your life purpose.

Exploring your obstacles from the point of view of your Observer Self often releases creative energy much the same way as when we take a trip and "get away from it all" for a while. Observing our problems from some distance—either internally, or externally by taking a vacation—helps us gain perspective. *Observe,* for a moment, one of your limiting beliefs, such as "I never have enough time" or "I should be further ahead by now." Notice how easily you condensed energy into the belief or thought-form. Notice that you created a negative energy pattern with your choice of seeing a particular problem. Where was that energy before you just created it?

Negative thought forms take even more energy to create than positive ones. Actually, as you become more conscious, it becomes harder to hear yourself making negative comments. You naturally shift away from spending energy on negativity. With each new insight, you have a greater amount of psychic energy available, which naturally increases intuition and synchronistic flow. Begin to observe yourself shaping potential energy—into *positive* beliefs or *negative* worries. Being "negative" literally puts your energy bank account in the red!

Remember, the Observer is the core, eternal essence of you. The Observer is not the same as the *act of dissociating from an event to split off from painful feelings*. Dissociation is a defense mechanism created to deny the trauma of an event. The Observer, on the other hand, is the You who existed before you were born, and the You who exists after you leave the body.

Accept the Obstacle and Learn to Love It as the Perfect Teacher

Natalie Goldberg, in her book *Long Quiet Highway,* tells how she wanted to persuade her Zen teacher to let her attend the training period even though she could not come for the Monday night lecture because of a teaching commitment. She spent hours thinking how she could talk the roshi into letting her do this.

> I began the recitation of all my carefully planned tactics. After I had completed only a sentence or two, he turned and looked out the window. I felt ridiculous . . . I rattled on until I was finished. I didn't know what else to do.
>
> When I was done, he turned to me: "What do you want?"
>
> "I want to sit this fall's training period, but I have to teach Monday nights and I can't come to lecture," I said.
>
> "I'll lecture on Tuesday nights," he said.
>
> "You can't do that!" I was startled.
>
> "Why not? You said you can't come on Mondays; can you?"
>
> "No," I shook my head.
>
> He opened his calendar book. "Yes, I can do Tuesdays."
>
> I left discombobulated. . . . The man was empty; Roshi was empty. He came from no angle. Not better or worse than I, not Zen master. From no time, no way it was done in the past dictating the present. At that moment, he came from nothing. No identity. No hierarchy. No schedule.[7]

PRINCIPLES AND PRACTICES
FOR WORKING THROUGH OBSTACLES

Working creatively to see what an obstacle might have to teach us requires us to use the same principles we have already learned in pursuing our life purpose. Write these principles down on three-by-five-inch cards to keep handy in times of stress.

- *Bring yourself and your attention into the present moment.* If you are worrying, you are either in the past or in the future. When you are deep into your problem, you have lost contact with your center, and your awareness is not in present time. *You* are not present. To regain your center, focus on your breathing for a few minutes.
- *Pay attention to body signals.* Feelings such as happiness, a stiff neck, or a sinking feeling in the stomach are intuitive signals about the direction you are going. Pay close attention whenever you feel a loss of power—whenever you feel *drained*. To regain your center, put the palm of your hand against your solar plexus. Command your energy to drop into your pelvic area.
- *Be clear about what you want.* Remember your purpose and priorities. Write out any problem on a piece of paper and ask for help in resolving it. Take the attitude that the solution is already in progress.
- *Pay attention to coincidences.* Are events giving you, in general, a "yes" or a "no" signal?
- *Be willing to see the truth instead of tolerating something that is going nowhere.* It's your life. Ask yourself, "How do I ultimately want to feel?" or "What am I trying to accomplish here?" "What is true for me?" (Not "What should I do to please others?")

Symbol Meditation—Going Inward for the Answer

Try this simple meditation to explore what your obstacle has to teach you. Choose a quiet place where you won't be interrupted. Meditation music may be helpful.

Read through the following instructions and then close your eyes and allow your images to arise. As soon as you are finished, jot down the information you received.

Close your eyes, take a few deep breaths, and allow your body to relax for a few minutes. Don't rush your process.

When you are relaxed, ask that your obstacle appear as *a symbol*. If nothing appears, *pretend* that your obstacle looks like something.

Next, ask the symbol four questions:

"What is your purpose in my life?"

"What is my belief that caused you to come into my life?"

"What are you teaching me?"

"What do I need to know or *think* to move on?"

Keep your inner focus on the symbol. As you ask the last question, "What do I need to know or think to move on?" imagine that you see another symbol, word, color, or energy pattern inside the first symbol or emerging from it. You are asking to be shown the solution *already present* in your problem.

Try to release any need to have the problem stay, go away, or turn out in a certain way. End your meditation by flooding your symbol with radiant, white light and allowing it to dissolve back into potential creative universal energy. Write down anything that you learned from the meditation.

Your work for the moment is done. Do not give any more thought to this issue, and do something that is relaxing and fun for a while.

Symbols Answer Questions

Janice did the meditation above. The problem she brought to the meditation was that she didn't have a car to travel to the city where she thought she should look for a job. Her *symbol for the problem* was a big, black hole in the ground. When she asked *the purpose of her obstacle*, her inner guidance said, "You are already in the right place." That surprised her because she could see no way to earn a good living where she was outside the city limits in a fairly run-down part of town.

Her question about *what belief caused this obstacle* was answered by, "You believe that you grew up on the wrong side of the tracks because of certain things that were said to you in early life and certain experiences that you *attributed to that idea.*" On reflection, Janice said she had always accepted that she was somehow inferior because she had never had any "breaks" like other people seemed to have. Her *foundation belief* was that she was *destined* to be poor all her life. By re-creating her original belief in being "on the wrong side of the tracks," she assumed, without question, that she would have better luck working somewhere else than where she was — in the city. This inner belief that somehow she was automatically born to be less than others had become an accepted fact in Janice's inner reality.

When Janice asked *what the obstacle (not having a car) was teaching* her, she finally heard the sentence, "Let them come to you." She really did not know what to make of this, but wrote it down in her journal, hoping to understand the meaning at a later time.

Her last question, "*What do I need to know or think to move on?*" engendered the following symbols: an unraveling bale of wire fencing material, and two flags, which emerged out of the black hole of her first symbol. Janice said, "I had absolutely no understanding of what these symbols might mean. I figured I simply was not getting any information on how to get a car. It wasn't until a few months later, when I came across my notebook again, that I had to laugh. About four months after I did that meditation, I happened to run into a woman in a Laundromat who was looking for someone to work for her. She had a kennel about two blocks from my house, and I went to work with her. One of the first things I had to do was help rebuild the fencing for the dog run. She had two checkered flags in front of her house, to help clients find the business. She and I are now becoming business partners. I am so thrilled to be working with the animals, and am much happier than I would have been doing office work or waiting tables in the city. I guess I'd say that I had to learn that there is no innate reason that I have to fail in life based on my early experiences of being poor. When I remember that, I feel like I have an open door in front of me."

Janice's story shows us that even though we may not understand the significance of a symbol at the time, it does contain helpful information regarding the state of our consciousness. *Not only that, but the psychic energy we invest in our quest for information is part of the intention that manifests our solution down the road.* We don't have to have total, logical clarity about what we need to do, but to trust that we will be given the opportunities to make choices consistent with our ultimate desires. Persistent attention to our root assumptions is the single most effective mental activity we can do for ourselves.

Resistance

I suspect that just about now, your natural resistance to this material may be starting to surface! Don't be surprised if you start thinking something like "Well, this is all easy for *her* to talk about. But *she* doesn't have *my* problems. My problems aren't just going to go away that easily." Be aware that in working through obstacles, one of the biggest obstacles of all is the resistance to change itself. Physicist David Bohm cautions us not to label a psychological state as a "problem" if it contains contradictory presuppositions (e.g., "I want to succeed but I can't because I am inherently inadequate"). Instead, he sees such a conflicted inner state as a paradox, which can never be treated as a simple problem to be solved. The paradox, by definition, keeps us from facing the unbearable root belief. He writes:

> More generally, one can say that when something goes wrong psychologically, it is confusing to describe the resulting situation as a "problem." Rather, it would be better to say that one was confronted by a paradox. In the case of the man who is susceptible to flattery, the paradox is that he apparently knows and understands the absolute need to be honest with himself and yet he feels an even stronger "need" to deceive himself, when this helps to release him from an unbearable sense of inadequacy and to substitute instead a sense of inward rightness and well-being. What is called for in such a case is not some procedure that "solves his problem." Rather, it is to pause and to give attention to the fact that his thinking and feeling is dominated, through and through, by a set of self-contradictory demands or "needs" so that as long as such thinking and feeling prevail, there is no way to put things right. It takes a great deal of energy and seriousness to "stay with" an awareness of this fact, rather than to "escape" by allowing the mind to dart into some other subject, or otherwise lose awareness of the actual state of affairs. Such attention, going immensely beyond what is merely verbal or intellectual, can actually bring the root of the paradox into awareness, and thus the paradox dissolves when its nullity and absurdity are clearly seen, felt, and understood.[8]

Common thinking says, "Releasing entrenched beliefs is not going to happen overnight." Maybe. Maybe not. We have been conditioned to believe that we must work hard to make changes. However, remember that our new collective vocabulary now contains the words "quantum leap"! We also now have a collective thought form that says, "I create my own reality." In addition, even science now tells us that time and space really do not exist and intention is communicated instantly. Therefore, it behooves us to . . . stay open. Once we experience a few synchronicities, we may really believe that anything is possible!

Stream-of-Consciousness Writing

If you feel more comfortable capturing your intuition in writing instead of meditation, use the stream-of-consciousness method. Use the same four questions that were used for the symbol meditation on page 253 and then let the answers pour forth. Do not censor any thoughts that emerge. That is, just let your pen start with any word that comes out on the page. Continue to let the words flow out without trying to control the message. When your unconscious sees that you really want information, you'll be surprised at how much information you receive internally as intuition — and how many new opportunities you receive in the outer world. All kinds of unexpected coincidences will come to you with time.

Mind Mapping

Another powerful way to explore your obstacle is to use a simple technique called "mind mapping," developed in the early 1970s by Tony Buzan. Try mapping the different facets of your obstacle.

Take a blank sheet of paper. In the center of the page, write a definition of your obstacle as briefly as possible. Then draw a box around your obstacle statement.

Next, draw a vertical line going *up* from the center box and then draw a horizontal line. On the vertical line write "Goals." On the horizontal line write whatever goals you'd like to achieve, listing as many goals as you want on separate horizontal lines.

From the *bottom* of the center box, draw another vertical line. On this line, write, "Roots of My Problem." Draw as many horizontal lines as you need to list the roots of your problem.

From the left side of the box, draw a line and label it "Beliefs I Have About My Obstacle." Make a separate horizontal line for each belief that you discover.

From the right side of the box, draw two lines. Label one "Things to Check Out" and one "Things to Do."

Feel free to create your own pattern for mind mapping this obstacle. There is no right or wrong way to do it. You may want to make a separate map for the things you want to experiment with or do to

MIND-MAPPING YOUR OBSTACLE

GOALS

Have my own business
Need to make $35,000/year
Would like an experienced business partner
I want a beautiful, serene atmosphere
I see myself standing near the front door, greeting people

OBSTACLE
"Fear" "Uncertainty"

My dream is to own a small teahouse, but I don't have any business experience. I'm not sure it's the right goal.

THINGS TO DO/CHECK OUT

Who do I know who can counsel me about business?
Put ad in newspaper for business partner. See who shows up
Get info: Treat like another "assignment from my boss"!
Share my dream with positive people
How is "being rejected by my father" an advantage in getting what I want in my present situation?

ROOTS OF MY PROBLEM

I've always worked for others
I felt invisible as a child
My parents both had "victim of life" mentalities
My father was disappointed I was born a girl and not a boy
Neither parent was in business

All these experiences had a purpose!

BELIEFS I HAVE ABOUT MY OBSTACLE

My family thought making money was greedy
I'm not good at business
I'm lacking something
I won't make enough quickly to live on
I'm not organized

Am I willing to believe something different/positive?

solve your problem. Each day, you can make a map of tasks you want to do, highlighting the ones you will do for sure. Once a task has been completed, mark it with another color.

Reminders for Attracting Solutions

If you wish to move forward even though a move seems scary, consider the following ideas:

- *Check to see what you are afraid would happen if the obstacle was not there.* One woman talked about always being on the edge with her business, but was unwilling to hire someone for even one day a week to help her stay organized—which in the long run would have helped her create more business. After some time, she discovered that her underlying belief was that being in business for oneself is risky. Nobody in her family had ever been an entrepreneur. She was afraid to hire a new person because that would have increased her *perceived risk*.

- *You can always make another choice tomorrow.* If fear paralyzes you, do *something*. One thing we know is that life constantly changes. Sometimes making *any* choice is preferable to continuing to wait until we have absolute certainty.

- *Expect the outcome to be even better than what you had wanted.* Relax! Remember, you don't have to control anything or anybody. What a relief!

> "Maintaining an attitude of playfulness may at first seem inappropriate for problem-solving, but intuitive problem solving is basically a creative process, and is more easily activated when critical judgment is suspended."
> Frances E. Vaughan[9]

The more relaxed and spontaneous you can be in everyday consciousness, the more easily you unblock any frozen energy. Remember that working with your inner forces is a *process*, and answers emerge unexpectedly, *over time*. Your work definitely continues outside of the meditation or the writing. The *journey* to your solution is your path of spiritual discovery, and is the real pot of gold.

Finally, it's important not to expect yourself to move any faster than you are ready to. Be patient, and know that each time you work with your inner world, things will change outside.

TALES OF OBSTACLES OVERCOME

You are about to meet three people who have truly lived by the seat of their intuition. Each of them has grappled with major setbacks and obstacles. Today each of them can look back at their hard-won triumphs and attest to the value of allowing synchronicity and intuition to lead them to their next encounter with the richness of life. Karen McCall's story shows us how early childhood deprivation and later financial woes became the foundation for helping herself and others achieve mastery over self-defeating behavior. Not only did she gain financial balance herself, but the outcome of her struggle helped develop a whole new field of financial counseling as well. In the second story, Angela (not her real name) shares how she has made peace with deep betrayal and grief. In the last story, we see how synchronicity moved Philippa's life forward just when life seemed darkest.

Turning Adversity into Life's Work

"Intuition and synchronicity have constantly been my guides as I found my career path," said Karen McCall, founder and director of Financial Recovery, a consulting firm in San Anselmo, California. "In 1986, I was employed by a large computer hardware company," Karen said. "I had job security, a company car, benefits, everything. The only thing was, I hated the job. And yet I could not imagine leaving it, either. I knew very little about computers, and I always had this inner feeling that I was going to be 'found out.'

"I started having stomach problems and I was very depressed. I couldn't face going to work, and started not showing up, or hiding out, which was easy to do because I was doing outside sales. After going to a therapist, I got a medical disability. It was during that period that I signed up for a career class. I asked myself, 'What would I *like* to do?' not 'What *could* I do?' "

What had preceded this turning point in Karen's life was crucial to her answering this question.

"Money has been my greatest teacher," she said. "And my greatest problem. When I was a little girl, I used to sit on the floor of my grandmother's house and pore over every page of the Montgomery Ward catalog. I would fantasize about what I would buy from the catalog to fix the lives of the people in my family. For example, my grandparents didn't have indoor plumbing, so I would think about the bathroom fixtures I would buy. One of my lifelong patterns has been fantasies about always fixing someone else. I did not know how to focus on my own needs. This failure to know myself set me up for the compulsive behavior of spending money on other people — expensive presents for my children or my friends, clothes to make me acceptable and attractive to others. Since I was continually trying to either impress others or take care of them, I was unconscious of how to really take care of myself. For years, I did not have a clue that I was doing this.

"The catalyzing event for me happened when I was shopping in Saks Fifth Avenue with my American Express card. I was standing at the Chanel makeup counter buying makeup when the clerk asked for my identification. She had been notified that I had spent over thirteen hundred dollars on the card in an hour, and they were afraid the card had been stolen.

"My spree had been precipitated by having been asked out on a date. I was buying a black silk evening outfit with a jeweled purse, and I had no idea of how much I had spent. And this shopping was doing nothing to improve the very real deprivation in which I was living. Here I was shopping like this, and I had no furniture in my apartment. I was eating fast food or cereal for dinner on the breadboard in the kitchen while sitting on a stepladder. The reason I had no furniture was that a couple of years before that, in a desperate attempt to raise money for taxes, I had sold everything I owned.

"After this wake-up call in Saks, I began to realize that I had a problem. Up till then, I had just thought it was normal to feel overwhelmed by my creditors, to be living from hand to mouth, and to have this feeling of shame about it all.

"I was lucky. I was led by coincidence to a self-help group, where I found, first of all, that I was not alone. I began to understand that my self-defeating money behaviors had an emotional and a practical component, and that *I could change my life.*

"I started working very hard to take control of my finances and get more conscious of my addictive behaviors. A couple of years went by, and one day I happened to attend a seminar for women in business. The speaker was saying some things that I strongly disagreed with, and I suddenly heard myself thinking, 'I would do this whole lecture differently.' I suddenly knew what I wanted to say, and I got incredibly excited. On the way home on the bus, I was writing so furiously in my notebook that when the bus came to the end of the line, the driver told me, 'Lady, I've never had anybody miss the BART station before!' I was completely oblivious as the ideas began pouring out.

"So I suddenly had this newborn idea that I wanted to have a private practice, counseling people about how to manage their spending by looking at the emotional reasons that drove their behavior in unconscious ways. After having wrestled with these issues of underearning, overspending, chronic debting, and managing money, I knew what I wanted to do. Because of my own work, I felt strongly that we don't have to suffer forever if we are in debt and feel lousy about it. There is something we can do.

"I knew, instinctively, that this system would work, but I was embarrassed to say it. At first, my idea of being a financial counselor seemed so grandiose that I was afraid people would think I was crazy. I think my intuition helped me by guiding me to talk about the idea to the two people who would be most supportive. After listening to my idea, my friend John actually came up with the name for the business. He said, 'Oh, you want to do financial recovery.' And secondly, my friend Theo said, after I told her about it, 'Yes. What can I do to help?' From that time on, I was in the flow."

One Person's Work Affects Us All

Karen now has a thriving business that exists solely on word of mouth. This type of financial counseling, taking into account the underlying beliefs and emotions along with the day-to-day practical management of income and expenses, did not exist as a professional field before. The emergence of Karen's pioneering lifework seems to have depended on at least four major factors. First, her early *personal experiences* had set the stage for her later encounter with these ideas. Second, the *timing* had to be right. Culturally, the 1980s were a time of great emphasis on money and materiality. There was a hunger for *more* of everything; it was a time when the collective consciousness of America received the big mental implant telling it, "You can buy what you want *now*" with credit cards. Third, there was also a collective movement toward the idea of self-examination and taking responsibility in the various recovery groups that developed out of the original Alcoholics Anonymous model. Fourth, the United States is a country where roughly only 10 percent of the people have a savings account, and credit card debt is out of control. The time had come, collectively as well as individually, to learn how to have a healthy relationship to money. While we traditionally have passed laws and regulations bearing on all aspects of governmental budgeting, fluctuation of interest rates, and financial institutions and regulatory systems, we have not up till now looked at money in terms of its psychological, emotional, mental, and spiritual aspects. Karen's own life learning, thus, serves a greater purpose.

No Experience Is Ever Wasted

A woman I'll call Angela, a successful interior designer, took one of my classes several years ago. Her witty, point-blank assessment of people and situations and unflagging sense of humor instantly endeared her to the class and to me. She has struggled with some of life's hardest challenges, and has managed to exhibit absolutely no trace of the victim about her. In her early sixties, she looks no more than forty-five. Three years ago, her daughter, a thirty-eight-year-old mother of two teenagers, suffered severe head injuries from a fall from a horse. I called Angela for an interview and asked her to share some of the experiences that led her to her current happiness as a designer.

She began by telling me that what most sustains her now is her design work and her ability to help people create a nourishing environment for their own health and tranquillity.

COMPOSTING

"It's hard to express in words the fulfillment I feel from working with my design clients. We may start out on an intellectual basis, maybe just remodeling a kitchen. But our relationship might span eight or ten years. The process is such a total intuitive collaboration. We don't know where we're going, and when we get to the end, we are all in a state of amazement with what we have achieved together. We bring out something beyond what we knew would be created.

> **"I wanted a beautiful home, a beautiful life, and security. I was gorgeous and wanted all the trimmings."**

"When I was a little girl, I guess I wanted to be a movie star and a dancer. I wanted to be popular and to be a star. I was Miss Idaho in 1953, and was a contestant for Miss Universe the same year. Afterward, I was offered a movie contract. But at that time, my mother, at age forty-three, started dying of cancer, so I immediately got married to a guy that she had always liked. Soon I discovered that the marriage was not going to work. That began my arduous years of single child raising.

"I supported myself and the girls for years. I was driven by a goal to find a man with money and not to have to work so hard. I wanted a beautiful home, a beautiful life, and security. I was gorgeous and wanted all the trimmings. But I see now that I was never willing to compromise myself. In the 1960s, I moved from Idaho to San Francisco, found a good job, and immediately tripled my income. I married the catch of San Francisco and had a dream wedding. We went into business together. Within months, I discovered he was a gambler, who even gambled away our till in the store. I bought him out and stayed in that business until I met the man of my dreams. He was an Adonis. He owned his own home, and he loved my children. We had a Cinderella wedding. However, in about six months, he started putting on dark clothes at night, and would come home with equipment he had stolen. Before I knew what was happening, he had our house robbed for the insurance money. When I discovered all of this, he turned violent. He was a true psychopath because he had no conscience and was not afraid of anything. I filed for divorce, and during all this also had a hysterectomy and bladder surgery. I was a mess!

"Of course, now when I think back, I know all of these trials gave me great, great strength. What I see now is that it caused me to really focus on wanting a deeper meaning in my life. I had to learn to trust myself.

"After recovering from all this for some time, I went to a country club, overtly looking for a man with money. I met a wonderful man, and we bought

> "I have learned to live with the expectation of not being happy all the time. I'm not trying to make believe anymore. I have learned to live with the way things are. What I really want now is quiet and deep, deep beauty. I want the preciousness of life."

and remodeled our house. Six months before our wedding, he went out jogging and dropped dead of a heart attack. I was nearly suicidal for a year and a half, because I had still not developed enough trust in the universe. My fiancé's death was the beginning of my spiritual path. We had an honest relationship and he was a guiding light. Before that I was religiously oriented, not spiritually.

"Because of the remodeling I did on our home, it was put on local house tours and in *Sunset* magazine, and that's what started my career. I am eternally grateful to him. My work is very strong now, and I just trust my intuition to do what's next. My children and my work have been the most fulfilling parts of my life.

"After my daughter's accident, there was enormous pressure to give up my vocation and move to take care of her. I was very conflicted about what to do, so I got into therapy. I came to realize that I'm not as good spiritually as I wanted to be and professed to be. That is a bitch. It's like being two people. Part of me absolutely adored my children, and the other part wanted a life. Being only a mother wasn't enough. I wanted to be creatively appreciated and wanted the feeling I have now. I like it. I'm no longer covert about it. For many years, I never admitted this truth. Vicki's accident pushed me into admitting this.

"Her condition absolutely devastated my life and the rest of my family's lives. It has forced me to learn about something that affects our whole society, and I feel a strong need to help educate others about the way the medical field treats traumatically brain-injured people instead of letting them die a peaceful death. These people lose all quality of life and are left to suffer more than a person in a concentration camp. In the last four years, I have left no stone unturned trying to help Vicki or find help. But there is no hope.

"Because of my daughter's tragedy, I carry with me horrible pain all the time, but I don't see myself as victimized. Her accident has actually pushed me to become better and better. But I have learned to live with the expectation of not being happy all the time. I'm not trying to make believe anymore. I have learned to live with the way things are. What I really want now is quiet and deep, deep beauty. I want the preciousness of life. My heart is broken and I miss her terribly, but I cannot change her situation.

"I'm proud of my choices. Each setback drove me further into understanding what it is never to give up.

"And I have to tell you one more thing that I enjoy in my life right now," she said with a big smile. "My compost pile. Composting has returned me to my roots in Idaho. I experience this deep satisfaction that can only be felt and really not talked about. I like getting the manure to put in the compost, and having my brother help me with the truck. I put my leftovers in there and know that I am helping care for the earth. I like the worms and the sweet smell as I put it on my garden vegetables. I am so conscious of the no-waste cycle. I wish I could explain in words how life-changing it is."

Synchronicity Is Always Available

Another story comes from Philippa (not her real name), a friend I have known for several years. I have watched her go through some incredibly hard times with health and finances. For example, on the same day in 1993, she was hired as art director on what turned out to be a blockbuster film, and was diagnosed with a serious illness that prevented her from taking the position. On the heels of recovering from that illness, Philippa was rear-ended in an automobile accident, and suffered serious brain damage. Philippa's spirit is indomitable. She has a gift for accepting every hurdle as a spiritual lesson, in spite of the pain. In her mid-fifties, she has long, dark-reddish hair and a vibrant manner. For our interview, she wore brown silk lounging pajamas and copper-colored metallic shoes.

PEACE DESPITE PAIN

"Only four years ago I was out there in the world inventing new products," Philippa began. "I was in the forefront of my career as a designer. Everything shifted when that lesson came to an end. Now I am still inventing, but I'm a different character. I don't have to be out in the world like I used to.

"My life is very peaceful at the moment. I can't drive too much because I get tired, but I love the peace and harmony of my life. I have so much love—from my husband, my spiritual teacher and my spiritual family, all my friends—and my two dogs.

"Even now with all that's happened to get in the way of 'my plans,' I feel absolutely on track. I feel almost like the gates of heaven have opened on the earth plane for me. All the answers to the questions I have been asking in my life seem to have been laid out for me. Questions like, Who am I? Where am I going? What am I supposed to be when I grow up?

"For me, this stage of understanding has come through pain and suffering. This peace, oddly enough, has come through the last two serious illnesses when I had to go deep within. Over a period of time, it gave me a deeper view of what was truly important to me. Before that, I was always wanting more of the material things, even though my spiritual development was strong from childhood. It's so deep it's hard to put into words, but a transformation came over me when I was in a life-and-death situation. A more grounded self came out.

"Before the auto accident two years ago, I was a designer of fashion, interiors, and products. I also worked in the film industry. I was at the doctor's office as he was telling me that I was seriously ill and would have to be hospitalized, when my secretary called me there to tell me that I had been called to work on a film by Steven Spielberg. I had waited for that call for so long, and here I was about to have surgery and be hospitalized for a month! When I got back from the hospital, I came home for rehabilitation for about eighteen months. At that time, I still had my desires to go back out into the world and accomplish. I was deep into my spiritual growth, and looking at my entire life after I had recuperated: "Who am I?" "What should I do?" "Where do I start again?"

"Just as I was coming through that search with some new direction, I was sitting at a stop light one day, and an ambulance rear-ended me. I suffered a closed-head brain injury and for two and a half years struggled with memory loss, problems with motor skills and speech, and stuttering. I had to learn math, and reading, and how to drive all over again. I had to learn to be a whole new person.

"For example, I used to have a gift for being able to imagine and create designs and images of interiors in my mind's eye and move them around. I didn't know this was such a gift until I woke up from the accident and it was all taken away. I have sequencing problems. I can't go from A to B to C. Sometimes I forget to butter the bread after it's been toasted. I don't have a visual skill like I used to. All of my creativity for design work, based on the theory of adding to—designing a room, designing fabric, etc.—was all taken away. But the gift that came to me was to become a sculptor. Sculpting is the art of taking away—minus.

"I just woke up one morning and I had a feeling that I needed to sculpt. All my life I've gotten messages like this from my intuition—

and I have acted on them. Doing the sculpting really carried me through the healing process. Each stone I worked was larger and more intricate. The more I took away, the more the beauty came out. Someday, I hope to have an exhibition to show people that they should never give up. There's always a tomorrow.

"I have learned that God doesn't love you any more whether you are sick or healthy or successful or rich. Life is so rich when you take the view that everything is teaching you something and causing you to grow in certain directions. You have to listen very carefully, and not be depressed or sorrowful because the lessons come whether you're dancing for joy or lying in bed."

Philippa's story continues with a remarkable synchronicity. Even though she had spent two years in her bedroom isolated from "life" and apparently suffering major setbacks to her career, universal intelligence seems to have provided, *effortlessly*, just what she needed to move ahead with one of her inventions. This example helps us to see that even when we are feeling down in spirit, we are still within the universal flow that moves us forward.

ON THE BUS

"Two months ago, my mother died," Philippa said. "I had to go down to Los Angeles to take care of her things, and also make some arrangements for my disabled sister. After finishing up there, I took the air porter to the Burbank Airport. I was so tired and drained! I was the only person on the air porter, and was glad because I didn't feel like talking. We stopped for what turned out to be the only other passenger. A woman got on. She immediately turned to me, and said, 'Are you going to San Francisco?' I said yes, and let it go at that. Then she asked, 'Are you going to the show?' So I said, 'What show?' She replied, 'The Fancy Food Show.' I was somewhat surprised and said, 'No, but I would like to.' I explained that I had just invented a chocolate candy, and that the show would be a good place to meet chocolatiers. Well, we wound up sitting together on the plane, and talked the whole way home. She realized that she had known of my boutiques in Los Angeles in the 1980s, and known of me indirectly. We had a lot of the same background. We became instant friends. It turns out that she is a food broker in the gourmet market. She invited me to San Francisco the following day, and introduced me to all of the chocolatiers I needed to meet."

TALKING TO YOURSELF

Autobiography

In order to get a sense of how you have handled problematic situations in the past, *write down significant events that had to do with money or work*. At first, just jot down the events, such as: "Age eight, got my first allowance, but lost it in the snow. Didn't tell anybody." "Age ten, Dad lost his job. I had to get a paper route. I hated getting up so early. I felt good giving Mom my earnings, but I felt guilty one time when I kept ten dollars for myself." "Age twenty-one, went in the service because I couldn't pay for college."

Once you have your list of events, *choose the one that has the most energy for you*. Write it as a short story starting with "In the beginning," and ending with any insights you now see. Be sure to write out what your *feelings* were at the time. *Does this story speak to anything in your current situation?*

Doing this exercise can help you release the energy that has been locked up in negative memories, regrets, or resentments, as well as remind you of past victories.

PART FOUR

BEING THERE

CHAPTER 13

Doing What You Love—and Were Meant to Do

⟨∞⟩

I feel that something vast and mysterious is at stake, something known only to me, important only to me.

JEAN MARTINE[1]

Finding your place in the world is a little like riding the subway. You are going somewhere. You made a choice to ride a certain train. You get on and off the train, and you ride with strangers and friends. Each time you change directions, you have made a new choice. You come home. You leave again. In life, you may never really grasp the entirety of your journey—until you reach your destination in the spiritual dimension after leaving this life. Once again in spirit form, you and your soul group will review every moment of your physical life. The true meaning of events and relationships will be revealed. Your soul eyes will be opened to what you have *really been doing* down here on earth in the life you are now living.

HOLDING A POSITIVE VISION

One day, my old friend contractor Michael Conroy and I were discussing life, and he said to me, "There comes a point where you just have to have faith that things will work out, even though you might be completely discouraged over your rate of progress." He told me he has always loved Leonardo da Vinci's comment about patience: " 'Sir, being truly patient is being patient when you no longer thought it was conceivably possible to do so.' " Michael continued, "I've given up wanting to be famous for anything. Now I just build houses, and people seem to want me to do that. Over the years, I have learned that I am not alone. I have learned to look for the lessons in every situation, and when you realize you are in a life lesson, it really frees you. I've also learned not to have expectations and not to let fear stop me from doing new things. One day, I suddenly thought, 'Why am I not struggling so much anymore?' Of course, I still have problems, but I'm not as worried as I used to be. Then I think, 'Have I fallen off the edge? Or am I finally getting it?' It's like finally getting sober and life actually starts to work. You click on at a deep level. At least I feel that now I'm in the right ballpark."

One spring day, I was sitting at a weathered wooden table underneath an ancient oak tree in the sun-dappled backyard of another good friend, Dr. Selma Lewis. Selma is a psychotherapist who commutes weekly between practices in Los Angeles and Fairfax, California. I know why she returns each week to Fairfax. Her rustic cottage is nestled at the end of a country road beyond which lies a wooded area, a grove that seems charged with spiritual energies. Earlier in the day, we had walked a mile or so up the path to a waterfall, and had been talking about the subject of this book. Friends such as Selma, and acquaintances such as the people who have contributed their wisdom and their stories to this book, are a big part of what makes my own life worthwhile. Long, quiet morning talks are one of the joys of life for me, and this day was no exception. While we sipped tea and listened to the twittering of birds, I asked Selma what "uncommon sense" meant to her.

"Uncommon sense is what we trust when we take a leap of faith," she said. "Uncommon sense comes not from the obvious, or the ordinary, or the expected. It comes as a result of knowing who we are and trusting that to take us where we need to go. It's a deep knowing of who we are and trusting our intuition to be on our side.

"Knowing yourself takes time. You have to learn, 'Am I a person who likes chocolate or vanilla ice cream?' 'Am I a person who needs to live in the country or by the sea?' 'Am I happier designing graphic layouts or building tree houses?' 'Am I good at running a business or am I an inventor?'

"Uncommon sense, it seems to me, pulls from a deeper level of wisdom—of what's right *for us*. Not in a way that has to upset the world so that our own egocentric desires are fulfilled, but so that we can give the world what's ours to give. Uncommon sense is listening to the voice that says, 'Slow down,' when we're late and the last thing we want to do is slow down. There's sometimes an oddness to uncommon sense, particularly for people who don't rely on using intuition very often or who don't see any significance in 'coincidences.'

"Our culture, no matter what religion we may be, is overlaid with the Puritan ethic. We are raised and trained to stop ourselves from our impulses. We feel guilty over the simplest things like eating a bowl of ice cream before dinner or needing to take a nap even when we're at the office. We don't allow ourselves to trust our uncommon sense, because we have stifled so many aspects of ourselves and squashed so many of our dreams."

COMPANIONS IN SPIRIT

You are living the life you chose for the specific challenges and opportunities it would afford you. Before you were born, you and your spiritual guides selected a life in which you would be able to work on tendencies that had previously challenged you in other lifetimes or that would further develop your consciousness. Your purpose each moment is to make choices that advance your evolution as a soul. These choices contribute to the overall evolution of human consciousness. Each day, you have the opportunity to connect to this deep track of purpose through what you pay attention to—through your passions, in what gives you joy, and where you meet despair. Your purpose is also present in each of your commitments. Each of the key players in your life is part of a contract that you all agreed to work through in this lifetime. For example, someone may have agreed to show up at a certain time in your life and introduce you to your soul mate, or to open up a new direction of work, or to enlighten you about a social problem that needs attention. Our mates in our peer soul group come and go throughout life, stimulating us to learn about compassion, love, responsibility, integrity, reliability, courage, the fruits of failure, the struggles of advocacy, or the balance between humanitarian and individual goals. We are never alone. We are in constant contact with our physical and nonphysical soul groups. Our job is to be more conscious when we are physically interacting with one another, and more telepathically open when we are dispersed or when we need guidance. Even though we receive intuitive assistance, we still must make our own choices and live our own lives. Spiritual growth comes from the consequences of using free will.

Why do we not consciously remember more of our prebirth choice about our life purpose? According to reports from people who have undergone hypnotic regression and tapped into their nonphysical state as a soul (between earth lives), amnesia of previous lifetimes is a prerequisite of incarnation. When we choose a body and make a plan about the life we are about to undertake, we make an agreement with our spiritual advisers not to remember the details of our previous lives. Dr. Michael Newton, a therapist and author of *Journey of Souls: Case Studies of Life Between Lives*, has studied the interlife through the deep-level hypnotic states of his clients. He quotes a patient who says:

> "We agree . . . not to remember . . . other lives. Learning from a blank slate is better than knowing in advance what could happen to you because of what you did before. . . . If people knew all about their past, many might pay too much attention to it rather than trying out new approaches to the same problem. The new life must be . . . taken seriously . . . without having old memories, our advisors say there is less preoccupation for . . . trying to . . . avenge the past . . . to get even for the wrongs done to you."[2]

Evidently, our advisers do sometimes break through our amnesia to assist our spiritual growth when it seems we are in need. When Dr. Newton asked a client if a total blackout of our eternal spiritual life is essential to our progress, the client replied, "Normally, yes, but it's not a total blackout. We get flashes from dreams . . . during times of crisis . . . people have an inner knowing of what direction to take when it is necessary. And sometimes your friends [entities from the spirit world] can fudge a little . . . they give you hints, by flashing ideas." We begin to see, then, that our intuitive hunches, our uncommon sense, may be originating from a higher dimension that holds our original birth vision, assisting us to stay on track with what we came to do. These intuitive flashes may come spontaneously. We may step back from our normal routine and spend more time in reflection, attuning ourselves to deeper sources of knowledge. Or, we may consciously decide to seek therapy or spiritual counseling to become aware of our patterns. Dr. Newton writes:

> When the time in our lives is appropriate, we must harmonize human material needs with our soul's purpose for being here.
> Our eternal identity never leaves us alone in the bodies we choose, despite our current status. In reflection, meditation, or prayer, the memories of who we really are do filter down to us in selective thought each day. In small, intuitive ways—through the cloud of amnesia—we are given clues for the justification of our being.[3]

After physical death, when you return to your nonphysical state in the interlife dimension, you will become aware of how closely you hit the mark in interpreting and acting upon your chosen life role. In the spiritual dimension, you will have complete recall of the tiniest detail of your present life. Depending on the level of perception your soul has developed, you will review and analyze, along with peers in your soul group and your more advanced soul guides, what this life has been about.

The reason you have taken the time to read this book—to quest for your place in the world—is the desire to "hit your mark," that is, to fulfill your original, inherent destiny. In order to review your life from that higher perspective, spend some time in quiet reflection in the next few days. Imagine that you have a spirit guide nearby who is holding your vision. Can you feel, even just for a moment, the core lessons of your life so far? The greater your intention to know that core purpose, the closer you move toward receiving spiritual guidance.

There are two essential principles in receiving inspired guidance and direction. The first is that we *must ask* for guidance to help us achieve our higher purpose. Second, we must be *willing to make the changes required* to follow our highest path. We grow through conquering our fear-based negative emotions (envy, self-indulgence, self-pity, violence, bigotry, intolerance, denial, domination, etc.) in life. The opportunities that we are given stimulate and challenge us to wake up to our destiny. Our spirit guides know exactly where we are and what we are doing in relation to our original motivation. While Westerners may speak about these spirits as guardian angels, many indigenous cultural traditions also believe spirit guides not only assist us in choosing a particular life path, but also hold that vision for us in the spiritual dimension while we are living on earth.

> "None of us comes here alone; it is not permitted. We're sent off by senior advisors and arrive in good company. The Holy Spirit has a multitude of emissaries whom we often refer to as 'guardian angels.' Many times, a so-called guardian angel is in fact a lifetime guide."
>
> Leah Maggie Garfield

We are at a time in history when the barrier between the material and spiritual dimension is being opened more and more frequently in the lives of thousands of individuals. In the last few years, there have been a plethora of books concerning angelic intervention and direct communication with non-physical beings. According to shamanic teachers such as author and shamanic practitioner Leah Maggie Garfield, in her book *Angels and Companions in Spirit* coauthored with Jack Grant, guides are always present, but not necessarily omniscient.

> Everything you know about interacting with other people applies to working with guides. . . . Guides can do favors for you, but you return the favor. . . . We tend to treat guides as if they were so much more perfect than incarnate beings, as if they were all-knowing deities rather than helpful friends in spirit form. . . . Even master guides don't have a handle on the whole universe. The validity of their information varies with the area of expertise. . . . Some guides — usually life guides — are particularly attentive to your wants and needs. They notice that you're hunting for a bit of information, and either they volunteer it to you directly or they arrange for you to bump into some manifestation of it as you pursue your daily routine. You must keep in mind, even so, that while guides can broaden your informational base and support your intentions, it's still you who has [sic] to make the choices and decisions regarding the course of your life. Your guides cannot and will not live your life for you. Nor do they have all the right answers ready-made.[4]

RECLAIMING YOUR DREAMS

How are you helping to take care of the world? How have your priorities shifted in the last few years? Our work together in this book has been geared to help you awaken to the core purpose you chose for this lifetime. At the deepest level, you know what you have to do. What would it take for you to start down the path to a dream you have long cherished? Only you know the answer to that question.

Even though instantaneous global communication has alerted us to the dangers of our current level of exploitation of the earth's resources as well as of our brothers and sisters, we may not take heed until a problem affects us directly. If we truly desire to know and live our life purpose, we must look around at where we have *been stationed*. What is our work to do — right where we are? Vision without action is only empty verbiage. Action without vision may also miss the mark. As we pursue our individual goals, individually and collectively we are continuously creating a field of consciousness — a consensual philosophy, which must, for our survival, remain richly diverse in content and process. This field of consciousness creates our earthly reality. Since each unit of humanity (which is you and I) participates in the unified field of universal energy, we can make it part of our individual purpose to deepen our sense of responsibility for caring for one another and our earthly home. This commitment to a *spiritual* process of transformation of our earthly concerns and problems, that is, a transformation of our consciousness, is the biggest purpose with which any of us could align. Collectively, this commitment *is* growing stronger every day despite the catastrophes we continue to create. It takes only 15 percent of humanity to shift collective consciousness.

When I was interviewing Roy Doughty for this chapter about his consulting work with businesspeople, he mentioned a concept from the new physics that caught my attention, and seemed to resonate with the work of consciousness that we are all engaged in.

"There's something called the *strange attractor* in quantum theory," he said, "that is sometimes used by analysts, for example, tracking a weather system or the stock market. They will log in all the parameters and factors, and that data makes different shapes on the computer. No matter what the shape of the data, there is always a hole in the middle of it. This hole is called the strange attractor.

Nobody knows why the hole is there. No one can define it. The only thing that defines the strange attractor is the things around it. So I see this when I go into business to consult with executives about what they want to achieve. We talk about everything around the strange attractor, but we don't talk about the people making choices. That's the part that's never talked about. Looking at yourself and at your business this way requires a huge shift in identity. Instead of seeing yourself only as a person who walks around making decisions, paying bills, and doing all the ordinary stuff, you become an infinite spirit who is on purpose."

In this last chapter, we hear the stories of four people who have taken some kind of leap of faith, following their soul's need for an uncommonly rich life experience. We meet Elizabeth Ferris, who left a comfortable suburban life and career in real estate to work in a refugee community with Tibetan nuns. We hear from Stephen Simon, whose dream of making spiritually based films is coming to fruition. Roy Doughty shares how his move from corporate life has allowed an early interest in literature to blossom into a consulting practice that helps others deal with moral and ethical issues. Last, Cynthia Schmidt describes the intuitive process that has allowed her to create seven successful businesses over the last two decades.

Perhaps, however, *your* dream is the true last story in this chapter.

LIVING THE ADVENTURE

Elizabeth Ferris has found a way to make a big difference in the world. Doing it has taken her from a comfortable life as a real estate agent in Marin County, California, to the challenging rigors of a Tibetan refugee settlement in India. Elizabeth, an attractive and vivacious fifty-three-year-old, was an acquaintance of mine years ago. She recently returned from her new home in Dharamsala, India, to visit friends and bring back word of her new life as a volunteer teacher of English with the Tibetan Nuns' Project at Dolma Ling Nunnery. Fascinated by her dramatic lifestyle change, I asked her to share her adventure.[5]

Leaving Home and Coming Home

"There is so much to do with helping the Tibetans establish a new life," Elizabeth told me. "But it's not work to me. Yes, things have to get accomplished, but it's a pleasure. It's fun! I can't wait to get started each day. I'm jazzed all the time. People say to me, 'You're looking younger,' and I do! I feel vitalized because what I'm doing is just exactly who I am. Everybody should live this way.

"Two of my English students have organized a new language school, run by Tibetans for Tibetans who already have a ninth-grade education in the Chinese or Tibetan language. They have started a multilingual education center that is teaching Tibetan, Chinese, Hindi, and English. I'm heading up the English program, writing grant proposals, and helping organize the whole school. We are getting funding and are growing and serving the people in a way that's really needed. It's exciting and tangible. Every day, I see how motivated these people are. Living there [in the resettlement village] makes me feel alive and real with every breath I take, and it's that way for them, too. As long as my health holds out, I will live there and work there. It's what my life is about.

"This all started two years ago when I went to a lecture on the Tibetan Nuns' Project. When the presenter mentioned that there was a need for someone to teach English at the refuge shelter in Dharamsala, I instantly thought to myself, 'I could do that.' Of course, I immediately had all kinds of fears about such a drastic change. I gave myself a couple of months to think about it. In the end, I rented my house, put my stuff in storage, and moved to India with the commitment to work there for a year and then reconsider a continuing commitment after that."

"People talk about 'sacrifice,' " she said. "But I haven't sacrificed at all. I am so grateful to be living and interacting with the Tibetans on a daily basis. It's such a reward.

"Living and working with people who have undergone such harrowing experiences can be very overwhelming. It's so overwhelming, in fact, you just kind of give up and try to do the little bit you can. The country is raw and harsh. Scarcity is everywhere. Life happens in front of you, and you can't ignore it. Nothing is shielded like it is here—where I lived in my suburban neighborhood.

"The Buddha said, 'Who you are and what you do should not be a hairsbreadth apart.' " Elizabeth said, "Before I left for India, I was selling real estate, and doing pretty well at it. But it was really out of sync with my true nature. After a while, that schism became so uncomfortable, I just had to change my life. Even if you're successful at what you're doing, if it's not really in tune with who you are or that voice that calls you, I think you have to find the courage to listen to that voice. It will get you back to what you should be doing with your life."

Looking at a small portfolio of pictures of her Tibetan friends, I was immediately struck by the joy I saw in their smiling faces. Besides teaching the 145 nuns, Elizabeth teaches (also for free) a few private students. Most are orphans or members of small families who have had to leave loved ones in Tibet. Learning English will perhaps give them an advantage in finding work and being able to start new lives.

"The escape from Tibet takes fourteen to twenty-seven days on average through the mountain passes," she explained. "They have to walk through the freezing, steep, and very dangerous mountains. They may spend ten to twelve days in this windy, cold, harsh environment. The only possessions and food they have is what they can carry themselves. When they get to Kathmandu to the Tibetan reception center, they may be in very bad shape."

Elizabeth was overjoyed when she had a chance to meet the Dalai Lama when he visited the nunnery. She was struck by his simplicity and humility when he received the small band of volunteers. He told them, "I'm just a monk and you are doctors and teachers, so I just want to have an informal chat. We are all the same." He thanked them for sharing their time and energy with his people. Elizabeth recalled, "He asked us if we had enough blankets and sweaters, and it was very sweet how concerned he was for our well-being.

"The nunnery at Dolma Ling is a new model," she said. "Traditionally, nuns took vows of chastity and poverty and spent all their time in religious study and prayer. But being in exile has changed things. Now they are needed in their community."

As life takes us up and moves us around, our purposes expand, our priorities shift, our search continues for what is ours to do.

HEARING THE CALL—THE POWER
OF COMMITMENT

In 1975, Stephen Simon was a lawyer who had no intention of practicing law, but had always wanted to be in the movie business. I had come across his name in Los Angeles when a friend suggested I call him for an interview since he seemed to be a person who was pursuing his life dream. Oddly enough, two months after I interviewed my friend Eleanor Coppola (Chapter 9) I found out that the movie she was considering making a documentary about—was the same movie Stephen Simon was producing, about which he talks in the interview below. When I interviewed Eleanor, I didn't know that that was the movie she was involved with! The synchronicity continued last week when I mentioned this train of events to my daughter, Sigrid Emerson, who lives in Los Angeles and, while trained as an actress, makes her living as a personal trainer. One of her clients, Bernard Williams, a movie producer, had given her the same script for this movie to read. Unbeknownst to me, she had had it with her when she visited me the previous month.

But back to Stephen's own story. I called him for an interview to find out how he broke into making metaphysical films.

"Well, let me go back a little," he began. "About 1976, I happened to go into a bookstore one day, and someone gave me a book called *Bid Time Return*. I can't explain it, but after reading it I suddenly knew that it was time to make this book into a movie, and that I was going to do this. Next, I begged my way into producer Ray Stark's office.

"I called Richard Matheson, the book's author and one of the deans of fantasy literature [*The Incredible Shrinking Man*] and asked him for a meeting. I met with him at lunch and essentially told him, 'I got into the film business so that I could make this book you wrote into a movie. If you trust me, I'll make this movie.' He stuck out his hand, and we had a deal, although it took me three years to make it—it's called *Somewhere in Time* with Christopher Reeve. It came out in 1980, and it was not a big financial success, although it has since become a cult classic in this genre.

"There was a long period of time after *Somewhere in Time* came out that was very difficult. In retrospect, I now think that there was an audience for the movie, but there was not enough collective consciousness built up yet around this type of subject. Richard Matheson, in the meantime, back in the 1980s, gave me a new manuscript about a man who is searching for his wife in the afterlife. Trying to get this produced has been an eighteen-year odyssey, and we are just now going forward with this project. It's called *What Dreams May Come* with Robin Williams. The film takes place in several fully realized afterlife settings, and its main theme is about creating your own reality.

"But getting to this point has been a major odyssey. Following *Somewhere in Time*, I got very discouraged. I had varying degrees of success but I always felt I was getting farther and farther away from my path. Then in 1990, I went through a painful divorce and bankruptcy. In 1993, I helped make a film called *Body of Evidence* with Madonna, which was about as far away from what I came in to do as you could get.

"In January of 1993, a friend said to me, 'Stephen, the man who started off making *Somewhere in Time* should not be making movies like *Body of Evidence*.' I had an epiphany at that moment. I knew what she had said was true. By August of 1993, I had left my job, left my relationship, and had begun immersing myself in metaphysics. During that time, I met my business partner, who shares my spiritual values and interests. All of my friends changed.

"I recognize now that it was better in the long run for this current film project to take this long to come into being. For one thing, films such as *Ghost, Forrest Gump*, and *Phenomenon* have helped create a market. We have a much better chance of doing it properly. For another, the right technology is now available and less expensive.

"Our company, Metafilmics, is so far the only company who has come out and said, 'We are spiritual beings.' We think *What Dreams May Come* will be a powerful leader, and I believe that these kinds of films will be made in the future in the same numbers that action films are made—ten or fifteen a year. We're not trying to replace action films, but we think this kind of film should have a place.

"The entertainment industry has such a unique ability to affect how people feel about themselves. Done right, it is a magical way to shift consciousness. So many films have made people feel ashamed of being human. They reinforce the idea that we are a debased species, that our basic instincts are to kill, humiliate, and dominate. While that *is* a part of humanity, we are not *by nature* a debased species. We have a unique ability to consciously love. *Forrest Gump,* for example, made people feel better about being human. When you uplift how people feel about themselves, you have taken your art form to the highest level.

"Our main theme is to show how we create our own reality, which we have been doing as a culture, but doing it without much reflection about the consequences of our beliefs. The big shift now is in understanding how to create our reality *consciously* — how to create a positive future.

"I think that as we get close to the millennium, films will have more power in presenting new levels of understanding of what it is to be human. As we come to understand that we do indeed create our own reality, then it makes sense that a collective experience such as millions of people going to the movies can affect our future reality.

"Besides producing, I've been drawn to work with others who want to pursue their own dreams in this field. Teaching for me is a way of integrating what I believe with how I live. It helps me see who I am. I get an enormous amount of joy from sharing my own struggles and listening to people's responses. In the fall of 1995, I was inspired for reasons that I can't even tell you to present a proposal to teach a twelve-week class at the University of California in Los Angeles. I thought I would get maybe twenty people, but seventy showed up. There were people who had never before had any consensual validation for their metaphysical beliefs. In twelve weeks, we formed an extraordinary resonance together that had amazing aftereffects. At the end of the class, for example, we did a meditation together, visualizing each other manifesting our dreams. Several people went out and got jobs in the industry or met other people on the same wavelength. One guy is an electrician who always wanted to be a writer, and he's now actually pursuing a writing career. Two people met and fell in love and are still together. Others formed business partnerships that are still flourishing. In less external ways, people seemed to confirm within themselves that it's okay to be who they are. They got support for not letting other people define who they are and tell them what to do. It was enormously empowering.

"In my case, I firmly believe that it was the resonance that emerged from that class that allowed me and my partner to get the financing for our project within three months. We are so used to impact-causation, and this was resonance-causation. It's incredibly synergistic."

VICE PRESIDENT OF ETHICS, CREATIVITY, AND BEAUTY

I interviewed Roy Doughty after hearing how he uses literature and poetry with business executives to stimulate meaningful discussions about such topics as ethics and creativity. An inspired method for bringing the full panorama of life into the daily round, this work lifts people's thinking to a higher order. For those not used to speaking with a psychological or spiritual vocabulary, discussing the themes in literature serves as a starting point for exploring their own aspirations and common human frailties, and tapping into higher wisdom.

Doughty explained that this program was first developed by Brandeis University at the request of judges to make them more sensitive to dealing with moral and ethical issues. Doughty became interested, he said, because it united two of his passions: literature and business. He was trained by Bill Maier, former director of the Bay Area Ethics Consortium.

"We present a range of stories for people to reflect upon," Doughty said. "Most of us, especially those inundated with the details of everyday business, spend very little time — and I mean, very little — in reflection. During these seminars, people are asked to read short novels or stories that force them to reflect on the meaning. When they come together in the seminar, their ideas are challenged, expanded, and deepened by the shared conversation."

"One of my favorites is Tolstoy's, *Ivan Illych*. It's the story of a judge from an upper-class family in Russia. He lives his whole life within the confines of his social class. His life is totally conventional. He spouts the same opinions as his friends. One day, he is promoted. He becomes excited and decides to redecorate his office. While he is doing that, he falls off a ladder. His life starts to unravel around the symptoms that begin to appear after the fall. In this process, he has to go back and look at all the life assumptions that he has swallowed whole hog. He asks himself questions such as, Why am I here? How should I treat other people?

"We all have these questions about how we are going to live in the world. We get conditioned early to accept our lot. In my own case, I started work early with heavy manual labor. It was hellish working so hard and being in school all day. I'll never forget one day when my dad picked me up after work. He said to me, "Son, unless you're born with a silver spoon in your mouth, you're going to have to work every day of your life, and you're going to have to work for somebody else." I'll never forget the certainty of his statement.

"At that moment, I knew that I was not going to be an artist. I was not going to be a poet. I was not going to be a writer. I immediately put all this stuff on the side, and thought only of how I was going to have to get a job that would pay the rent. I didn't think the world had a place for the things that I cared about. For me, the world took on this huge heaviness. So I committed myself to taking any odious situation.

"I did that for twenty years and had all sorts of addictive problems. I started leading a double life. There was a private me that was doing things that you could call purposeful or meaningful — writing poetry and dabbling in art. There was a public me that was getting married, paying the rent, and working in corporations. Everybody saw that public me as the only me, and I despised that person! I didn't like the personal self, either, because he was too wimpy to live out his dream. So I was basically hating and denying myself every day *to pay the rent* [emphasis added].

> "Perhaps I need to ponder the meaning of work in general—in other times as well as in our own—and as I ponder, I sense a kinship between the words 'work' and 'worship.' I begin to suspect that man is physically organized in exactly the way he is, just so that he will need to work in order to live; and it seems possible that the substance required for his own transformation and for the maintenance of the universe is created as a direct result of his work."
> Jean Martine[6]

"One day when I was on the road, I had a realization. I was staying in hotels and taking meetings my predecessor had set up, and I suddenly saw all these other executives just like me. But they looked twenty-five years older. They were eating cheesecake and drinking brandy every night to reward themselves. These guys were the winners and they looked like they had been run over by cars. There was something wrong with this picture. I thought if I worked really hard I could have a heart attack in a year!

"I started becoming a vegetarian and stopped drinking and using caffeine and started meditating. I'd be sitting with people after work and they would be talking about their sexual conquests and their hunting and finally, I would say, 'What's really going in your life?' and they would break down and blubber and blurt out that their son was a drug addict, or that their wife was having an affair. One guy said to me that he went to a therapist because his son was a drug addict and he told me in disbelief while he was drinking his scotch, 'The therapist looked at me and said I was the problem.'

"I'd go back to the hotel room and stare at the ceiling and think, 'What am I going to do?' I found myself starting to tell the truth in whatever context I would be in. Even as a manager, I started speaking out about how I really saw situations. I was at that time a vice president of a company, and had to give a motivational talk to all the salespeople. Instead of talking about being motivated by the goal of merely making money, I gave a talk on clarity of purpose and non-attachment. I knew this worked because I had been practicing this myself, and had tripled sales in my territory. I attributed my success to my new mode of being honest and straightforward with clients, *and* unattached to the results of each sales call.

"I found that being unattached to any specific outcome is a major part of the success of this path. Of course, this idea is totally radical in sales because all sales are predicated on finding what the customers' desires are, and then trying to motivate them through that desire. My new clarity and sense of personal purpose precipitated a chain of events which eventually took me out of the corporate world.

"I had to decide how I wanted to be in the world. When I started acting on my principles, one of the things I found out was that the corporate environment was not about just being successful and providing goods and services. To me, it seemed mostly about dominance and control. All of these insights caused a big shift in my life, and I finally started working for myself as a consultant. Now I get hired for the very things I used to get fired for. I guess I finally managed to break through the belief that I got from my dad—that a person has to work for other people.

"For me, being on purpose is when I can feel that what I value about myself is also valued by the world. What I most value about myself is creativity and connection to spirit. Now that I am working with the corporate ethics seminars, I'm using language and literature to connect people back to spirit. I am so involved that I lose track of time. I am so energized by the end of the day because I have seen people transform their thinking or come to know something important about themselves.

"Through these vivid stories, we examine a wide range of ideas, including such topics as racial conflicts. For example, we asked people to read James Baldwin's book, *Sunny's Blues*, which centers around a black algebra teacher. The character finds a path out of the ghetto, but at the cost of doing everything he was "supposed" to do. The story is about his struggle between conventionality and a truly meaningful life.

"This kind of material promotes a lively conversation. It forces people to look at their own lives. For example, in one workshop, a business executive began talking about one of the books, and within about five minutes, he said, in an almost parenthetical way, 'When my daughter was killed in a car accident . . . ' and then went right on to his ideas about the novel. The next speaker went on as if the first man had said nothing unusual. I noticed one woman who had a pained look. She broke in and said, 'How can this person mention such a life-changing event [having a daughter killed in an accident] and we don't even talk about it? So her comment got us talking. This particular group had a lot of doctors and lawyers in it. It was fascinating to see that there were doctors there who had never thought about death and all the related issues and feelings.

"Discussing literature sets a whole different tone for dialogue than if you just start with a normal conversation. When you start with a story by Tolstoy, you're dealing with the work of a genius who has spent his life thinking about the deepest issues of what it means to be human. Most of us look at literature as entertainment rather than as a possible path to catharsis and healing. We keep art at the periphery of our lives, whereas in indigenous cultures, creativity and spirituality are at the very center of things. Reflecting on and discussing these themes touches something in people so deeply, they come out a different person.

"We've been trained by circumstances to hide ourselves. We use the light of the story to look into the nooks and crannies of own lives. When someone's old life falls away, a new realization rushes in. Moral guidance becomes not just 'the good thing to do,' but the only thing that makes sense to the soul. Then your life begins to take on a sense of connection and purpose.

"Why *shouldn't* there be a vice president of ethics, creativity, and moral choice in a corporation?" Doughty laughed. "I like to think of morality the way the Greeks did. For them ethics and aesthetics were not two unrelated subjects. Morality was the good, the beautiful, and the true. We've stripped this description away from morality, and instead defined it as what is useful. So we live impoverished lives, working in cubicles, hammering out actuarial tables about life and seeing life-and-death decisions as just a set of numbers."

LET IT BE SUFFICIENT TO BE WHO YOU ARE

With time and attention to where *your* path lies, and the courage to live your calling, you reach a stage where you have become yourself — unique and interesting. You become willing to invest your energy in broader goals. According to social scientists and psychologists, there is an ongoing dance between differentiation and integration. Professor Mihaly Csikszentmihalyi, author of *The Evolving Self*, says about this oscillating path:

> It is not a circular motion that returns to where one started, but rather, it resembles an ascending spiral, where concern for the self becomes steadily qualified by less selfish goals, and concern for others becomes more individualistic and personally meaningful. At its best, this process of spiraling growth results in someone like Albert Schweitzer, the philosopher who played Bach superbly on the organ, and spent most of his life running a free hospital ... The same spiral ascending between the alternating poles of personal and community values is found in other cultures, as well. The ideal career of a Brahmin male, for instance, is expected to oscillate between these same poles: first he is supposed to be a dutiful son, then a religious scholar, in middle age a successful farmer and family man, and finally in old age a monk who withdraws from active life to meditate in the wilderness. What is perhaps even more interesting is that this pattern of how individuals learn to value different goals as they mature may actually mirror the evolution of the self in the history of the human race.[7]

DREAMING BUSINESSES INTO REALITY

Cynthia Schmidt, an entrepreneurial businesswoman, had just turned in her resignation as vice president of marketing for the software business she founded six years ago, when I called to interview her. During twelve years in the fields of human resources and sixteen in marketing, she has started seven different businesses, from employment agencies and recruiting firms to software manufacturer and a Southwest art gallery and spiritual center. Cynthia has been literally following her dreams and bringing them to reality over and over again, and seems to have mastered the intuitive process of: (1) receiving an original vision and testing it over time for validity, (2) setting an intention to manifest the vision, (3) asking for support for the way to unfold, (4) recognizing and acting upon synchronicities, and (5) trusting universal wisdom (uncommon sense). In our interview, Cynthia said:

"I founded this software company, six years ago, and have reached what I call a pinnacle. That's why I've resigned. My goal was to take the business public, and I've done that. My inner wisdom tells me that I'm complete, and has started showing me something completely new.

"I intuit my businesses long before they show up in my life. They come in the form of mental pictures, and they show up in dreams or vivid daydreams. I've learned to pay attention to them rather than say, 'Oh, that's just a dream.' I write about them in my journal and determine, over time, if the intuitions and dream images are trustworthy. I've dreamed in all my businesses this way, and I've come to know the capabilities of my mind. I've already started dreaming in my next business, which tells me that I'm complete with the current one.

"My intuition comes through pictures, rather than intellectual concepts. For about a year before I opened my Southwest art gallery, I had dreams of gorgeous minerals. After six months of these dreams, I said, 'Something is going on.' Synchronistically, I went to Santa Fe, New Mexico, and recognized some of the elements of my dream. Once I saw how the elements were coming together, I started to create the business and it evolved in a normal way.

"Before I started the software business, I had visions that were global and international, and about processing information in a new way. The business developed following a vision I had after seeing a video on the Global Brain. I literally saw this business, and spent six months envisioning it. Then, synchronistically, three software engineers came to me with a proposal for a product which exactly fit my vision. I knew this was no accident. My strength is being both visionary and practical. My practical side comes from the good, solid upbringing I received from my mother and father.

"Currently, the new vision that is coming in is about creating a spiritual conference center with an emphasis on body and spirit for businesspeople. Businesspeople know very well how to have conferences, but they don't usually have balanced lives. I want to be a catalyst for introducing the many balancing techniques available. But my vision also has a broader scope. I want to define and build self-sustaining communities for people for the twenty-first century. Serendipitously, at a retreat about six months ago, I met a man who has exactly the same intention of building self-sustaining communities.

"I do think that more and more people are starting to connect with others who have similar purposes or visions. But in order to take advantage of these synchronicities, we have to be conscious of it and not treat these meetings lightly. Once I realize that I have a vision with value, I open my mind to any possibility. First, I have a strong intention to create, and then I utilize the energy of the universe proactively by praying, by being an eternal optimist, and by trusting that the universe is watching over my intention and vision. I think most people don't remember to ask for help. Everyone has this creative power within them, but we have to constantly remember to ASK—shout it out in the shower.

"Most of the time I feel I truly have an inner sense of knowing, and I trust that I will be okay. I rarely now fall into fear or worry about outcomes. But this has come after about ten years studying the Course in Miracles, and learning about myself. At the same time, going through a transition is never easy for anyone, and certainly no easier for me. It's often very frustrating. For example, I know that I have chosen to resign my current position in order to create an opening for the next event, which is probably one to three years away. I know that part of the process is to rest, rejuvenate, and enjoy, but I get impatient! It would be nice to allow the pace to be what it needs to be, without being impatient. All I can say is that when I was younger, it was much worse. Patience does seem to come with age.

"As a young girl, I wanted to be a fashion designer, and then as a teenager I decided I wanted to be an industrial psychologist. I read about industrial psychology in a book and dreamed about it. It was my first big dream and I held on to it for a long time, which is why I wound up in human resources for twelve years. I have to laugh because even though I did not have the title or function, I have used my therapeutic skills in all my work. But my real excitement comes from being creative and having the freedom to express that creativity. I always went for positions that gave me one or the other. In each of my seven businesses, I've been responsible *and* creative—whether in building the company, hiring people, or doing multimedia programs. It didn't matter what form the creativity took. For example, I had never been in an art gallery in my life, but I came back from Santa Fe, sat down, and drew up a plan for one following my visions.

"For me, creativity flows from my ability to paint a visual picture. To do that I get very centered, close my eyes, and ask for a picture to show me what I need to know. I use this technique in my writing. I'll clear my mind and become quiet, and ask for the words to come that will not be from my ego, but from creative, universal thought. I give it a few minutes, and then start typing. I know I can bring in the right communication just by asking. If I don't do that, I can get in trouble. Then I have to start all over, and ask again.

"In the process of owning my art gallery and spiritual conference center, I had the opportunity to work with a lot of wonderful teachers. Over the last ten years, I attribute my success to a combination of meeting some very good spiritual teachers, working steadily with the Course in Miracles, reading books like *The Celestine Prophecy* and *The Tenth Insight* [both by James Redfield]. This work opens you up. Most of the people in the business community haven't had this much exposure to spiritual principles, and they don't know how to trust.

"One of my roles in the software company is to look at alternative products and make recommendations on whether to merge, acquire, sell, et cetera. Now that I have learned to trust my inner sense of knowing, and trust that what I need will show up, I know that I don't have to depend only on myself to get the information we need. For example, I might see a news flash on the Internet that draws my interest. If there is something I'm supposed to do, I will get another synchronicity. Related events will happen. All of our recent negotia-tions have been absolutely synchronistic. People ask me, 'How did you identify the key players?' I didn't. I've asked for information to come, and I've asked that it be easy. Everyone in business expects you to go through a linear process of analysis and research and I truly do very little of that. I have cultivated my inner knowing so well by now that I know the best way to be on track is by asking, by being receptive, and by trusting. I certainly couldn't do this as easily ten or fifteen years ago. I didn't have the solid sense of knowing and trust that I have now. I have a department of sixteen people, and they are in awe of this process, but they are considerably younger. In order to know the reality of this process, you have to experience it yourself. The intuitive path is a difficult lesson to teach just through mental concepts because you really only feel the excitement and truth of it as you go.

"I guess you could call this path, the path of following uncommon sense. I just trust that what I'm supposed to know and do will be available to me."

ON THE ROAD AGAIN

People who lead fulfilling lives generally have found a sense of "home" in what they do. They have a philosophy of life that connects them to a larger vision. They accept that life is a continuing challenge. More often than not, they are able to live according to their own schedules, choosing work that is interesting and complex enough to keep them engaged. They get excited about being effective and about being stretched to learn new things. They have a few good friends who understand their vision and perhaps even share common aspirations. They are not driven by urgency, competition, or the demands of the ego. People who are happy have found an internal harmony by participating fully in the world from the platform of their strengths and passions, having come somewhat to terms with their foibles and weaknesses. For the most part, they do what they do best. They tend to be wholly involved and present in the moment, and not diminished by pride, envy, fear, or self-loathing. They usually know when they have made choices that are in alignment with their inner sense of moral rightness. They look forward to what life will bring each day, and, at the same time, honor their commitments and

AS YOU GO FORWARD . . .

- Embrace the moment, and accept where you are *now*.

- Remember that, before birth, you carefully considered the opportunities offered by this lifetime, and chose to take this body and this experience.

- Reconnect to your purpose by learning new skills and working *with* obstacles.

- When in doubt or fear, look for your underlying opinions and assumptions about *everything*.

- Keep your focus on that which gives you energy, and move with trust in that direction.

- Give up the need for certainty.

- Strengthen your faith in the truth that you are born with an inherent purpose, and that purpose *must and will* be revealed to you through your own intention, intuition, synchronistic meetings, and the uncommon wisdom of your spiritual guidance.

do what they say they will do. They care about the little things of life, and they also feel a part of the universal order.

AS YOU GO FORWARD . . .

You have your own place in the world. By now you should have a larger vision of what that place might be and where it is taking you after you close the covers of this book. As you go forward, review what you have learned here, and keep your sight, like a mariner on the sea, on the star of your inner guidance. Let that light shine on all that you do, showing you the next step.

In all things, use your intuitive, phototropic sense: Turn toward the Light.

TALKING TO YOURSELF

Make a list of what makes life worth living to you.
What is it you want to do next?
Review the main concepts of this book, and write down on an index card any idea that touched you. Keep your stack of cards handy, and draw one out anytime you need support.

Meditation—Imagine You Are a Tree

You are a great and powerful field of energy expressing the qualities of your soul's essence. Sometimes it will be helpful to quietly imagine yourself as another magnificent creation of the holy order. Experiencing the different qualities of other life-forms may help you find your own place in the world. This last meditation comes from writer and psychotherapist Deena Metzger. It is found in her book *Writing for Your Life: A Guide and Companion to the Inner Worlds*:

> Close your eyes and imagine yourself as a tree. Imagine that your feet, planted firmly on the ground, are roots extending deep into the earth, that your torso is a trunk stretching upward, and your arms are branches reaching into the sky.
>
> Become the tree.
>
> Now this is the difficult part: let it be sufficient to be a tree. After you have come to know the tree deeply, you can practice this meditation as a bird, a stone, a star, until you can become one with all life, with all forms of being.[8]

NOTES

INTRODUCTION

1. Leonard Laskow, *Healing with Love: A Breakthrough Mind/Body Medical Program for Healing Yourself and Others* (New York: HarperCollins, 1992), p. 70.

CHAPTER 2: YOU ARE A SELF-ORGANIZING SYSTEM

1. Margaret J. Wheatley and Myron Kellner-Rogers, *A Simpler Way* (San Francisco: Berrett-Koehler Publishers, 1996), p. 98.

2. Mihaly Csikszentmihalyi, *Flow: The Psychology of Optimal Experience* (New York: HarperPerennial, 1991), p. 218.

3. Margaret J. Wheatley, *Leadership and the New Science: Learning About Organization from an Orderly Universe* (San Francisco: Berrett-Koehler Publishers, 1996), p. 50.

4. Wheatley and Kellner-Rogers, *A Simpler Way*, p. 73.

5. Thomas Moore, *Care of the Soul: A Guide for Cultivating Depth and Sacredness in Everyday Life* (New York: HarperCollins, 1992), p. 185.

6. Joseph Jaworski, *Synchronicity, The Inner Path of Leadership* (San Francisco: Berrett-Koehler Publishers, 1996), p. 79.

7. Jeanne Achterberg, "Humanity's 'Common Consciousness,'" *Noetic Sciences Review* (Winter 1996), p. 19.

8. Mihaly Csikszentmihalyi, *The Evolving Self: A Psychology for the Third Millennium* (New York: HarperPerennial, 1994), p. 292.

CHAPTER 3: TAKING A STAND MOVES YOU INTO PLACE

1. Greg Anderson, *Living Life on Purpose: A Guide to Creating a Life of Success and Significance.* (New York: HarperCollins, 1997), p. 21.

2. Quoted in William Elliott, *Tying Rocks to Clouds: Meetings and Conversations with Wise and Spiritual People* (New York: Image Books/Doubleday, 1995), p. 126.

3. Susan Ferriss and Ricardo Sandoval, "The Death of the Short-Handled Hoe," *San Francisco Examiner Magazine*, April 13, 1997, p. 28.

4. Dalai Lama and Jean-Claude Carrière, *Violence & Compassion* (New York: Doubleday, 1996), p. 33.

5. Quoted in William Elliott, *Tying Rocks to Clouds*, p. 126.

CHAPTER 4: ANYTHING IS POSSIBLE

1. Caroline Myss, Ph.D., *Anatomy of the Spirit: The Seven Stages of Power and Healing* (New York: Harmony Books/Crown Publishers, 1996), p. 67.

2. Gary Zukav, *The Seat of the Soul* (New York: Fireside/Simon & Schuster, 1990), p. 98.

3. Peter Senge, Introduction to Joseph Jaworski, *Synchronicity, The Inner Path of Leadership* (San Francisco: Berrett-Koehler Publishers, 1996), p. 3.

4. Fran Peavey, with Tova Green and Peter Woodrow, *Insight and Action: How to Discover and Support a Life of Integrity and Commitment to Change* (Philadelphia: New Society Publishers 1994), pp. 94–95.

5. Greg Anderson, *Living Life on Purpose: A Guide to Creating a Life of Success and Significance* (New York: HarperCollins, 1997), p. 69.

CHAPTER 5: THE MAGNETIC FORCE FIELD
OF YOUR LIFE PURPOSE

1. Wayne Dyer, *Manifest Your Destiny: The Nine Spiritual Principles of Getting Everything You Want* (New York: HarperCollins, 1997), p. 24–25.

2. Gary Zukav, *The Seat of the Soul* (New York: Fireside/Simon & Schuster, 1990), p. 93.

3. Kathleen Norris, *The Cloister Walk* (New York: Riverhead Books, 1996), p. 382.

4. Quoted in William Elliott, *Tying Rocks to Clouds: Meetings and Conversations with Wise and Spiritual People* (New York: Doubleday, 1996), p. 88.

5. Ibid., p. 218.

CHAPTER 6: SYNCHRONICITIES UNFOLD YOUR PURPOSE

1. Margaret J. Wheatley and Myron Kellner-Rogers, *A Simpler Way* (San Francisco: Berrett-Koehler Publishers, 1996), p. 75.

2. Stephen Larsen and Robin Larsen, *A Fire in the Mind: The Life of Joseph Campbell* (New York: Anchor Books/Doubleday, 1991), p. 317.

3. Marie-Louise von Franz, *On Divination and Synchronicity: The Psychology of Meaningful Chance* (Toronto: Inner City Books, 1980), p. 8.

4. Joseph Campbell with Bill Moyers, *The Power of Myth* (New York: Doubleday, 1988), p. 196.

5. Peter Senge, Introduction to Joseph Jaworski, *Synchronicity, The Inner Path of Leadership* (San Francisco: Berrett-Koehler, 1996), p. 12.

6. Leah Maggie Garfield and Jack Grant, *Angels and Companions in Spirit* (Berkeley, Calif.: Celestial Arts, 1984, 1995), p. 54.

CHAPTER 7: INTENTION AND NONATTACHMENT

1. Joseph Jaworski, *Synchronicity, The Inner Path of Leadership* (San Francisco: Berrett-Koehler Publishers, 1996), p. 48.

2. Frank Zappa, "All About Music," in *Creators on Creating: Awakening and Cultivating the Imaginative Mind,* ed. Frank Barron, Alfonso Montuori, and Anthea Barron (New York: Jeremy P. Tarcher, 1997), p. 196.

3. Ibid., p. 197.

4. Margaret J. Wheatley and Myron Kellner-Rogers, *A Simpler Way* (San Francisco: Berrett-Koehler Publishers, 1996), p. 44.

5. Reprinted from Carol Adrienne, "It Comes to Me," in *The Celestine Journal,* May 1997.

6. Jaworski, *Synchronicity,* p. 38.

CHAPTER 8: USING INTUITION TO FOLLOW THE MOVEMENT
OF YOUR LIFE PURPOSE

1. Gary Zukav, *The Seat of the Soul* (New York: Fireside/Simon & Schuster, 1990), p. 82.

2. Laura Day, *Practical Intuition: How to Harness the Power of Your Instinct and Make It Work for You* (New York: Villard Books, 1996), p. 87.

3. Dan Millman, *The Life You Were Born To Live: A Guide To Finding Your Life Purpose* (Tiburon, Calif.: H. J. Kramer, 1993), p. 50.

4. Quoted in Stephen Larsen and Robin Larsen, *A Fire in the Mind: The Life of Joseph Campbell* (New York: Anchor Books/Doubleday, 1991), pp. 61–62.

5. Ibid., p. 67.

6. Jean Houston, *The Possible Human: A Course in Enhancing Your Physical, Mental, and Creative Abilities* (Los Angeles: Jeremy P. Tarcher, 1982), p. 36.

7. Quoted in Larsen and Larsen, *A Fire in the Mind,* p. 69.

8. Day, *Practical Intuition,* p. 94.

CHAPTER 9: INCREASING CREATIVITY AND
DEVELOPING YOUR ABILITIES

1. Deena Metzger, *Writing for Your Life: A Guide and Companion to the Inner Worlds* (San Francisco: Harper San Francisco, 1992), p. 55.

2. Neale Donald Walsch, *Conversations with God* (Charlottesville, Va: Hampton Roads Publishing Co. 1995), p. 118.

3. Anna Halprin, "The Process Is the Purpose," in *Creators on Creating: Awakening and Cultivating the Imaginative Mind,* ed. Frank Barron, Alfonso Montuori, and Anthea Barron (New York: Jeremy P. Tarcher, 1997), p. 49.

4. Rainer Maria Rilke, "Letters to Merline" in "The Process Is the Purpose," in op. cit., p. 53.

5. Natalie Goldberg, "Writing Fearlessly," in *Ordinary Magic: Everyday Life as Spiritual Path,* ed. John Wellwood (Boston: Shambhala Publications, 1992), p. 95.

6. Eleanor Coppola, *Notes on the Making of Apocalypse Now* (New York: Limelight Editions, 1995), p. 165.

7. Mihaly Csikszentmihalyi, *Flow: The Psychology of Optimal Experience* (New York: Harper & Row, 1990), p. 158.

8. Stephen R. Covey, *The 7 Habits of Highly Effective People: Powerful Lessons in Personal Change* (New York: Fireside/Simon & Schuster, 1989), pp. 268–269.

9. Dan Millman, *No Ordinary Moment: A Peaceful Warrior's Guide to Daily Life* (Tiburon, Calif.: H. J. Kramer, 1992), p. 274.

CHAPTER 10: IN THE VOID

1. Tony Schwartz, *What Really Matters: Searching for Wisdom in America* (New York: Bantam Books, 1995), p. 418.

2. Stephen Wolinsky, *The Tao of Chaos: Essence of the Enneagram* (Bearsville, N.Y.: Bramble Books, 1994), p. 33.

3. Quoted in Schwartz, *What Really Matters,* p. 418.

4. Quoted in William Elliott, *Tying Rocks to Clouds: Meetings and Conversations with Wise and Spiritual People* (New York: Image Books/Doubleday, 1995), p. 199.

5. Jon Kabat-Zinn, *Wherever You Go There You Are* (New York: Hyperion, 1994), p. 90.

6. Gary Zukav, *The Seat of the Soul* (New York: Fireside/Simon & Schuster, 1990), p. 218.

7. Thomas Moore, *Care of the Soul: A Guide for Cultivating Depth and Sacredness in Everyday Life* (New York: HarperCollins, 1992), p. 39.

8. Natalie Goldberg, *The Long Quiet Highway: Waking Up in America* (New York: Bantam Books, 1993), p. 99.

9. Jean Martine, *A Way of Working,* ed. D. M. Dooling (New York: Parabola Books, 1979), excerpted by John Welwood in *Ordinary Magic: Everyday Life as Spiritual Path* (Boston: Shambhala Publications, 1992), p. 148.

10. Sanaya Roman, *Spiritual Growth: Being Your Higher Self* (Tiburon, Calif.: H. J. Kramer, 1987), p. 84.

CHAPTER 11: THE SHADOW AND LIFE PURPOSE

1. Thomas Moore, *Soul Mates* (New York: HarperPerennial, 1994), p. 234.

2. Anthony Storr, *Churchill's Black Dog, Kafka's Mice* (New York: Ballantine Books, 1990), p. 191.

3. John R. O'Neill, "The Dark Side of Success," excerpted in *Meeting the Shadow: The Hidden Power of the Dark Side of Human Nature*, ed. Connie Zweig and Jeremiah Abrams (New York: Jeremy P. Tarcher/Putnam Books, 1991), p. 107.

4. Storr, *Churchill's Black Dog*, p. 193.

5. Robert Bly, *A Little Book on the Human Shadow* (New York: Harper San Francisco, 1988), p. 24.

6. Ibid., p. 25.

7. James Hillman, *The Soul's Code: In Search of Character and Calling* (New York: Random House, 1996), p. 278.

8. Wayne Dyer, *Manifest Your Destiny: The Nine Spiritual Principles for Getting Everything You Want* (New York: HarperCollins, 1997), p. 134.

9. John P. Conger, *Jung and Reich: The Body as Shadow* (Berkeley, Calif.: North Atlantic Books, 1988), p. 112.

CHAPTER 12: TRANSFORMING OBSTACLES

1. James Hillman, *The Soul's Code: In Search of Character and Calling* (New York: Random House, 1996), p. 203.

2. Ibid., p. 211.

3. Frances E. Vaughan, *Awakening Intuition* (New York: Anchor Books/Doubleday, 1979), p. 165.

4. John P. Conger, *Jung and Reich: The Body as Shadow* (Berkeley, Calif.: North Atlantic Books, 1988), p. 89.

5. Vaughan, *Awakening Intuition*, p. 168.

6. Dalai Lama and Jean-Claude Carriere, *Violence & Compassion* (New York: Doubleday, 1996), p. 160.

7. Natalie Goldberg, *Long Quiet Highway: Waking Up in America* (New York: Bantam Books, 1994), p. 157.

8. David Bohm, *On Dialogue*, ed. Lee Nichol (London: Routledge, 1996), p. 63.

9. Vaughan, *Awakening Intuition*, p. 153.

CHAPTER 13: DOING WHAT YOU LOVE—AND
WERE MEANT TO DO

1. Jean Martine, *A Way of Working*, ed. D. M. Dooling (New York: Parabola Books, 1979), excerpted by John Welwood in *Ordinary Magic: Everyday Life as Spiritual Path* (Boston: Shambhala Publications, 1992), p. 148.

2. Michael Newton, Ph.D., *Journey of Souls: Case Studies of Life Between Lives* (St. Paul, Minn.: Llewellyn Publications, 1997), p. 67.

3. Ibid., p. 68.

4. Leah Maggie Garfield and Jack Grant, *Angels and Companions in Spirit* (Berkeley, Calif.: Celestial Arts Publishing, 1984, 1995), pp. 63–64.

5. Excerpted from Carol Adrienne, "The Spirit of Giving," in *The Celestine Journal*, December 1996.

6. Martine, *A Way of Working*, p. 149.

7. Mihaly Csikszentmihalyi, *The Evolving Self: A Psychology for the Third Millennium* (New York: HarperPerennial, 1994), p. 235.

8. Deena Metzger, *Writing for Your Life: A Guide and Companion to the Inner Worlds* (San Francisco: Harper San Francisco, 1992), p. 239.

ABOUT THE AUTHOR

Carol Adrienne lives in El Cerrito, California.

To obtain information about a personal twenty-five-page numerological analysis (Life Chart), please send a self-addressed, stamped envelope to: The Spiral Path, 6331 Fairmount, #422, El Cerrito, California, 94530; telephone (510) 527-2213 or fax (510) 528-2295.